ISLAM AND THE MUSLIM WORLD

No. 6

General Editor: JOHN RALPH WILLIS
Centre of West African Studies, University of Birmingham

ISLAM
BELIEFS AND INSTITUTIONS

ISLAM

Beliefs and Institutions

BY

H. LAMMENS

TRANSLATED BY

SIR E. DENISON ROSS

FRANK CASS & CO. LTD.
1968

Published by
FRANK CASS AND COMPANY LIMITED
67 Great Russell Street, London WC1
by arrangement with Methuen & Co. Ltd.

First edition 1929
New impression 1968

Printed in Holland by
N. V. Grafische Industrie Haarlem

CONTENTS

FOREWORD

A BOOK written in good faith! This work seeks to be no more, no less. Neither controversial, nor polemical; *sine ira nec studio.* An entirely objective account, as its sub-title announces, of the beliefs and institutions of Islām. Otherwise, a manual—that is to say, a popular work. But I venture to hope that Islāmists and Orientalists will recognize that it is a popular work which has drawn its information from the fountain-heads of the Qorān, of Islāmic tradition, of the *Sīra*, etc. To these sources let me add a prolonged contact with Muslim circles. In the matter of references I have been content to limit myself to the Qorān.

It is first and foremost contemporary Islām which is here considered, Islām as formed by the evolution of thirteen centuries. But the details supplied enable the reader to follow its historical development. I take for granted a knowledge of the outline of its political history from the death of the Prophet onwards. I have omitted vanished sects, also the description of the quarrels of Muslim scholasticism, those which gave birth to the schools of the Mu'tazilites, the Ash'arites, the Murjites, etc., contenting myself with such brief allusion to them as the account of the beliefs requires. As regards private institutions, marriage, slavery, etc., the author has confined himself to essential elements, sacrificing picturesque detail.

Beyrout, 1926

ISLĀM

BELIEFS AND INSTITUTIONS

I

THE CRADLE OF ISLĀM: PRE-ISLĀMITE ARABIA

ARABIA presents the picture of a rectangle terminating in the south of Nearer Asia. This gigantic screen of inhospitable territory intervenes between the fabled lands of India and the classical East, the cradle of our civilization. Western Arabia alone in its mountainous complexity will claim our attention in this survey. There, to the east of the Red Sea, about half-way between Syria and the Indian Ocean in the province called Ḥejāz, Islām was born. From this region, bounded on the north by Syria, the east by Nejd, the south by Yemen and the west by the Eritrean Sea, sprang the impulse which resulted in the Muslim conquests and expansion. It is, then, to the Ḥejāz that we shall devote our first pages: to the Ḥejāz, the cradle of Islām.

I. THE ḤEJĀZ

CLIMATE. The climate of this province is tropical and the heat oppressive, except in certain mountainous regions situated on the borders of Nejd and of Yemen. In this region the picturesque district where the town of Ṭāif stands about 1,500 metres high, and especially its southern extension, the mountain chain of Sarāt reaching a height of 10,000 feet, might pass for an Alpine resort. The climate of the Ḥejāz, intemperate during the summer, is rigorous, even in winter, especially on the exposed steppes of the interior, where at night the thermometer then falls below zero. Everything in Arabia is harsh and decisive : the weather, the colours of the landscape, the character of the inhabitants, their constitution all nerves, muscle and bone—their language possessing so poor a gamut of vowel sounds, side by side with a veritable debauch of consonants and gutturals—and finally their alphabet in which more than half their characters are only distinguished from one another by diacritical signs.

Rain falls at very long and irregular intervals during the winter and at the beginning of spring only. Periods of complete drought, possibly extending over a period of three years or more, are also known. On the other hand, there are sometimes exceptionally rainy years. Rainstorms of short duration—but of extraordinary violence—occur, veritable water-spouts and cloudbursts, which in a few hours send flowing down the hollow valleys temporary rivers as wide as the Nile and the Euphrates, sweeping away whole encampments with their flocks and herds. At Mekka the rains penetrate into the Ka'ba and overthrow it. These cataracts put new life into the steppes : reduce the excessive salinity of the soil, and develop in a few days the hardy pastoral flora of the desert.

It is the *rabī'* or the festival of nature for the flocks and their watchers. 'Milk and butter, as an Arab author says, flow in streams. The emaciated little Beduin children grow fat-bellied and fill out in all directions. Their shape, tubby and full to bursting, makes them look like puppies gorged with mother's milk.' In ordinary times the camels do without water for four or even five days at a time : but now, full-fed on grass and succulent plants lush with sap, they no longer need be led to the distant watering-place, and can endure thirst for nearly a month at a time.

The Arab too can supplement the usual meagre fare with an abundant crop of truffles, wild artichokes and other uncultivated plants.

The Beduin, according to Sprenger, is the parasite of the camel. This picturesquely brutal phrase means that when the camel is full-fed all the Saracen people cease to be hungry ! Nothing is better justified than the nomad's solicitude for this noble animal, his foster-parent, his means of transport, and his wealth in barter.

The Qorān (**16**, 5–7) rightly regards it as a gift of Providence. Its milk, its flesh and hair furnish him with food and covering : its hide makes leather bottles and other domestic utensils, even its dung is used as fuel and its urine as a specific against malaria and lingering fevers.

Nefūd. It is a popular misconception to imagine Arabia as buried under a shroud of moving sands. This description applies only to certain provinces, happily not numerous, which are called the *nefūd*. This term is unknown in the literary language, in which the *nefūd* correspond to the Desert of Dahnā. They consist of ranges of white or reddish sand-dunes covering an area of hundreds of square miles and sometimes attaining a height of over 150 feet. In summer these dreary wastes of waterless sand are the traveller's nightmare.

But when the winter has been rainy they become the camel's paradise. According to the explorer

Charles Huber, 'to possess a corner of land in the nefūd is considered as a source of wealth'. The first rains cover the earth with a carpet of verdure; euphorbiæ, which love a sandy soil, spring up in the midst of a multitude of humble plants, vigorous creepers and strongly aromatic and savoury herbs.

Oases. The Ḥejāz, then, has the aspect of a broken and hilly country, interspersed with barren steppes, except after the winter rains. The greyish, ashen appearance of the landscape is relieved by tracts covered with black rocks, thrown out by old volcanoes. These are the *ḥarra*, and are found principally towards the east in the direction of Nejd. There are some small oases. The principal ones going from north to south are Tabūk, Taimā, Al-'Olā, Fadak, Medina and Khaibar. The old palm-groves strung out near the watering-places down the long corridor of Wādi 'l Qorā between Medina and Tabūk have disappeared to-day as well as the oasis of Fadak. Some have deduced from this that the climate of the Peninsula has been modified. But in Arabia, since the Hijra and especially since the advent of the 'Abbāsids, there has been no change except a recrudescence of anarchy and insecurity, going hand in hand with a lessening human activity in the struggle against a rigorous climate. The most important of the oases cover a bare ten square miles of surface. Khaibar, which is situated in the middle of the *ḥarra*, owes its existence to the abundance of its water-supply and the disintegration of its volcanic rocks. It has always been famous for its fertility, no less than for its unhealthiness and for the torrid heat of its climate. At the time of the Hijra all these oases, with the exception of Tabūk, were occupied and their value enhanced by the Jews, although it appears that in Medina the Arabs had obtained a slight numerical superiority over their

Jewish fellow-citizens. But apart from Medina, which became the cradle of Muslim tradition, the population of the oases has exercised only a very slight influence on the evolution of primitive Islām.

II. THE POPULATION

THE BEDUINS. The population is divided into two classes: the Beduins or nomad shepherds and the settled peoples who were once Beduins. Language, customs and religion are everywhere the same. The settlers occupy the oases and three agglomerations worthy of the name of towns: Medina, Mekka and Ṭāif. The agglomeration and the port of Jeddah (present population 30,000) date from the Hijra.

The Beduins then constituted the great majority of the population as they do to-day, when they are in the proportion of 83 per cent. It was they who were to accept Islām from the townspeople, and maintain in strength the armies of the Arab conquest, until such time as the conquered peoples came forward to fill the gap. On this account alone they would be entitled to claim our attention, but also because it is amongst them that the type and character of the race are best preserved. The same cannot be said of the settlers. Notwithstanding constant renewal by influx from the desert, the townspeople show undeniable traces of foreign influence and even of the infiltration of non-Arab blood. Ṭāif was near the Yemen. Mekka had become a cosmopolitan centre, frequented by foreign merchants, and also an important slave-market, the slaves being principally imported from Africa. It possessed a colony of Abyssinians and Medina was half Judaized. No such influences affected the Beduins, protected by their isolation and the bitter harshness of their deserts from the invasion of exotic manners and customs.

THEIR PRINCIPAL CHARACTERISTICS. What picture should we form of the Arab, that is to say of the Beduin ? For when speaking, for the sake of brevity, of the Arab, it is the Beduin we mean and not the neighbouring populations of Arabia, Syria and Egypt, upon whom the idiom of the desert was eventually imposed by the Muslim Conquests. How was it that these people, previously unknown to the Old World, came to make such a resounding entry on the stage of history ? 'Nothing is more false,' says Renan, 'than to imagine the Arabs before the advent of Islām, as a rude, ignorant and superstitious people.' They are a pre-eminently open-minded race with a receptive intelligence. Even on a first encounter, the Beduin, in spite of his rough appearance, can never be mistaken for a man of primitive or barbarian stock. His resolute bearing, his virile appearance—the inclemency of the climate, the privations of a desert life, bring about natural selection and ruthlessly eliminate the weaklings—the shrewdness and point of his replies, the ease of bearing with which he receives a guest, rather produce the impression of some gentleman fallen on evil days, some belated descendant of the Biblical patriarchs. Everything about this poverty-stricken fellow, even to his picturesque rags, his solemn exterior and his sententious speech, goes to complete the illusion. Placed under favourable conditions, which he can only find outside his own country, he is able to assimilate our progress, and the most advanced conquests of civilization. We may recall Philip the Arab, a Syrianized Arab of Ḥaurān—Zenobia—and the great buildings of Palmyra and Petra.

THE ARABIC LANGUAGE AND POETRY. From the sixth century A.D. onwards, the Beduin possessed in his national tongue a marvellously flexible literary instrument, capable of becoming, and which did in fact become, a scientific idiom. These illiterate people love poetry and cultivate it with passion, the women sharing in the general enthusiasm. If we may judge by fragments dating from the century before the Hijra, some of them touched up under the 'Abbāsids, which have been handed down to us by literary tradition, it appears to be a poetry of skilful construction and varied prosody. If it is rich in sententious expression and overflowing with energy and passion rather than with ideas, yet it lacks neither harmony nor picturesqueness and possesses a surprising profusion of formulæ. This poetry is poor in figurative expression, in original and thought-provoking imagery, still more so in moral or religious themes—these are, as it were, set aside. Filled with eloquent tirades, it has no emotional appeal and no gift of dreams.

It confines itself to the representation of external life, which it depicts with vigorous realism and with a construction as monotonous as the desert : it strives to give by means of words the impression of forms and colours. It does not bear translation well. Possessed of a sonorous idiom, keen powers of observation and a passionate temperament, loving independence up to —and beyond—the point of anarchy, the Arab had everything that made for the development of eloquence. But his rudimentary social organizations did not help to that end either before or after the Hijra. If a highly perfected language can be considered as a reflection of the soul and spirit of a nation, then the very advanced evolution of the Arab idiom should preclude the possibility of regarding the pre-Islāmic Beduins as a primitive people.

ARAB CHARACTER. Where the moral qualities are concerned, we must speak with some reserve ; they are not on a level with the intellectual faculties or with the literary development attained by the Beduins.

Justice forces us to protest against the wild enthusiasm of romantic admirers, in love with the exotic, or local colour. There is reason to contest the accuracy of the idyllic picture painted by certain Orientalists of this fundamentally positivist and realist specimen of humanity.

Renan, for instance, says, ' I do not know whether there exists in the whole history of ancient civilization a more gracious, pleasing or animated picture than that of pre-Islāmic Arab life, especially as it appears to us in the admirable type of 'Antar.' Renan's excuse is in too shallow a knowledge of ancient Arabic literature. He had not taken the time to examine how much historical truth is contained in the legend of 'Antar, created by the romancers of Baghdad and Kūfa. When we call the Beduin an individualist, we have pointed out the principal source of his failings and summed up in a word the gravest deficiencies in his moral nature. He has never raised himself to the dignity of a ' social animal ', never established any stable or regular form of authority. Ibn Khaldūn had already noted this in pages of his *Muqaddama* or Prolegomena which have become classic. We must not be deceived by the history of the Caliphate. First this adventure completely removed the nomads from the disastrous influence of their surroundings. Then, under the Omayyads, it was the Syrians, and in Baghdad the Iranians, who organized a form of agreement and permitted the rule of the Caliphate to function, although not without incessant jolts.

Only individualism can adequately explain the Beduin's lack of devotion to the general good, of kindness, or even of mere humanity. The harsh and depressing climate of the desert aggravates his individualistic tendencies. It forces him to live in isolation with his family and to wrangle with his neighbours over the scanty water supply and meagre pastures, essential to the existence of those flocks on which depends the life of him and his.

The nomad possesses all the defects of individualism, and also its doubtful and troublous qualities—self-confidence, dogged determination, tenacious egotism and rapacity. On the other hand, solitude, by forcing him to rely upon himself alone, by heightening his natural faculties, by straining them to give the last ounce of which they are capable, has saved him from lapsing into the commonplace.

HOSPITALITY. Egoistic, self-seeking and with a heart closed to altruistic sentiments, the Beduin has an instinctive horror of bloodshed, not from mawkish sentiment but because he fears the consequences of the inexorable law of the '*thār*' or vendetta. He considers this as the most sacred of all the institutions of the desert, a veritable religion with its hard consequences which the legal avenger, that is, the nearest relative of the victim, will not attempt to avoid. But he feels no scruple in robbing a traveller, strayed without an official protector into the territory of his tribe. *Hospes, hostis.* The property of a stranger, even though he be an Arab, if not protected by the ægis of the small tribal community, is regarded as *bonum nullius*, or, as it is called, '*māl Allah*', 'the goods of Allah', and therefore fair game and the prey of the strongest. In a good year when copious rains have brought life to the solitary places and swollen the udders of his flocks, the descendant of Ishmael resembles Abraham. He suddenly becomes a great lord and fulfils the duties of hospitality nobly, especially should there be a poet near by to blazon to the four corners of Arabia—where the poet acts as journalist and arbiter of opinion—the proofs of his munificence. For he is vainglorious and is sensible of the charms of good verse. He maintains that 'fame is worthy to be bought at the price of gold'.

COURAGE. He has been called courageous. Scholars have even attributed the success of the first Muslim conquests to the exceptional quality of his valour. We may well hesitate to share so flattering an opinion, and the reasons for this reserve will appear later in our second chapter when we have to survey briefly Muḥammad's military career. The Beduin hates to fight in the open—especially since the use of firearms. What we should call courage he merely considers as recklessness and gratuitous bravado. In the matter of warfare he only practises raiding, if in his struggle for existence raiding can be said to merit that name. Ruse plays a predominant part; like the beasts of prey, he prefers to surprise his enemy, and flight seems to him a simple stratagem of war. Finally, he does not esteem anonymous courage, that of the soldier fighting in the ranks or dying in the trenches, the obscure victim of an order, or of honour. It used to be customary for the women to come and weep over the tombs of the departed. 'Go not far away, noble shade!' they cried. 'A fine consolation!' replied the Beduin poets, whom any one wishing to understand fully the mentality of the nomad must not weary of citing—'Will the elegies of our women call me back to life?'

TENACITY. The most indisputable quality of the Beduin—yet another fruit of his individualism—is his *ṣabr*. This word must not be translated as 'patience'. It is something quite different. It is an indomitable tenacity in struggling against his enemy—nature—against the implacable elements, against the desert beasts of prey, and above all against man, a hundred times more menacing to his flocks, his sole fortune, than the wolf and the hyena. This tenacity has given him a temperament of steel, at once supple and resisting. It enables him to live and even to prosper under a sky and in an environment where everything pines except the Beduin and his *alter ego*, 'the ship of the desert'. Sensation pierces like a lancet-point that angular and bony frame, perpetually bathed in a hardy, dry air. Hence his fits of rage, his lusts, and his unbridled sensuality.

ANARCHY. Ishmael, the Biblical ancestor of the Arabs, is thus described in Genesis (**16**, 12) :—'*manus ejus contra omnes et manus omnium contra eum et a regione universorum fratrum suorum figet tabernaculum*' —'His hand shall be against every man and every man's hand against him ; and he shall dwell in the presence of all his brethren.' In his aggressive persistent isolation the Beduin has remained the true descendant of the son of Abraham and the desert still remains the country of *bellum omnium contra omnes*. Incapable of rising unaided above the clan idea, or of conceiving any higher form of social organization, the Arab's political scheme inevitably falls to pieces the moment some 'iron hand' is withdrawn and he is left to follow the bent of his own anarchical temperament.

THE TRIBAL CHIEF. Of the modern demagogue it has been written : 'While refusing to admit that any man is above him, he finds it intolerable not to be superior to others.' This further trait fits the Beduin marvellously. The chief of the tribe was formerly called *Seyyid*, Master, Lord, but this title has in modern times been replaced by that of *Sheikh*, since *Seyyid* has been reserved for the descendants of Ḥusain, the grandson of Muḥammad. The Caliph Mu'āwiya one day asked a nomad on what conditions it was possible in the desert to obtain the title of *Seyyid*. The answer is worthy of consideration : 'Keep open house : be gentle of speech : make no demands on anyone :

show the same cordiality to rich and poor alike—in short, treat all men as equals.' This is to demand the continuous exercise of heroic self-abnegation, and popular wisdom bears witness to the same thing in these proverbs : *Sayyidu 'l-qawm ashqāhum* and again *Sayyidu 'l-qawm khādimuhum,* 'The *Seyyid* of the tribe must make himself a slave, the most humble of all men.'

The choice of the *Seyyid*, then, depends upon the free election of the tribe. The choice rests on the principle of seniority. The precarious authority of the chief is transmitted—so says the formula—(*kābir 'an kābir*) 'from elder to elder'. These haughty democrats, these heads stuffed with aristocratic prejudices, these fighters, incessantly called upon to defend against aggression the handful of goods which they possess, flatly refuse to bow to the edicts of an inexperienced young man. The word '*Sheykh*', 'senior', old man, in itself suggests these prejudices. With total disregard for the services of the dead chief, and for the merits of his sons and brothers, they are supremely unwilling to be bound in allegiance to a family. Thus authority may pass from uncle to nephew : it may migrate from clan to clan. The case of chiefs whose ancestors to the third degree were successively *Seyyid* are quoted as phenomenal. The transmission of power, succession in the direct line, in short, the dynastic principle as the Omayyads inaugurated it, revolted the Arabs. It can readily be imagined whether their political habits permitted the stabilization of authority, and the softening of the individualism and anarchical instincts of the race.

MEKKA. Let us now turn our attention to the settled peoples, or better, the townspeople. In order to study them we shall consider Mekka, the religious and commercial metropolis of the Ḥejāz, as it appears to us at the end of the sixth century of our era, on the eve of Muḥammad's appearance on the scene.

Mekka seems to correspond to the *Macoraba* of the Greek geographer, Ptolemy. The name is thought to be derived from the Sabbean *mukarrib*, sanctuary, which would imply the antiquity of the Ka'ba. The chief and ruling tribe in the city, that of *Quraish*, were originally nomads but had been settled there for about 200 years, and wielded full authority. They governed by means of a sort of guild of merchants, and formed, as it were, an oligarchical republic. Mekka owed its economic prosperity to its geographical position and to its relations with the important trade route to India. This strange city was fortunately encamped at the extremity of white Asia, opposite Africa of the blacks, at the cross-roads leading from Babylonia and Syria towards the plateaux of Yemen, the 'Arabia Felix' of the Classics—towards the provinces of the Indian Ocean and of the Red Sea. From Babylonia, from the ports of the Persian Gulf as well as from the Yemen, flowed the rich products of the Middle East and of India: from Syria those of the Mediterranean world. We see Mekka opening negotiations with the neighbouring states, obtaining safe-conducts, free passage for her caravans, and concluding the equivalent of commercial treaties with Byzantium, Abyssinia, Persia, and the Emirs of Yemen.

THE GOVERNMENT OF MEKKA. We have used the word republic, for want of a more suitable term. It is true that we find at Mekka a vested authority, a form of government, but it is precarious and difficult to define. It is the *Mala'* of the Qorān (**23**, 34, 48; **26**, 33; **27**, 29, 38), something like a gathering of notables, of chiefs of the clans. It included representatives of the richest and most influential families.

Thus *Abū Sufyān*, father of the future Caliph Mu'āwiya, of the illustrious Omayyad family, is called ' Sheikh of Quraish and its head ' (Kabīruhum). We must be careful not to look too closely at this high-sounding title, accorded, moreover, to other contemporary Quraishites. Even at Mekka, we still meet with the manners and prejudices of the individualist Arab. Abū Sufyān was merely the foremost of the merchants, of the Mekkan financiers, the richest of them perhaps, but certainly the most intelligent, the most patriotic, and possessing more than any other a feeling for the common weal. In these qualities lies the secret of his real authority and of his influence for good. Against him and his colleagues of the merchants' guild, the heads of the Quraish families jealously guarded their authority and the right of veto, which they did not hesitate to use, as any decision taken must be unanimous. Without interfering with the autonomy of particular clans, however, the general assembly or *Mala'* knew how to exercise discreet pressure when the public good or the interest of the city demanded such intervention. It was this interest which was cited at first as cause for opposition to the religious propaganda of Muḥammad. The *Mala'* began by counsels which were succeeded by threats. There came outlawry, that is, the recalcitrants were placed under the ban of the tribe, which thenceforth refused them its protection. This instinct of solidarity, continued with constant resurgences of the anarchical spirit native to the Arab, constituted the originality of the Mekkan Government.

This conservative spirit was fostered by the desire to exploit commercially the protection of the holy months—a sort of truce of God—as well as the attraction exercised by the sanctuary of the Ka'ba, and the annual pilgrimage, with its stations near Mekka, which were the sites of fairs visited by the majority of Arabs. The Quraishite guild strove to utilize these advantages, unique in Arabia, in order to make them a source of economic benefits. Considerations of trade always came before everything else in Mekka.

Commercial Life. A close study of the rich and picturesque literature of the *Sīra* and *ḥadīth* conveys an impression of the intense and overflowing life of 'this unfruitful valley' of Mekka, as the Qorān (**14**, 40) calls it. It is as if we caught the humming of a human hive or found ourselves in the vicinity of a modern Stock Exchange. There is the same constant agitation, the same money-fever, the same frenzied speculation, and also the same succession of rapid fortunes and sudden catastrophes. Mekka became the Paradise of stockbrokers, of middlemen, of bankers with their money-loans placed at rates of interest which were usurious or appear so to those who will not take into account the enormous risks run by capital at that time and in such a place.

In the money-changers' books, men speculated on the currency exchange: they gambled on the rise and fall of foreign monies, on caravan freights, on their arrival and also their lateness. The influx of Byzantine, Sassanid and Yemenite coins, the complications of the old monetary systems and the knowledge necessary for their manipulation, gave rise to an infinity of operations and to the most lucrative transactions.

Caravans. According to Strabo, all Arabs are stockbrokers and merchants, *κάπηλοι μαλλον δί "Αϱαβες και ἐμποϱικοί*. At Mekka 'esteem was professed only for the merchants'. *Man lam yakun tājiran fa laysa 'indahum bishayin.* This infatuation spread even to the women. They put their wealth into banks and commercial enterprises: they took shares in them sometimes for trivial amounts. Thus few caravans set forth in which the whole population, men and women, had not a financial interest. On their return, every one received a part of the profits proportionate to his stake and the number of shares subscribed. The dividend was never less than 50 per cent., and often amounted even to the double. On departure the caravans carried leather, spices, precious essences, and metals, particularly silver, from the Arabian mines. Given this business activity there is no cause for astonishment if we find at Mekka merchants who in our day would be classed as millionaires. I may here refer the reader to the special study which I have devoted to them.[1]

THE SITE OF MEKKA. And yet it would be difficult to meet with a more forbidding site, even amongst the ruined rock-masses of Tihāma, the lowest-lying and most desolate part of this stern province of Ḥejāz. Gripped, as it were, in a vice between two steep and naked mountains, the town occupies the bottom of a depression, a veritable basin, where in winter the rains of the formidable Tihāma thunderstorms were stored. Such was their violence that periodically they devastated the city and overthrew, as has been seen, even the sanctuary of the Ka'ba. In the badly-ventilated corridor, scorched all through the endless summer by the pitiless sun of Arabia, without the shelter of a single palm-tree, the population in order to slake their thirst were reduced to the uncertain flow of the well of Zamzam, near the Ka'ba. But this hollow, swamp and furnace by turns, coincided with one of the most important stations on the ancient spice route, with the cross-roads of the continental routes linking up Yemen, Africa and Syria, and leading to the rich markets of India, coveted and striven for by every nation. This

[1] Cf. *La Mecque à la veille de l'hégire*, p. 222, etc.

coincidence accounts, in spite of the heavy drawbacks of its climate, for the rôle played in Arabia by this strange city destined to shelter the cradle of Muḥammad and that of Islām.

III. RELIGION

Orientalists continue to discuss at length the reality and also the depths of religious feeling which should be attributed to the Saracens before the Hijra. A perusal of the oldest monuments of Beduin literature, that is to say, what remains of pre-Islāmite poetry, which Renan has aptly described as *légère et indévote* —'light and irreligious', yields to the student, as we have seen, no trace of real, religious preoccupation.

THE KA'BA. We have already mentioned the cult of the Ka'ba. It is a rectangular building, originally roofless. It serves as a casket for the Black Stone, which was the great fetish, the principal though not the only divinity of the Quraish clan. The actual length of the Ka'ba, frequently altered and reconstructed—the last restoration dates from the seventeenth century—is 39 feet by 33, with a height of 49½ feet. The Black Stone is built into the south-eastern angle 5 feet above the ground. On the eve of the Hijra in all nomadic Arabia, particularly in the Ḥejāz, religion shows, behind this *practica multiplex*, and throughout the varying local observances, one characteristic trait; the predominance and popularity of *litholatry*, the cult of sacred stones or *baetuli*. They were called '*bait Allah*'—'The House of God'; they passed for the representation and also the dwelling-place of the divinity, and none attempted to examine or discuss these traditional ideas. The Ka'ba, originally a Beduin sanctuary, served, with this sacred well of Zamzam, as centre to the agglomeration of settlers which grew into Mekka.

No Idols. In spite of the absence of a real mythology recalling that of Greece, Arab paganism possesses a sort of Pantheon in which figure gods and goddesses whose relationships have been insufficiently studied. But it knew no idols properly so-called, no formal representations of divine beings. Its divinities were, as we have just seen, stones which took the most varied forms: oddly-shaped blocks, monoliths, erected or strangely sculptured by atmospheric erosion, assuming sometimes the appearance of men, of columns or pylons. Some remained attached to the rock where they had been discovered. Others, like the Black Stone, were preciously enclosed in a small building when the worshippers were not content to surround them with a circle of stones. Usually there was a well in the neighbourhood which served for ablutions, and often also a sacred tree, itself a god or the habitation of a divine being. On this were suspended the trophies of war, votive weapons, the offerings of visitors, sometimes a bit of stuff or a fragment of clothing.

All round stretched the *ḥaram*, sacred territory affording the right of sanctuary to all living things, men and animals. Even the trees of the *ḥaram* must be religiously respected, and no branch must be plucked from them. These rustic open-air sanctuaries were deserted during the greater part of the year. The tribe—each tribe or group of tribes possessed its own special gods—assembled there on solemn occasions—for example, the beginning of autumn or of spring—to offer up sacrifices, principally of camels. Those present had to undergo purification and ritual abstinences.

The Biblical holocaust was unknown. The blood of the victim, sometimes replaced by libations of milk, was poured out on the *baetulus*, or into an opening made at the foot of the god-fetish. After that came ritual repasts—a sort of communion, in which the flesh was eaten by the participants, who had all shaved their heads. After this ceremony they came out of the *ḥaram*, the state of holiness, to enter the *ḥill*, the profane state: in other words, to resume their ordinary occupations.

Certain *baetuli* were carried into war, when the nomad community was engaged in a struggle where its very existence was at stake. This also happened during certain religious ceremonies: for example, those of the *Rogations*, '*istisqā*', following prolonged droughts, or at the time of the pilgrimages. On these occasions the *qubba*, a kind of pavilion-tabernacle, made of red leather, was used. These processions ended by the sevenfold *ṭawāf*, the ritual circumambulation of the sanctuary. The guardianship of the *qubba* was entrusted to an escort of women, who accompanied with clashing of timbrels the liturgical chants and shouts of praise and thanksgiving. During the pilgrimage similar processions conducted the participants to its various stations, or linked-up neighbouring sanctuaries. Divination was also practised, in front of the *baetulus*, by means of ritual arrows with which the *Kāhin*, or accredited soothsayer, drew lots. These furnished the affirmative and negative answer to the question asked. A *Kāhina*, or female soothsayer, often replaced the *Kāhin*.

The cult of the Quraish clan and the whole ritual of the Mekka pilgrims, with its halts, *mauqif*, at 'Arafa, Minā, etc., its circumambulation and processions to Ṣafā, Marwa and other urban sanctuaries, sprang from this extremely primitive fetishism. Of this complex mass of archaic ceremonies, the Islāmic *ḥajj* has preserved the principal practices.

It has summarily destroyed all traces of their origin. In order to destroy their polytheistic significance it has attached them to the cult of Allah, and ascribed their institution to Abraham, founder of the Kaʿba. Incurable fatalists, the Beduins had never retained any precise idea of a future life or of the immortality of the soul. They admitted the existence of *jinns*—ill-defined beings, half-demon and half-man, reproducing in the same way as mortals. They are feared because they have the power of rendering themselves invisible: nevertheless, they are subject to the law of death. In the century which saw the birth of Muḥammad, Allah began, however, to emerge from the mass of tribal deities and from the group of *baetuli*. They still continued to be honoured, but it was acknowledged that '*Allah akbar*'—Allah is the greater.

There was no real *clergy* or *priestly caste*. Its place was filled by hierophants, dancers of an inferior kind, soothsayers, augurers, diviners, officiating priests, guardians of the *baetuli* and the sanctuaries. The *Kāhin* and his feminine counterpart, the *Kāhina*, uttered oracles, questioned the sacred arrows, presided at the *istisqā*—the object of which was to bring rain. The *sādin* were mere keepers of the sanctuaries. The *ʿāif* and the *qāif* interpret omens and decide knotty questions of civil status and genealogy. The *Kāhin* were at the head of the ill-defined hierarchy; the office was not hereditary like that of the *sādin*. They accompanied the armies and the *qubba* tabernacle and by virtue of their prescience must give information about the movements and plans of the enemy. They exercised also the functions of *ḥakam*—judge-arbiter. They were credited—especially the *Kāhina*, or pythonesses—with secret powers, such as that of drawing down rain, of conjuring spirits, maladies and spells, and that of rendering the arms and strategy of the enemy powerless by means of mysterious formulæ, as did Balaam in the Bible.

There is nothing to prove that infanticide was prevalent in Arabia, except in the Tamīm tribe, which appears to have practised it during a severe famine. This imputation, too easily admitted by Orientalists, is based upon the disregard of the Beduins for their female children. This has been associated with a rhetorical question in the Qorān (**16,** 61) which was too literally interpreted by poets in the first century of the Hijra.

THE JEWS. We have already spoken of the occupation of the oases of the Ḥejāz by the Jews. They were to be found in more compact colonies in Medina, where they monopolized the most profitable spheres, commerce and industry, and had permitted the Arabs —those who were soon to be called the *Anṣār*—to instal themselves as their customers. These customers, having finally acquired numerical superiority, aspired to become the sole masters. After the Hijra Muḥammad came sharply up against the hostility of the Jews of Medina, a fact to which the Qorān bears eloquent testimony. Ṭāif also possessed a Jewish colony. At Mekka they were only represented by passing merchants. In Yemen they succeeded in founding a Jewish state, and came into conflict with the Christians of the country.

They had rabbis, synagogues, schools, in short all the organization and the exclusive prejudices of Talmudic Mosaism. To them the Arabs were '*ommiyyūn*', Gentiles, not ignorant people, or solely in the sense that they did not possess a *Kitāb*—a revealed book. The Jews looked down on them from a great height, although they were themselves for the most part proselytes of Ismaelitish origin. This scorn told against them in their struggles against Islām; but at any rate it did not prevent them from cultivating, and with success, Arabic poetry in the style of the

Beduins. They were all town-dwellers; there is no record of a single Jewish nomad tribe.

THE CHRISTIANS. The position of Christianity in the Ḥejāz was much less favourable from the point of view of diffusion and especially of cohesion, and it did not, like Judaism, enjoy the advantage of being concentrated in the oases. It was nevertheless widely spread amongst the Beduins living near the Syrian frontier, also in the States of the Ghassānids and in the Yemen, where it struggled successfully against Judaism. In the corridor of Wādi 'l Qorā and in the neighbourhood of Syria groups of ascetics and Christian hermits were to be found. Ancient poetry bears witness to the popularity of these monks and the echo of that sympathy lingers in the Qorān (**5,** 85; **24,** 35, etc.; **57,** 27). At Mekka we can only prove the existence of a tiny handful of native Christians, that is to say Quraishites. Like the Jews, the Christians in Arabia were addicted to commerce, principally to pedlary in the towns, the oases and the Beduin encampments. Abyssinian Christians, both merchants and slaves, appear to have been numerous at Mekka. All these foreigners were upholders of old heresies. They belonged to heterodox states, principally to Jacobitism, and after that to Nestorianism and to the Christianity of Abyssinia, heavily intermingled with elements of Judaism. Muḥammad seems to have sought their company (**16,** 105; **25,** 8).

Intercourse with such informants, persons of vague conceptions and speaking a foreign language (Qorān **16,** 105), knowing their own religion very imperfectly and filled with disagreements and doctrinal divisions, —all these circumstances contributed towards a lack of finality in Muḥammad's judgment of the dogmas and value of Christianity. In the early days he failed to distinguish it clearly from Judaism. This was also the mistake of the small contemporary group of *Ḥanīf*—monotheists, but neither Jews nor Christians. Before his arrival at Medina, Muḥammad believed himself to agree in principle and on broad lines with the two *Scripturary* religions.[1] He appealed constantly to their testimony (Qorān **16**, 45; **21**, 7, passim) and found in the agreement with monotheistic dogma the proof of the reality of his mission to work amongst his compatriots for the triumph of monotheism. He cordially desired (Qorān **30**, 4) the victory of the Byzantines over the Iranian polytheists. It was at Medina, in disputing with the Jews, that he discovered his misconceptions and became firmly convinced of the bad faith of the Scripturaries.

[1] The author employs the very convenient word *scripturaire* when speaking of the *ahl-al-kitāb*, or 'people of the Book', i.e. the Jews and the Christians. This has been rendered in English by *Scripturary*.—(Translator.)

II

MUḤAMMAD: THE FOUNDER OF ISLĀM

IT was in this anarchic Arabia, in the cosmopolitan and pagan atmosphere of Mekka, that Muḥammad—the original form of the anglicized name 'Mahomet'—was born. The Qorān (**61**, 6) also calls him 'Aḥmad'. His date of birth should be fixed not towards 570—the traditional date still commonly admitted by Islāmologists—but towards 580, if it is true that he barely passed his fiftieth year.

His life is known to us through the Qorān and from a traditional compilation, the *Sīra*, the matter of which was collected and later edited by Muslims from the end of the first century of the Hijra onwards. During the last half-century this prolix documentation has been subjected by Orientalists to a severely critical examination. The least well-known, and certainly the most often debated part of the *Sīra* is that dealing with the Prophet's life in the Mekkan period. After the Hijra the principal data grow more precise.

I. MEKKAN PERIOD

YOUTH. Muḥammad came of a good family, that of the Ḥāshimites, which belonged to what one might call the citizen-aristocracy, but had fallen on evil days. At Mekka, Muḥammad's enemies alleged these origins and the lowliness of his social station as arguments against his prophetic mission (Qorān **17**, 96; **25**, 8;

43, 30). His father was called 'Abdallah and his mother Āmina. He never knew his father, who died abroad prematurely, and scarcely Āmina, carried off before her time. *Sūra* 93 states that he became an orphan at an early age and passed his childhood and youth in penury. These details are all we know with certainty of the first twenty-five years of his life. He is reputed to have been esteemed for his loyalty, was of a thoughtful turn of mind and interested himself in questions of religion which were treated with indifference by his sceptical fellow-citizens. His journeys outside of Mekka and even of Arabia offer nothing improbable, as all the Quraishites were engaged in trading by caravan. The Qorān frequently alludes to these travels and even to sea-voyages. In the course of these expeditions the *Sīra* has it that he came into contact with Christian monks.

MARRIAGE, VOCATION. The Ḥāshimite orphan is said to have been taken under the care first of his grandfather, 'Abdalmuṭṭalib, and afterwards of his uncle, Abū Ṭālib, the father of 'Alī. At about the age of twenty-five, he married a rich Mekkan widow, Khadīja, of very ripe age—she was over forty. He had several children by her, of whom only the daughters survived. His daughter, Fāṭima, outlived him. Married to 'Alī, her cousin, she became, through her sons, Ḥasan and Ḥusain, the ancestress of numerous families of Sherīfs, or descendants of the Prophet.

The question of a future life hardly exercised the Mekkans at all. It was while debating this that Muḥammad, towards the age of thirty, passed through a religious crisis, which, following on nocturnal visions (Qorān **44,** 3; **73,** 1, etc.; **74,** 1, etc.; **97,** 1), brought about the conversion of this serious-minded man. Disgusted with the crude fetishism and materialism of the Quraishites, he embraced monotheism and belief in the dogma of the resurrection. He found himself in agreement on these points with the Jews and the Christians, and being persuaded that if there exists only one God, there can be only one revelation, from which it is impossible that the Arabs should have been excluded, he felt himself called to preach these eternal truths amongst his compatriots. The exact date and precise circumstances of his religious evolution—how he gradually came to believe himself exalted to the rôle of Prophet, remain unknown ; we have no information on this subject except the mysterious allusions of the Qorān (**96**, 1–5 ; **74**, 1–10 ; **81**, 17, etc.), which are transcribed and elaborated by the *Sīra* in innumerable and picturesque anecdotes.

First Preaching. He began to preach his new faith, at first in an atmosphere of indifference, but soon in face of the hostility of the sceptical Mekkans. His social demands on behalf of the poor irritated the rich, the oppressors of the weak. The chief weapon used against him by his adversaries was sarcasm, which they directed for choice against the dogma of the resurrection, unwearyingly preached by the innovator ; also against his prediction of an imminent catastrophe, and the eschatological arguments that the Preacher deduced therefrom. To escape from these vexations, several of the earliest Muslims emigrated to Abyssinia. The discussions in question are set down at length in the Mekkan *Sūras*. There also is to be found the description of the *isrā*, his 'nocturnal journey' from Mekka to Jerusalem. It forms the solemn beginning of the 17th *Sūra* : 'Glory to Him who by night transported His servant from the holy sanctuary (Mekka) to the far-away sanctuary, in the country that men have blessed (the Holy Land), that He might reveal to him His marvels. Allah hears and sees All.' Since that time Islām has regarded Jerusalem as its third holy city.

FAILURE, THE HIJRA. The Prophet was soon convinced of the impossibility of converting his fellow-citizens. His firmness was not, however, shaken, nor his faith in his mission, which he held fast to the end. He began by communicating it to a small band of followers, amongst whom we distinguish men of resolution such as Abū Bekr and 'Omar, who later became his most devoted helpers. After an unprofitable propagandist journey to Ṭāif, the luck of chance meetings put him in touch with some Medinese Arabs passing through Mekka whom contact with their Jewish fellow-citizens had rendered more susceptible to religious ideas. They invited Muḥammad to take up his abode in their native town. He was then about 40 years old—or 50, according to the traditional version.

His exodus from Mekka inaugurated the Hijra, that is to say, migration. This forms the starting-point of the Muslim era, instituted seventeen years later by the Caliph 'Omar. It is reputed to have begun on 16th July, A.D. 622. The Hijra marks in Muḥammad's career a no less interesting change; it started the political evolution of Islām; the Prophet became the ruler of a State. In the old Arab law, the Hijra did not merely signify rupture with his native town, but was equivalent to a sort of declaration of war against it. The Mekkan guild were under no misapprehension. Up to that time the watchword for Muḥammad's disciples had been to 'Stand fast' in the midst of contradictions; the *jehād* was a spiritual war. At Mekka the period of action began; they were enjoined to take up arms until Islām should have gained the ascendency, and the 'infidels be brought low and forced to pay the tribute' (Qorān 9, 29).

II. MEDINESE PERIOD

At Medina. Some hundreds of Medinese readily accepted the new doctrine. These were the *Anṣār* (Qorān **9**, 101), that is to say, 'the Helpers'. Some Muslims of Mekka had gone before the master to Medina. They and their fellow-citizens who later followed their example are designated by the name of *Muhājir*, 'Refugees' (Qorān, *loc. cit.*). *Helpers* and *Refugees* were to form the ranks of the future aristocracy of Islām. By a convention, *'ahd*, very cleverly drawn up, Muḥammad tried to play the part of arbiter between the Muslims, Jews and pagans of Medina and bring all disputes before his tribunal.

He would no doubt have succeeded, given the malleability of the Medinese, had it not been for the obstinacy of the Jews of the oasis. His early contact with them had at least permitted him to become familiar with the Biblical history of Abraham, from which he learnt the genealogical relationship of Ishmael to the Arab people. Later on he used these facts to render Islām independent of the two Scripturary monotheisms, Judaism and Christianity, with which he was not slow to discover his doctrinal disagreement. Muḥammad related Islām to Abraham considered as its religious ancestor, and by proclaiming this patriarch the founder of the Ka'ba, he was confident that he could depaganize the old Mekkan sanctuary and consecrate it to the worship of Allah.

After having tried to conciliate the Jews, at least by means of a political agreement, he was forced to realize that they had nothing in common with him and were, in fact, profoundly hostile. Postulating that prophecy was the exclusive privilege of Israel, they refused to recognize the claims of the *ommī*, 'gentile' Prophet. Their rabbis never ceased to harass him with their disputations and their gibes; their poets riddled him with epigrams. Provoked beyond endurance, Muḥammad declared them 'the worst enemies of Islām' (Qorān **9**, 85). Having renounced the idea of convincing them, he thought at first to intimidate them by the murder of their principal chiefs. Later, when he felt secure as regards Mekka, he adopted still more radical measures against these obstinate opponents.

Battles, Badr. Some months after his installation at Medina, Muḥammad sent forth armed bands against the caravans of Mekka. It was an answer to the petty persecution of those few adherents who had remained in his native town, also an attack on its most vulnerable point. The Quraish guild became alarmed. The traffic, that is to say, the prosperity of the city, was endangered: it depended on the security of the trade routes.

In the meantime an important Mekkan caravan had set out on the road to Syria. It was to bring back about 50,000 dinars in goods and bonds. Muḥammad determined to intercept it on its return. This news spread consternation in Mekka when the leader of the caravan, Abū Sufyān, managed to give the alarm. Amidst scenes of disorder a contingent of several hundred men was organized, merchants and townsmen snatched from their counting-houses: improvised soldiers ill-prepared to stand up against resolute adversaries, whom they made the mistake of despising. This mob imagined that the enemy would disperse at the news of their approach.

In spite of the counter-order sent by Abū Sufyān, who had contrived to outdistance the Medinese and save his caravan, the Mekkans advanced in the greatest disorder towards Badr, the theatre of an annual fair. And so as to be prepared for all emergencies the Quraish merchants had brought their trashy wares in order not to miss a good opportunity. It was in the market-place of Badr that they came unexpectedly into collision with the Medinese troops, accompanied by Muḥammad in person. It was a lamentable stampede. Notwithstanding their very great numerical superiority, the Mekkans counted several dozen dead and as many prisoners, whom they were compelled to ransom at a heavy price. This was the miracle of Badr (year 624) celebrated by the Qorān (**3**, 119). It exalted the pride of the Muslims, and was widely bruited throughout Arabia.

OḤOD. The humiliation and consternation in Mekka were great. For a whole year, preparations were made for a military revenge, and to these the proud republic devoted the whole of the profits realized by the caravan of Badr, which the skill of Abū Sufyān had snatched from disaster. The Mekkans took their revenge on the day of Oḥod (625). The Muslims were completely defeated and Muḥammad himself was wounded. The conquerors did not dare to attack Medina, an open town, stripped of its defenders. Their indecision turned the success of Oḥod into a fruitless victory. As for Muḥammad, this serious defeat did nothing to abate his courage, and some months after the day of Oḥod he had re-established confidence amongst his followers. He renewed his attacks and forays against the commerce of Mekka, which was soon reduced to the last gasp.

THE WAR OF THE 'TRENCH'. Mekka called up the levies of her allies, the Beduin tribes, and mobilized her mercenary troops, the 'Aḥābīsh', so called because the majority were of Abyssinian extraction. The new army, about 10,000 strong, marched, in 627, to attack Medina. This episode figures in the *Sīra* under the name of the 'War of the Trench' or *Khandaq*.

To eke out the inferiority of his military forces, Muḥammad had conceived the idea of protecting by means of a very modest ditch—*khandaq*—the most vulnerable part of the city. This slight obstacle sufficed to break the rush of the assailants. The understanding between Muḥammadans and Beduins broke down and Muḥammad's skilful manœuvres succeeded in dividing them. They fought at a distance, principally with stones and arrows, and at the end of a month, the allies decided to raise the blockade of Medina (cf. Qorān **33**, 9–27). Adding the losses on both sides, it is impossible to make up a total of twenty dead. This practical illustration goes to confirm our theoretical estimate of Beduin courage (see p. 10).

Diplomacy. After this success Muḥammad might have considered the game as won. Instead of exploiting it by means of arms, he preferred to have recourse to diplomacy, in which he excelled. Under pretext of accomplishing the pilgrimage, he set out at the head of 1,400 Muslims and, for form's sake, submitted to a reverse; he allowed himself and his followers to be stopped on the borders of the *ḥaram* by the armed Mekkans. But he, the *ṭarīd*, the political exile, knew how to wrest from their negotiators what he had set his heart upon, by means of the Pact of *Ḥudaibiyya* (628). In it he treated with Mekka on equal terms, and in the capacity of head of a State. Islām gained thereby in prestige, and won over new adherents amongst the Quraishites. The most remarkable of these recruits were beyond question the two future captains, Khālid ibn al-Walīd and 'Amru ibn al-'Aṣī.

Whilst preparing by force of arms and diplomacy to compass the surrender of his native town, Muḥammad had worked since Oḥod to secure the sole possession of his base of operations, the oasis of Medina. A group of influential Medinese had consented to embrace Islām, but they meant to remain masters in their own house, instead of being governed by Mekkans. It is they whom the Qorān calls '*munāfiqūn*', hypocrites and 'infirm in heart'. Muḥammad overcame without much difficulty this nationalistic movement, the leaders of which were lacking in resolution.

EXPULSION OF THE JEWS. The Jews of Medina gave him more trouble. He had tried in vain to win them over. They, also, were lacking in decision; instead of uniting resolutely, first amongst themselves and afterwards with the enemies of Muḥammad, they were content to provoke him by their sarcasm. This stubborn though ineffective opposition finally drove him to exasperation. He began by expelling the weaker tribes. The last—that of the Banū Qoraiẓa—was vanquished. All the able-bodied men to the number of 600 were ruthlessly killed, and the women and children sold by auction. On their flourishing domains Muḥammad established the 'Refugees' of Mekka. The Jews of Khaibar and of Fadak were also compelled to submit and reconcile themselves to cultivating their fertile oases for the benefit of the Muslims now their masters.

THE DEFEAT AT MŪTA (629). The Muslims with their appetite whetted by these successes, but compelled by the Pact of Ḥudaibiyya (*v.* p. 31) to respect the Mekkan caravans, now turned their gaze in the direction of Syria. A strong column of 3,000 men set out to raid Transjordania. Muḥammad does not appear to have been confident of the success of this adventure, nor to have approved of it, any more than did his circle of intimates. There is nothing to show that he ever seriously envisaged conquests beyond the Arabian frontiers, otherwise he could not have refused to accompany this perilous expedition, in which Abū

Bekr and 'Omar, etc., also abstained from taking part. Muḥammad allowed himself to be replaced by Zaid, his adopted son. On arrival at Mūta, near Karak, on the east of the Dead Sea, the Medinese raiders came into collision with the *Musta'riba*, Arab Christians of Syria, attached to the Byzantine Empire.

As Muḥammad had feared, the Muslims were completely defeated (629). Khālid ibn al-Walīd succeeded in bringing back to Medina the miserable remains of this foolish expedition. In the interval Muḥammad had matured in his mind a plan which was particularly dear to his heart: the conquest of his native town.

CONQUEST OF MEKKA. In that metropolis, all clear-sighted men judged the game irretrievably lost for Mekka. Without showing his hand, Muḥammad entered into relations with the fittest man amongst the Quraishites, Abū Sufyān (*v.* p. 14), whose daughter, Umm Ḥabība, sister to the future Caliph Mu'āwiya, he had just married. Having hastened to Medina on pretext of renewing the Ḥudaibiyya pact, the Quraishite leader undertook secretly to facilitate his son-in-law's entry into his native town. He would distract the attention of his fellow-citizens and prevent them from taking any military precautions. On his side, Muḥammad would give full amnesty for the past, and would respect the immunities and the ancient organization of Mekka, where the pagan cult was to be officially forbidden. Muḥammad seems even to have consented not to take up his abode there : an agent whom he would nominate would represent him, and apart from this the Quraishites could govern themselves according to their ancient customs. As for the ' Refugees ', Muḥammad's Mekkan companions, they would not demand the restitution of their property which had been confiscated.

This was the '*fatḥ Makka*', the conquest of Mekka.

Muḥammad occupied it without striking a blow. Everything happened according to the prearranged plan, with only one single hitch—the Prophet put to death half-a-dozen of his enemies from amongst those most deeply compromised. The population of Mekka paid homage, *bai'a,* to the conqueror: but it was lacking in conviction, with the result that on the death of the Prophet the first signs of defection at once became visible in the city.

LAST SUCCESSES. Muḥammad then set out from Mekka on the day of Ḥunain (cf. Qorān **9**, 25) to disperse a strong coalition of Beduin tribes. After that he proceeded to lay siege to the town of Ṭāif (*v.* p. 5), the outer defences of which he tried in vain to force. On returning to Medina, where he continued to reside, he received the submission of Ṭāif and the homage of numerous Beduin deputations. They hastened eagerly to lay before the victorious Prophet the allegiance of their tribes, but with several of them this step was purely political and did not carry with it the acceptance of Islām.

In the year 631, Muḥammad at the head of a strong army—the most numerous which had yet been mustered in Arabia—set out towards Syria, no doubt with the object of wiping out the painful memory of Mūta. But, on arrival at the oasis of Tabūk (*v.* p. 4), the limit of Byzantine territory, he hesitated to adventure further. From Tabūk he contented himself with sending out armed bands, which plundered the towns of the Nabatea, and the small ports of the Red Sea.

Since the surrender of Mekka, Muḥammad had abstained from reappearing there, even at the season of the pilgrimage. He was content to send a representative to the ceremonies; but he decreed that henceforward infidels should no longer be allowed to participate. It was only at the beginning of 632 that he decided for the first time to assume the leadership of the pilgrimage.

DEATH OF MUḤAMMAD. Three months after his return, he died very unexpectedly at Medina, on 8th June, 632. We believe that he had barely passed his fiftieth solar year. The conversion of Arabia had only made serious progress in the Ḥejāz. Medina alone could be considered as definitely won over to the new doctrine, much more so than the towns of Mekka and Ṭāif. Nowhere else had anything been done beyond paving the way for Islāmization ; its political power had in particular been recognized.

Always elusive, the Beduins deserved the reproaches levelled at them by the Qorān : the chief of which is want of sincerity (**9**, 89–100 ; **49**, 14), the profession of Islām by lip-service only. They hated the Holy War and no less the obligation to pay tithes. On the death of the Prophet several tribes, alleging that the homage, *bai'a*, was of strictly *personal* character, claimed freedom from the oath of fidelity taken to Muḥammad, and although calling themselves Muslims, refused to send the proceeds of the fiscal taxes to Medina. The wholesale defection of the Beduins showed how well founded was Muḥammad's distrust.

THE SUCCESSION. This unexpected death threw Muḥammad's immediate circle and the community of Medina into confusion. It reawakened party spirit and the dissensions between Medina and Mekka which only the strong personality and prestige of the master had been able to quell. Nothing had been prearranged about his succession, nor the future of the Muslim community. On these points the Qorān remains silent ; no doubt Muḥammad meant to deal with them later. The very recent loss of Ibrāhīm, the son he had had by the Coptic slave Māria, had troubled his spirit. He still had to complete the framework and organization of his work. In the rare moments of leisure which the wars and vicissitudes of his eventful career left to him, we see him modifying or even abrogating verses of the Qorān (**2**, 100; **16**, 103). We feel that he was preoccupied in adapting Islām to the ever-changing circumstances of the passing hour. May he not have thought to endow it with a hierarchy, charged to preside over its destinies? It is certain that death left him no time to do so.

Before ever troubling to inter the corpse which had remained for two days without burial Anṣār and Muhājir began to dispute over the succession. The first had their Medinese candidate; the Mekkans were divided. After violent discussion, the Quraish faction, centred round Abū Bekr and 'Omar, by a surprise manœuvre, installed their candidate in the *Caliphate* or vicariate of the Prophet. This was Abū Bekr, father of 'Ayesha, the favourite of the vanished master. The great influence of the latter and also the energetic intervention of 'Omar swept the wobblers off their feet, to the great disappointment of 'Alī, Fāṭima's husband, who never resigned himself to it, and this fact, together with the claims of his descendants, soon caused the schism of the Shī'as and the shedding of rivers of blood.

III

THE QORĀN: THE SACRED BOOK OF ISLĀM

THE doctrinal sources of Islām are contained in the collection called the Qorān and in the Corpus of the *Sunna*. The Qorān is the written revelation; the *Sunna* represents oral revelation transmitted through the channel of tradition.

QORĀN. 'Qorān' means not reading but *recitation* (Qorān **16,** 100; **17,** 95; **19,** 19; **73,** 20; **87,** 6). It is essentially a text designed to be read in religious ceremonies and to take therein the place held by the Bible 'lessons' in the liturgy of the monotheistic religions. To Muslims it is '*Kitāb Allah*' and '*Kalām Allah*', the book and the word of Allah. This is why a Qorānic quotation is always introduced by the preamble 'Allah has said'. As for the interpolation 'the Prophet has said', this always refers to something contained in the *Sunna*, never to a text in the Qorān. Throughout the latter it is Allah who is supposed to speak in the first person, when he is not addressing the Prophet, who is merely his mouthpiece.

Muḥammadan orthodoxy considers the Qorān as 'uncreated', in the sense not only that it reproduces a copy conforming to the prototype of the divine revelation, but that in its actual form, in its phonetic and graphic reproduction, in the linguistic garb of the Arab tongue, it is identical and co-eternal with its celestial original. Thus to assert that the fact of its recitation was a creative art is considered gravely heterodox. As to the date of composition of the various parts of the Qorān, this extends over the first three decades of our seventh century (between the years 610 and 632).

AUTHENTICITY. The Qorān, as it has come down to us, should be considered as the authentic and personal work of Muḥammad. This attribution cannot be seriously questioned and is practically admitted, even by those Muḥammadan sects who obstinately dispute the *integrity* of the text; for all the dissidents, without exception, use only the text accepted by the orthodox. Certain portions were revised and altered by the Prophet himself and in his lifetime a number of the *Sūras* were collected in writing. It seems, however, that the greater number of them were only memorized by the reciters or *qāri*.

In its present external form tradition attributes the edition which we possess to the Caliph 'Othmān (644–656). He realized the necessity for stopping in time the dangerous diffusion of editions and copies of an unauthorized character, and presumably ordered their destruction. His intervention assured, apart from some slightly variant readings, a text of remarkable uniformity. Beyond this uniformity, the editors of 'Othmān's Qorān do not seem to have been prompted by any critical considerations in the establishment of the text. The Shi'as in their hatred of 'Othmān, their great aversion, assert that the original text has been gravely changed and even mutilated. The Khārijites exclude the 12th *Sūra*, which they treat as a romantic story. But dissenters and orthodox all, as we have said, possess no text but that of 'Othmān.

The editors of the '*qirāv'a mashhūra*', or *textus receptus*, worked under the domination of a servile scrupulousness for tradition. Otherwise they would not have been able to resist the temptation to improve, by means of equivalents readily furnished by the lexicon, the poor rhymes terminating the verses. They would not have scattered broadcast through the collection, sometimes in the course of the same *Sūra*, groups of verses which have a logical connection. They would have tried to delete or tone down the principal repetitions and tautologies which make its bulk unwieldy. Revision after the author's death would have modified the verses relating to Zainab (Qorān **33,** 37), and brought into agreement the differing versions of the same prophetic legend. In the enumeration of the prophets it would have separated and distinguished between those of the Old and those of the New Testament, and such a re-editing would have brought consistency into the story of Abraham's relations with Ishmaël and Isaac, which are completely dissimilar as related in the Mekkan or the Medinese *Sūras*. In deciding what order to assign to the *Sūras* a critical revision would at least have adopted some criticism less primitive than that of length. Above all, it would have cut out the most glaring anachronisms: the confusion between the two Marys (**19,** 22), between Haman, minister of King Ahasuerus, and the minister of Moses' Pharaoh (Qorān **28,** 5–7, 38; **40,** 38); the fusion into one of the legends of Gideon, Saul, David and Goliath (**2,** 250, etc.); the story of the Samaritan (*sic*) who is alleged to have made the Jews worship the golden calf (**20,** 87, etc.). The Qorānic Vulgate has respected all this, and left everything exactly as the editors found it.

PRESENT FORM. This Vulgate is composed of 114 *Sūras* or chapters, of very unequal length, ranging from 3 to 280 verses. Certain verses contain only two words, others over half a page. The longest of the *Sūras* are, as we have seen, placed arbitrarily at the head of the collection, without regard for the chronology of these revealed utterances or the date when they are given. The names chosen to designate them, *Sūra* of the cow, of the light, etc., are ancient and already mentioned by St. John Damascenus, therefore anterior to 750. There are altogether 6,200 verses, each terminated by an assonance, serving as a rhyme. This rhyme of a special nature, called *saj'*, is much more loose than that allowed in the metres of prosody, and in the endless verses of the prosaic Medinese *Sūras* the author finishes by disregarding it altogether. The division of the Qorān into 4, 8 or 30 *juz'*, parts, or 60 *ḥizb*, sections, was introduced for a practical purpose; it is designed to facilitate public or private recitations of the work such as are customary on solemn ritual occasions, funeral commemorations, etc.

From the point of view of philology, the sentences run flowingly, especially in the post-Hijran *Sūras*, and this first prose work of Arabic literature achieves a remarkably finished style. Some Orientalists have alleged that it has been touched up in order to bring the language to the standard of perfection set by the pre-Islāmic poets. In that case we must suppose that these purists in their revision have paid no attention to the extremely primitive rhymes of the most recent *Sūras* and above all that they have passed over slight faults of grammar and style which it would have been so easy to rectify. (Qorān **20,** 66: *inna* followed by a nominative; **49,** 9, dual subject of a plural verb.) In **2,** 106; **4,** 40–41, the predicate is singular in the first clause of the sentence, and in the plural in the second although relating to the same grammatical subject. In **27,** 61; **35,** 25, *passim*, Allah speaks in the third person; then, without transition, in the first. Thus in **2**, 172, the celebrated philologist Al-Mubarrad read *al-barr* instead of *al-birr*, in order to avoid this singular construction : ' *piety* is *he* who . . .' In spite of all this there is no occasion for surprise in the fact that the Qorān, especially the Medinese *Sūras* with their more polished phrases, less interspersed with ellipses and anacolutha than the pre-Hijran ones, has served as the standard for fixing the rules of national grammar.

In our Qorāns the title of each *Sūra* is followed by the note *Mekkan* or *Medinese*, to indicate that they were given at Mekka, or, after the Hijra, at Medina. Instead of following chronological classification, beginning with the first, that is to say the earliest, the editor has adopted the order in use in the *divans* or poetic works, which always open with the longest pieces. He has also classed or retained in the Mekkan *Sūras*, and conversely in the Medinese, groups of verses belonging to other periods. This lack of order has been sharply criticized by the Shi'as, who unhesitatingly lay the blame on the Caliph 'Othmān, guilty, in their opinion, of omitting the verses relating to 'Alī and his family.

It is certain that the incoherence of the authorized version does not make it easier to understand a text often concise to the point of obscurity and filled with allusions to events of which the details are imperfectly known to us. Such difficulties are the *mubhamāt*, the problems whose solution constitutes a branch of the *Tafsīr* or Qorānic exegesis. The *Sūras* posterior to the Hijra are thick with allusions to the difficulties and discussions arising in the Muslim community and to the domestic affairs of Muḥammad, together with attacks on his adversaries, the Jews and ' hypocrites ' of Medina. Nevertheless, the prudent Prophet affected to preserve all the more meticulously a sort of *anony-*

mity and to avoid all personalities. He only forgets himself so far as to indicate by name his adopted son Zaid and his uncle Abū Lahab. As regards place-names he mentions only Mekka, Medina, Badr, Hunain, to which should be added the name of the Rūm, Byzantines, at the beginning of the 30th *Sūra*, a very discreet allusion to the prolonged struggles of Heraclius with the Persians. This is one of the rare chronological landmarks to be found in the Qorān.

EXEGESIS. The system of *Tafsīr*, exegesis, sets out to resolve all the problems of hermeneutics. To this end it draws principally on the vast collection of *hadīth* or traditions (cf. Chap. IV), the innumerable anecdotes of which profess to set forth in plain terms the cryptograms of the Qorān, or sometimes even to transmit a commentary emanating from the Prophet or his intimate circle. Some ' *qira'āt* ', *lectiones variae*, are to be met in the works of the Arabian grammarians and philologists, and these are collected and codified by what are called the ' seven schools of *qurrā'* ', considered as orthodox. Comparison with these variants is a very meagre help towards the establishment of a really critical test.

Of the versions anterior to 'Othmān's edition there subsist only slight traces; sufficiently numerous to show divergences in detail, but too few to modify perceptibly the substance and integrity of the accepted text. Certain variants spring from the imperfect paleography of the Arabic alphabet, and the rarity of accented letters in primitive manuscripts. The complete absence of vocalizations gives rise to dissimilar readings and orthographic renderings. There are also some intentional corrections. Some critics have proposed to soften in places the Qorānic text where it seems too harsh, or else to make its meaning clear by the adoption of synonyms or even the insertion of a very brief gloss. For instance, the practice of commerce is authorized during the pilgrimage (Qorān **2,** 194), 'and during fairs' adds a variant. The fasts omitted during Ramadan should be replaced by an equivalent number of days, 'successive', or 'following on' as a reading hastens to explain. In the first verse of the *Sūra* 'Ar-Rūm' a variant substitutes the active wherever the *textus receptus* uses the passive.

Throughout the Qorān God speaks in the first person. But Allah being 'omniscient' it is obvious that nothing can nor should astonish him. Impressed by this reflection, a *qāri* has therefore replaced (**37,** 12) '*'ajibtu'—I am astonished*—by '*'ajibta'—thou art astonished*—that is to say, thou, Muḥammad. The same inspiration brought to bear on the abrogated verses has suggested the substitution for '*nunsīhā*'—*we cause them to be forgotten* (the verses in question)—of another reading judged more inoffensive: '*nansa'uhā*'—*we postpone them*—we put them off until later. The Qorān complacently stresses the favour granted to the Arabs in the person of a fundamentally national prophet; '*min anfusikum*'—*sprung from your midst.* Thinking to enhance the prestige of Muḥammad and his relationship to Allah, a variant proposes to read '*min anfasikum*'—'from the most distinguished amongst you'. Add to all this the uncertainty in the use of the particles *bi, fi, li, fa, wa,* etc., and some idea may be gained of the resources available to textual criticism.

As long as no one of the copies said to have been destroyed by 'Othmān has been found, we must abandon hope of possessing a text different from the present edition. The Shi'a *Tafsīr,* when dealing with the question of the Caliphate and the privileges granted to 'Alī and his family, professes, as we shall see later (Chap. VII), to restore the integrity of the primitive text. In spite of this claim the Shi'a has not dared to introduce these restitutions into the Qorāns which the sect uses for liturgical ceremonies and which agree with the edition transmitted by the Sunni channel.

PRINCIPAL COMMENTARIES. The Sunni *Tafsīr*, fundamentally hostile to all attempts at subjective criticism, confines itself to a strictly traditional interpretation, such as is alleged to have been transmitted and laid down by Muḥammad, by his first Companions and by the masters of the *jamā'a*, or community of Islām. The object of this *Tafsīr* is not so much to pursue along progressive paths the study of the Qorānic text as to put forward nothing which does not bear the stamp of orthodoxy. The most brilliant commentator, and certainly the one most representative of this narrowly conservative method, is the celebrated historian and founder of a school of jurisprudence, Ṭabarī (922), the author of a *Tafsīr* in thirty volumes numbering about 5,200 pages of closely-written text. An excellent philologist, with a unique knowledge of the historical, religious and juridic literature of Islām, he has condensed into his monumental compilation the exegetic erudition of his predecessors, which he quotes and treats comparatively. It may be said that he voices the whole Qorānic learning of the three first centuries of the Hijra.

The '*Kashshāf*' of Zamakhsharī (1074–1143) represents a more progressive tendency. Zamakhsharī is as respectful as Ṭabarī of the Qorānic text and equally convinced of its divine origin, but as a disciple of the Mu'tazilite school he strives, by multiplying explanations more rational than rationalistic, to excise from the Qorān all traces of matter favourable to determinism, anthropomorphism, the intervention of *jinns* and other theories to which Mu'tazilism is opposed. Fakhr ad-dīn ar-Rāzī (1209), representing the anti-

Mu'tazilite and anti-Ẓāhirite tendency, has inserted in his rambling commentary literary, philosophic, juridic and other dissertations, veritable monographs having nothing in common with exegesis. He closes the series of great commentators who laid claim to produce original work. To Baiḍāwī (1286), well known in Europe thanks to Fleischer's edition, we owe a good manual or hermeneutic compendium, very conservative in tendency. Equally well known is the '*Tafsīr al-Jalālain*', so called because in it are combined the commentaries of two Egyptian scholars, Jalāl ad-dīn al-Maḥallī (1459) and that of his pupil, the indefatigable polygraphist Jalāl ad-dīn as-Suyūṭi (1505). From the pen of this same Suyūṭi we may mention '*Al-itqān fi'ulūm al-qor'ān*', a sort of introduction to the exegesis of the Qorān.

We shall speak elsewhere of Qorānic exegesis as practised by the Shi'a sects. It is the triumph of '*ta'wīl*', allegorical interpretation. The *ta'wīl* is practised with no less enthusiasm by the adherents of the '*taṣawwuf*', namely, the members of the *Ṣūfī* congregations. In addition, these Islāmic mystics find in the Qorān the confirmation of their esoteric doctrines. Let us borrow an example from the *Tafsīr* of the famous Andalusian *Ṣūfī*, Muḥiy ad-dīn ibn al-'Arabī (1165–1250), who died and was buried at Damascus. For him the 12th *Sūra*, that of Joseph, becomes the allegorical drama of the powers of the soul. Jacob represents the intellect, Joseph the tender heart, a prey to the envy of his ten half-brothers, who are held to represent the five internal and the five external senses.

MEKKAN SŪRAS. Our edition of the Qorān is satisfied, as we have seen, with distinguishing between Mekkan and Medinese *Sūras*. This fundamental distinction should be retained, but a comparative study of the text permits us to pursue it further and establish a less summary chronological distinction. Thus by studying the style, the mode of composition, and the subject-matter, we come to distinguish at least two categories in the *Sūras* which belong to the Mekkan or pre-Hijran period.

The oldest, those contemporary with or following closely on the opening of Muḥammad's prophetic career, are the most animated, the most lyrical, and also the most abrupt. Exclamations, interjections and striking images abound, and many sentences have remained unfinished. The same is true of certain arguments, where the conclusion is merely indicated. It is left to the reader to supply the premises or missing clauses, which have not passed beyond the speaker's mind. Another peculiarity characterizes the oldest *Sūras* of the Qorān, the multiplicity and piling-up of oaths. The author calls to witness the most dissimilar objects—the sky, the stars, the mountains, the trees, etc. This use of oaths grows less as the Prophet nears the Hijra, and ceases entirely at Medina.

In the least ancient *Sūras* of the Mekkan period appear the legends of the Biblical prophets. These reflect the vicissitudes of Muḥammad's preaching and his struggles at Mekka. It is also at that time that the name 'Raḥmān' to designate Allah came into use, as well as the Oratorical apostrophe 'O men!', which was replaced at Medina by 'O Believers!' The verses, very short, and as it were breathless in the earliest *Sūras*, begin to lengthen, the rhyme grows more commonplace, conventional phrases creep in and synonymous expressions jostle one another. As a whole, the style of these last *Sūras* already foreshadows that of the Medinese period. During the ten first years of his prophetic career Muḥammad only attacks the heathen, and refrains from falling upon the Jews and Christians with whom he believed himself to be in agreement on the fundamentals of his preaching.

MEDINESE SŪRAS. These are easier to recognize, as are the pericopes or Medinese fragments which have strayed into the Mekkan *Sūras*. This is due first to the style, which is more prosaic, especially in the numerous legal stipulations. The sentence unfolds more regularly, sometimes even to the point of becoming a period. The verses take on a greater amplitude and the parts of the syllogism are less often implied than in the Mekkan period. The tone differs completely from that of the pre-Hijran period ; it becomes more assured, more dominating even than at Mekka, where it exhorted a *pusillus grex* to endurance, *ṣabr*, in the midst of denials. Now we may divine the voice of a leader and lawgiver. Imperatives abound : 'obey the Prophet'; 'pay the tax of alms, *zakāt*', etc. This last word, and also others such as '*ḥanīf*', monotheist, belong to the lexicon of the Medinese period. The eschatological arguments which pervade the Mekkan *Sūras*—the approach of the Judgment, etc. —are abandoned ; Polemics against the heathen grow rare, and to make up for this the Jews, the Medinese enemies of Muḥammad, the 'hypocrites' and 'infirm of heart', are the subject of attack. Military addresses occupy a considerable place. Allusions to contemporary events, to current news, increase in number : incidents in the Prophet's domestic life, his marriage with the divorced wife of Zaid, his adopted son (Qorān **33**, 37), the accusation brought against 'Ayesha, his favourite (**24**, 10, 11), the statute imposed on his wives after his death, etc. Abraham is represented as the founder of the Kaʿba and Islām is called 'the Faith of Abraham' (**22**, 76, etc.). Muḥammad went back beyond Moses and Christ to claim kinship with the Biblical patriarch who 'was neither Jew nor Christian' (**3**, 60); in other words, he proclaimed Islām's independence of the Scripturary religions.

DOGMA IN THE SŪRAS. Ritual and liturgical stipulations,—prayer and pilgrimage—social and penal laws, all the canonic legislation by which primitive Islām was to live and which the juridical schools of the second to third centuries expounded, date from the Medinese period. On the other hand, it is the Mekkan section of the Qorān which contains the brief enunciation of the dogmatic ideas and simple theodicy of the author; concepts to which the Medinese chapters merely add a few superficial traits.

In the early days of his mission Muhammad besides preaching monotheistic dogma was much concerned with eschatology. He announced, if not the imminence of the last Judgment, at least that of a catastrophe which will smite all miscreants who resist his preaching. These ideas are reiterated with monotonous insistency, and without any very apparent effort to vary their expression, or replenish the stock of images and comparisons, generally quite unoriginal, applied to the existence of God, His attributes and relations with the world. Allah is the Creator, the only and unequalled Master. He knows no 'associates' or rival divinities, such as the pagans, whom the Qorān for this reason calls '*mushrikūn*'—*associators*—assign to Him. Before the Hijra Muḥammad at first directed his attacks only against the Quraishite and Beduin pagans. At Medina, after his rupture with Judaism, his polemics add to these enemies 'the peoples of the Book', that is, the Jews and Christians.

Angels are represented as the ministers of Allah. The angelology of the Qorān is not complicated; it developed only at Medina in intercourse and discussion with the Jews. It designates by name the archangel Michael, and particularly the archangel Gabriel (Qorān

2, 91, 92 ; **16,** 104). This latter, also called the *Holy Spirit* or simply the *Spirit,* is regarded as the authorized medium of prophetic revelations. Angels watch over man and are charged to write down his good and bad deeds. Satan (Iblīs or Shaiṭān) appears throughout as the enemy of man and the great tempter ; his fall dates from the day when he refused to prostrate himself with the angels before Adam (Qorān **18,** 48). The Qorān has adopted belief in the *jinns* (see p. 20) which are created from fire and are divided into good and bad. They try to steal the secrets of Heaven. A few of them have embraced Islām (**46,** 28).

Amongst books which are revealed and presented as such, only the Pentateuch (*Taurāt*), the Psalter and the Gospels are mentioned by name in the Qorān. Allah has predestined the eternal fate of men, but on the other hand he is shown as prone to be moved by compassion, by repentance and good works, ' which blot out evil ones '. The Qorān contains texts both for and against determinism, according as the author's aim is to show the full responsibility of man or to stress the omnipotence of the Creator. The texts unfavourable to freewill are, if not the more numerous, at least the more striking and seem best to render Muḥammad's inmost thought. Muslim tradition has seen this unerringly, and Sunni orthodoxy has therefore quite formally pronounced itself in favour of fatalism. It considers the absolute predestination of all human actions as an article of belief, and sees therein merely a simple corollary of the infinite power of Allah. Only the Qadarites and Mu'tazilites refuse to concur in this deduction. The former, considered by the orthodox community as heretics, have taken their name from the controversy, for they proclaim that man is left free to determine his ' *qadar* ', *fatum,* that is, his eternal destiny.

PROPHETS. God has not ceased to call men back to the profession of monotheism by the ministry of prophets. The Qorān gives no indication of their number, but tradition counts them by thousands. Their legends, indefatigably re-told, and re-edited, fill the *Sūras*, and the chain, unbroken since Adam, passes through Noah, Abraham, Lot, Ishmael, Moses—and Christ—to end in Muḥammad, 'the seal of the prophets' (Qorān **33**, 40). This Qorānic *apax legomenon* is generally translated as 'the last of the prophets' in the sense—the only one admitted by Islām—that after him no other will appear. But nothing precludes a different interpretation of the mysterious phrase—that Muḥammad was the last of the prophets because he *stamped*, as with a *seal*, the preaching of his predecessors. It is indeed a conception familiar to Muḥammad that his doctrine was not an innovation but the 'confirmation' of the Scripturary monotheisms, that is to say, of Judaism and Christianity (cf. **2**, 38, 71, 85; **3**, 2, 34; **4**, 50; **5**, 50, 52 *passim*).

'To Thee, O son of Mary, wherefore low
In attitude adoring should I bow?
Have I not wrought and builded to the sky?
Jesus of Nazareth a prophet was, as I
Whom after Him and Moses Heaven did send
The work begun to finish and extend.' [1]

THE CHRISTOLOGY of the Qorān is extremely characteristic and has been strongly influenced by the literature of the apocryphal gospels. The Christ, *'Isā*, is called 'Son of Mary', and the latter is confused

[1] *'O fils de Myriam, martyr mystérieux,*
Pourquoi donc, devant toi, baisserais-je les yeux?
Pourquoi? Mon édifice immense touche au faîte.
Jésus de Nazareth était aussi prophète,
Mais le ciel me fit naître après Moïse et lui,
Pour achever leur œuvre et pour l'agrandir.'
(H. de Bornier, *Mahomet*, Act II, Sc. 6.)

with Mary the sister of Moses and Aaron (**3**, 31; **19**, 29). His virgin birth is energetically attested and upheld against 'the calumnies of the Jews' (**4**, 155). From the cradle He incessantly performed the most astonishing miracles, an assertion the more surprising as Muḥammad confessed plainly that he himself was not a Thaumaturge (**13**, 8, 27; **17**, 95; **25**, 8; **29**, 44). Christ is 'the Messiah, the Word and spirit of Allah'. The Qorān seems here to retain an echo of the *Logos* of St. John.

The sense which it attached to '*Kalima*'—Word—remains enigmatic. No doubt he wished simply to convey that the Messiah had acted as an organ and intermediary to divine revelation: this realistic interpretation is in harmony with his conception of prophecy, for he alleges that the preaching of Christ dealt only with monotheism (**3**, 44; **5**, 117; **43**, 63), another favourite theme of Muḥammad. Jesus is only the 'servant of Allah', a mere mortal like the other prophets. He is said to have foretold the coming of Aḥmad; that is, of Muḥammad (**61**, 6). The latter was never able to admit the mystery of the crucifixion:

> '*In death I shall surpass Thee! Thy death was too sublime,*
> *O Jesus! for Thou gavest the victory to crime!*'[1]

The death on the cross was only an 'illusion', a legend propagated by the Jews (Qorān **4**, 155, 156). The Qorān expresses indignation against the Christians, who give to the Messiah the title 'son of God' (**5**, 116; **9**, 30; **43**, 59); it repeats indefatigably that Allah 'is not begotten and has not begotten'. This polemical attack went further than the Christians

[1] '*Je mourrai mieux que toi! Ta mort fut trop sublime,*
O Jésus! Tu permis le triomphe du crime!'
(De Bornier, *loc. cit.*)

and was also aimed against the heathen, who considered the angels as children of Allah (**21**, 26; **52**, 39, etc.). Incontestably the Christology of the Qorān accords to Jesus a place apart amongst all the prophets. It only avoids with the more solicitude, however, everything which would place Him above humanity to the detriment of monotheistic dogma.

ESCHATOLOGY. The eschatological concepts were chiefly expounded in the Mekkan *Sūras*. They affirm the reality of a future life, of paradise and hell, of the resurrection and the Judgment of all men. After death each will receive the reward of his works, the just in heaven, the wicked in hell, which place of torment is, together with heaven, to be everlasting. The Qorān enumerates certain deadly sins, '*Kabā'ir*', such as polytheism, the murder of an innocent person, etc., which are deserving of hell. Certain texts declare, nevertheless, that Allah can 'in His omnipotence' grant deliverance to the damned (**2**, 108–110); others insinuate that for Muslims hell will be temporary (**4**, 51, 116; **11**, 109, etc.; **92**, 15–16). This last conclusion, adopted by tradition against the Khārijites, has to all appearances been borrowed from the Talmudist Jews, whose right to claim a similar privilege the Qorān (**2**, 74) nevertheless disputes (**3**, 23).

The 'true believers will do no more than pass through the fire' (**19**, 71–72). It must therefore be equivalent to a *purgatory*.

These places of bliss or torment are depicted as material. The wine of Paradise, served by dazzlingly beautiful youths, 'shall not cause their brows to ache' (**56**, 11, etc.). The Medinese *Sūras* avoid reference to the paradisal 'houris' mentioned in the pre-Hijra verses (**55**, 72; **56**, 22). Women of the faithful, and 'the spouses' of believers, are admitted to heaven and take their place there, but these wives will then be freed from the infirmities belonging to their sex (**2**, 23; **3**, 13; **4**, 60). Nowhere is the beatific vision clearly mentioned; Allah remains 'inaccessible to human eyes' (**6**, 102). If on the day of resurrection 'their looks are turned towards the Lord' (**75**, 22–23), the orthodox commentators interpret this passage as referring to fleshly vision; while the Mu'tazilites only see it as a figurative and symbolic phrase. Otherwise, these latter argue, God would be in one place and would be limited.

Catastrophes and strange phenomena will precede and announce the end of the world: the invasion of Gog and Magog, the appearance of a mysterious beast, the splitting in twain of the moon, etc. Then will begin the Judgment of all men, called in the Qorān by very diverse names; 'the hour', 'the day of judgment', 'of the resurrection', etc. All the dead will arise; this point is the subject of some of the longest dissertations in the Mekkan texts, and on this subject the Prophet heaps up analogies and comparisons. All men will appear at the last Judgment, where their eternal fate will be finally settled.

But how are we to imagine the fate of souls during the period intervening between death and the Judgment? This problem has caused acute embarrassment to the Muslim schoolmen, no doubt because the *Sūras* furnish no clear solution. Certain verses, in conformity with ancient Arab beliefs, suppose the dead to be either sleeping or insensible in the tomb (Qorān **22**, 7; **50**, 18). The tradition of the Sunnī and Imāmites has seized upon this suggestion and deduced therefrom its theory of the 'Torment of the Tomb'. This theory does not succeed in making clear the nature of the sufferings which torment simultaneously body and soul, in spite of their separation and of the bodily insensibility which follows it. The same tradition goes on to discuss whether Muḥammad and the prophets enjoy a life of consciousness in their sepulchres. As far as Muḥammad is concerned, popular belief answers in the affirmative.

As for the martyrs, Qorānic texts proclaim them 'living in the presence of Allah and receiving from Him their subsistence' (**2**, 143; **3**, 152, 163; **4**, 76; **22**, 57; **47**, 5–7); an assertion which must by some means be reconciled with the fact of the resurrection which will come shortly before the last Judgment. A few privileged souls receive in the same manner and without waiting their eternal reward in heaven (Qorān **36**, 25, etc.). The wicked go straight to hell. There will be brought forth at the last Judgment 'the Book' containing an exact account of the smallest actions, together with 'the Balance designed to weigh them'. To this apparatus Muslim tradition adds the 'bridge as sharp as a razor-edge across which the souls must pass'. The *Mu'tazilites*, and in our day the progressives and modernists, see in 'the bridge' and in 'the torment of the tomb' which the '*'aqīdas*', professions of faith, have adopted, symbolic representation which it is better not to scrutinize too closely.

Such are the principal themes touched on by the theology of the Qorān. The author confines himself to asseverating them vigorously and to enumerating them time after time in the Mekkan *Sūras*. The Medinese pronouncements are overwhelmed by details and provisions of a practical nature which do not add to this exposition any new doctrinal element. In his character of prophet and *voice of warning*, '*nadhīr*', Muḥammad did not feel called upon to furnish demonstration. He was a messenger of Allah, whose mission was confined to '*balāgh*', or transmission of divine messages. The task of harmonizing and systematizing them was left to the theorists of the first three Muslim centuries, spurred on by the need to combat dissident sects. Just as Muḥammad admitted to ignorance of the future, it never occurred to him to pose as a dialectician. He referred his opponents, as we have seen, to the testimony of the Scripturaries, in whose 'Bibles', *Kitāb*, proofs of his mission and teaching would be found (*v.* p. 23). He felt that he possessed the truth, and that it was incumbent on sceptics and those who denied it to furnish arguments (Qorān **21**, 24). Sometimes he goes so far as to outline a syllogism bearing on certain dogmas either more hotly disputed by recreants or dearer to his heart than the others. Thus the existence of several divinities seems to him irreconcilable with the order of the universe (**17**, 44; **21**, 22). For the most part he confines himself to marshalling comparisons and analogies.

INFLUENCE OF THE QORĀN. It is difficult to overestimate the influence of the Qorān on the formation of Muslim mentality. All Muslims admit without question the miracle of the '*i'jāz*', that is, the insuperability of the Qorān. Not even the united efforts of men and *jinns* could succeed in composing a fragment comparable with it (Qorān **2**, 21; **17**, 90). It is in the mould of this divine book, existing in heaven from all eternity under the guardianship of the angels (**30**, 13–15), that the Islāmic conception of the world has been fashioned. That conception explains to us the general likeness existing amongst all Muslim communities, notwithstanding their ethnical differences.

The Qorān, learnt by heart from infancy, used as a textbook for the elementary school manuals, offers to the believer the easily assimilable elements of a philosophy at once positive and revealed. He finds therein the doctrine of the rule of providence, and the just estimation of all events, none of which can henceforth disconcert him. By showing him the Islāmic community as the object of Allah's favours, the heir divinely chosen to receive the inheritance of infidel nations (Qorān **6,** 165; **10,** 15, 74; **35,** 37), the Qorān flatters the believer's vanity and upholds him in the midst of his trials. It is for him an epitome of sacred and profane history; a manual of prayers, a code of the religious and social life, a reminder of daily conduct, in short, a collection of definitions and maxims of a practical nature. Its sententious style is conducive to reflection in the Muslim; he concentrates his whole attention on the power of God and on His incessant intervention in the government of the world.

THE FIVE PILLARS OF ISLĀM

Among the religious duties—'*'ibādāt*'—incumbent on every Muslim, are five which, by reason of their importance, are called 'the pillars of Islām'. These duties are at once binding on the individual believer, and in his default, on the community of believers at large. They are the profession of faith, prayer, alms, fasting and pilgrimage.

1. THE 'SHAHĀDA' or profession of faith is contained in the phrase: 'There is no God but Allah and Muḥammad is his Prophet'. In its brief compass this formula attaches Islām to the group of monotheistic religions by proclaiming the unity of God, and distinguishes it from them by affirming the prophetic mission of Muḥammad. Its recital admits the infidel to the Muslim community. Every Muslim must pronounce it at least once after he is considered as *mukallaf*, i.e. subject to religious obligations. In practice the customary offering of prayer, of which the *shahāda* forms an integral part, takes the place of this obligation.

Theodicy of Islām. We have already spoken (p. 24) of Muḥammad's prophetic mission and of how it is regarded by Islām. The first part of the formula, that which proclaims the unity of God, implies the existence of a Muslim theodicy. Its principal rôle consists in harmonizing the transcendence of the essence or '*Zāt*' of Allah, His ineffable divine unity, first with the multiplicity of His attributes, '*ṣifāt*' as mentioned in the Qorān—will, power, knowledge, etc.; secondly, with the innumerable qualificatives—seeing, hearing, sitting, speaking, and so on—associated by that collection with the name of Allah. It was essential to avoid the dissociation of essence and attributes; furthermore, a too laboured insistence on the Qorānic qualificatives produced a risk of falling into anthropomorphism. This problem exercised Islāmic theologians at an early date, and they sought for a solution.

We have already mentioned the Mu'tazilites. Their doctrinal activity and influence were specially marked during the caliphate of Māmūn (813–833) and of his two successors. They are known to us as the defenders of free will (*v.* p. 49). Anti-determinists and later opposed to any distinction between the essence and attributes of God, the Mu'tazilites called themselves 'the defenders of justice and unity'—'*al-'adl wa't-tauḥīd*'—as though their system alone safeguarded the concept of equity—by asserting the freedom of the will—and of unity as these attributes should be recognized in God. But how was it possible, while maintaining the reality of the attributes, to avoid the necessity of giving them co-eternal existence with God?

The school founded by Al-Ash'arī (965) believed it had found the solution, thanks to this formula of reconciliation and compromise: 'Allah *knows* through his knowledge; he *can* through his power, etc., which attributes are not really distinct from his divine essence.' Orthodoxy adopted theory and formula without, however, consequently condemning the Mu'tazilites as heretics. When the Qorān speaks of the 'face and hand of Allah', etc., Ash'arī takes these expressions in their literal sense, guarding, however, against the reproach of anthropomorphism by observing that they must not be visualized as human members. '*Bilā kaif*' should be interpreted as not troubling to understand the *how* or modality. The mystery of this modality passes man's understanding, and discussion should be avoided. These formulæ are designed to satisfy the intellectuals and the simple faithful.

2. PRAYER. Private and individual prayer, '*do'ā*', is subject to no sort of regulation, as opposed to the '*ṣalāt*', which is ritual prayer and must be in Arabic. Tradition has fixed the number, left indeterminate in the Qorān, of the five daily '*ṣalāt*' of dawn, noon, '*aṣr* (midway between noon and sunset), sunset and of nightfall, about an hour after sunset.

These prayers must be performed by the faithful, facing in the direction of the *qibla*, that is to say, of Mekka, and in a state of legal purity, '*ṭahāra*'. Alternatively, they must be preceded by ablution, '*waḍū*', of the face and hands, of the arms up to the elbow, and of the feet including the ankles. In case of necessity the '*tayammum*', or rubbing with sand, may be substituted for water. The procedure is similar in all other cases where legal purity is required; for example, in reciting or merely touching the Qorān. Before the public noonday prayer on Friday complete ablution —'*ghusl*'—is obligatory. The '*ṭahāra*' is destroyed by sleep, contact with things regarded as impure, e.g. corpses, wine, pork, dogs, etc., the needs of nature, conjugal relations, etc.

The ordinance of prayer is strictly regulated. It comprises two to four *rak'a*, according to the time of day: four at noon, at *'aṣr* and at nightfall; three at sunset and two only at dawn. These prayers can be recited at home and in the mosque. Each one is announced by the muezzin (*mu'adhdhin*) from the minaret of the mosque. If several persons are gathered together, they should place themselves under the direction of an *imām*, or president. As for the *rak'a*, it resolves itself into inclinations of the body (*rukū'*) and complete prostrations (*sojūd*), the forehead touching the ground.

Each prayer opens with the *takbīr*, or repetition of the formula, '*Allah Akbar*'; next comes the recitation of the first *sūra*, or *Fātiḥa*, followed by the *shahāda*; the whole being punctuated by *qiyām*, or the standing posture, inclinations of the trunk and complete prostrations. It finishes with 'the prayer for the Prophet' (*ṣalāt 'alān-nabi*), followed by the salutation (*salām*) to the congregation, which is recited turning to the right and to the left. This series of postures and formulæ may be prolonged, and an effort made to break the monotony by the interpolation after the *Fātiḥa* of further invocations, *sūras* or groups of Qorānic verses. Their number is determined by the devotion of the worshipper and regulated by the *rite* to which he belongs. The use of Arabic is strictly enforced. Abū Ḥanīfa admits an exception in favour of the foreigner, whose tongue cannot master the pronunciation of Arabic.

The Friday Prayer is obligatory upon all adult males. Women take no part in it. It is held at the mosque at noon with a congregation of at least forty of the Faithful and under the direction of a president, or *imām*. Before the prayer the president delivers from the pulpit two addresses (*khuṭba*) in

Arabic in which reference is made to the head of the State. He then performs two *rak'a* with the congregation. Friday is not regarded as a weekly day of rest, this observance being unknown to Islām.

A special '*ṣalāt*' with *khuṭba* solemnizes the two great canonical festivals of the year: that which ends the fast of Ramaḍan and that of the tenth day of the month of Dhū'l-ḥijja, which coincides with the sacrifices of the pilgrims at Mekka. The festivals instituted to commemorate the birth (*maulid*) of Muḥammad, his ascension (*mi'rāj*) to heaven, etc., are of more recent date.

3. THE ZAKĀT, or '*ṣadaqa*', is a kind of alms-tithe, or tax on capital. Its proportion, a tenth, twentieth, etc., is regulated in the books of *fiqh*, according to the nature of the goods taxed. Every year it is levied in kind on the Muslim's possessions. According to the Qorān (**9**, 60), it may only be spent for humanitarian purposes—redemption of slaves, aid to members of the community, travellers, debtors, volunteers of the Holy War, and also those whom, in conformity with the wish of the Qorān, it is important to win over to the cause of Islām. The distinction between the '*zakāt*' and other taxes, its exclusive use for the ends above-mentioned, has virtually fallen into desuetude. Everything is paid into the treasury. The '*sharī'a*' seems to recognize for Muslims no more than the strict legality of the '*zakāt*'.

4. THE FAST OF THE MONTH OF RAMAḌAN. This daily fast begins with the break of dawn and lasts until sunset. It comprises total abstinence from food, drink, perfumes, tobacco, and conjugal relations. During the night all these interdictions are raised. Dispensations in the case of illness, travel, the Holy War, etc., are temporary; the obligation is renewed when the reason for exemption has disappeared. The

deficiency must be made up by an equivalent number of fast days, and in cases of intentional omission, charitable deeds must be added by way of expiation.

5. Pilgrimage to Mekka. Minors, slaves, and poor persons are exempted from this obligation. Other causes of exemption are unsafe roads or times, and a state of war or public disturbances. But with the disappearance of obstacles the obligation is renewed. 'The pilgrimage is the sole centre of effective co-ordination, capable of giving a liturgical structure to Sunnism' (L. Massignon). It has adopted most of the ceremonies of the old Arabian pilgrimage (*v.* p. 19).

Essential features are the wearing of the *iḥram*, a seamless garment, the *tawāf*, circumambulation of the Ka'ba, the course, *sa'y*, from Ṣafā to Marwa, the halts (*wuqūf*) at the outlying sanctuaries of 'Arafa, Muzdalifa and Minā, with a sacrifice at Minā. This is the '*'īd al-aḍḥa*', or feast of sacrifice, celebrated on the same day, likewise by sacrifices, throughout the whole of Islām. For as long as he wears the *iḥram*, the pilgrim must submit to the abstinences imposed during the fast of Ramaḍan. In addition, he must abstain from hunting and from cutting his nails and hair. Certain schools authorize the vicarious performance of the pilgrimage. Others regard such vicarious performance as a strict obligation, if the pilgrimage has not been accomplished by the Muslim in his lifetime.

The *'omra* is a lesser pilgrimage, an optional but highly meritorious observance, not restricted to any particular time of the year. It comprises the same ceremonies and the same obligations—apart from the sacrifice—as the great pilgrimage, but is confined to the visit to the Ka'ba and the urban sanctuaries of Mekka. Held in no less honour, except among the

Wahhābis, is the visit to Medina, to the tomb of Muḥammad.

THE JEHĀD. The war against the non-Muslims, so frequently recommended in the Medinese *sūras*, almost became, as with the Khārijites, a 'sixth pillar of Islām'. Islām owes to it her expansion, in which 'the mission', properly speaking, has played an insignificant rôle. The '*sharī'a*' has always looked upon the Holy War as one of the principal duties of the Caliph. It continues to be regarded as a 'required duty' (*farḍ al-kifāya*), not an individual obligation, but binding on the community as a whole. Thus if a Muslim sovereign or state consecrate themselves to it, it is considered as accomplished; but in theory the Jehād should know neither intermission nor end until the whole world has been conquered for Islām. This is one of the most incontestably popular concepts of the Islāmic ideal.

It is to this theory that we owe the geographical distinction between '*dār al-harb*', or 'war territory', and '*dār al-islām*', or 'the land of Islām', governed by the laws of the Qorān. In the case of countries inhabited by pagan or Scripturary populations but independent of Islāmic rule, truces may not in principle be concluded for periods longer than ten years, but such truces may be renewed indefinitely. The Qorān (**5**, 56) forbids 'taking Jews and Christians as friends'. These regions belong by right to Islām and efforts should be made to enforce this right as soon as circumstances permit. The Muslim countries which have become European colonies, or passed under the rule of a protectorate, are likewise regarded as '*dār al-islām*'. It is understood that for these regions, too, the 'non-Muslim rule is an anomaly which should be suffered only while Islām is powerless to react' (Snouck Hurgronje).

To '*dār al-islām*' is related the idea of the 'forbidden territories'. No non-Muslim may openly penetrate within their confines, on pain of death. This prohibition comprises the sacred territories (*ḥaram*) of Mekka and Medina. It is an unwarrantable extension of Muḥammad's decree addressed to *pagans* only, and forbidding not their presence in Mekka but their participation in the ceremonies of the pilgrimage (*v.* p. 34). There is no doubt that in the first century A.H., non-Muslims obtained permission not only to visit the holy cities, but also to stay or even to settle there.

PERSONAL STATUTE. Regarded as a religious law and derived from the Qorānic prescriptions, the personal statute occupies the first place after the '*'ibādāt*', or religious obligations, enumerated above. In Chapter V marriage will be discussed as a contract. The Muslim may marry a Scripturary. This authorization is refused to the Muslim woman, whose choice is restricted to co-religionists. The right of a husband to pronounce a divorce against his wife is almost unlimited. After the first and the second pronouncement, '*ṭalāq*', it is still lawful for him to retract, but not after the third '*ṭalāq*', unless the wife has accepted another husband and been divorced anew. The distribution of inheritance has been minutely regulated by the Qorān, in accordance with ancient Arab law, but revised in favour of the wife, for whom a portion is reserved. The '*sharī'a*' has been obliged to conform strictly to these stipulations.

OTHER PRESCRIPTIONS. The absolute prohibition of the '*ribā*' excludes not only *usury*, or usurious interest, but all trading in money, all combinations of fixed interest, all compensation for the loan or temporary transfer of capital. In face of this severity, Muslim jurists have been forced to invent the '*ḥīla*'. These expedients make it possible, by devious ways, to evade the interdiction, to obtain credit and to prevent capital from lying idle and unproductive. It is thus that the insurance companies and savings-banks forbidden by the '*sharī'a*' as a form of gambling are to be found conducted on similar lines to joint-stock companies. At the present time fifty per cent. interest is looked upon as legal in Arabia.

The *penal law*, derived principally from the Qorān, sanctions the '*qiṣāṣ*', the law of retaliation, or an eye for an eye. For certain offences the Qorān fixes the penalties, '*ḥudūd*': flogging for adultery and drunkenness, hand-cutting for theft, capital punishment for rebels and highway robbers. These penalties are called '*ḥudūd Allah*', the laws and justice of Allah. This fact forces the civil authorities in Islāmic territory to have regard for this archaic penal legislation and so retards its evolution. This evolution will be studied in Chapter V.

IV

THE 'SUNNA', OR THE TRADITION OF ISLĀM

THE SUNNA. The second doctrinal source of Islām after the Qorān is, as we have said, to be found within the *Sunna*, that is, the 'custom'. How are we to understand and define this 'custom'? The Qorān (**17**, 79; **33**, 62) calls the conduct of God in His providential ruling of the universe the '*Sunna* of Allah'. The *Sunna* which we shall consider here is specifically called the '*Sunna* of the Prophet'. It is the custom in which this 'noble pattern' (Qorān **33**, 21) is said to have enacted positive rules for the religious and moral life, such as spring from his examples and extra-Qorānic teaching, or such, at least, as were sanctioned by his tacit approbation (*taqrīr*).

ITS IMPORTANCE. As early as the first century A.H. the following aphorism was pronounced: 'The *Sunna* can dispense with the Qorān, but not the Qorān with the *Sunna*.' Proceeding to still further lengths, some Muslims assert that 'in controversial matters, the *Sunna* overrules the authority of the Qorān, but not *vice versa*'. As an example, they quote the penalty of stoning, inflicted in the beginning on adulterers, although the Qorān (**24**, 2) had stipulated for flagellation only. It is true that a statement is attributed to 'Omar that the verse about stoning had at first figured in the Qorān. This text (**5**, 42) orders that thieves shall have the hands severed. The *Sunna* excepts stealers of sheep and dates. According to the Qorān (**2**, 176) a testator must leave a portion of his property to his parents and kindred. This prescription has been partially abrogated by this dictum of the Prophet: 'The infidel does not inherit from the Muslim, nor the Muslim from the infidel.'

On the other hand, Shāfi'ī, Ibn Ḥanbal and other eminent authorities have not failed to protest against the hypothesis that the *Sunna* abrogates the Qorān. But all admit that the *Sunna* completes and explains it. And before the growing mass of sometimes contradictory *ḥadīth*, final agreement was reached by considering the Qorān and *Sunna* as two factors of outwardly equal importance, destined to fix the rules of the religious life. The Prophet never acted or spoke 'from mere impulse' (Qorān **53**, 3). When, therefore, he laid down the detail of the Islāmic *Sunna*, he must have been inspired from Above (the theorists of Islām speak here of *latent* inspiration), as he was for the promulgation of the Qorān. The privilege of '*iṣma*, or infallibility, which must be conceded to him in both cases, entails for the Faithful the obligation of submission. This is why the orthodox Muslims affect the title of '*Ahl as-sunna*', people of the *Sunna*, or *Sunnis*.

Complement of the Qorān. In his lifetime, the Prophet was there to solve difficulties. After his demise it was soon discovered that the dead letter of the Qorān was a very imperfect substitute for the living oracle. The written text revealed obscurities and also gaps. As regards the obscurities, the Prophet had tried to diminish their number by re-editing certain verses with a view to their elucidation (Qorān **2**, 100; **16**, 103). But overtaken by death, he had not time to re-touch and complete the rough dogmatic and disciplinary summary begun during the Mekkan period. Thus the Qorān ceaselessly enjoins the practice of prayer. But nowhere does it describe the modality nor fix the number of daily prayers. It assumes that these practical details have been regulated, and it has only been possible to regulate them from the Prophet's example and directions.

At Medina Muḥammad found himself suddenly faced with a new situation. He had hastily to organize his community. Forced by circumstances to legislate, he did so, sometimes with astonishing prolixity, and on questions of secondary importance, such as wills and inheritance. On the other hand, the Caliphate and the hierarchical organization of Islām are never touched upon. In the matter of religious legislation properly so-called, and of the devotional life, the Medina *Sūras* have foreseen and solved only an insignificant number of problems. Again, these all-too-rare solutions envisage only a small community—the patriarchal society of Arabia. They have no thought for the countries of the old civilizations into which the new religion was to be rapidly carried by conquest, or for conflicts which could not fail to arise between the Qorānic prescriptions and the legislation of these countries on questions of landed property, commercial law, etc.

Distracted by the incidents of his domestic life, worried by the demands of his new functions at Medina, and finally by wars, the Prophet had to advance cautiously in his attempts at legal regulation. We may recall the phases which prepared the way for the definite prohibition of wine. Naturally a temporizer, he seems to have been afraid of using his authority, of discrediting beforehand by untimely action the dangerous expedient of '*naskh*', or *abrogation*. His intervention was provoked much more by circumstances than by the importance of any question. Thus, in cases where there was no settled usage, where nothing had been stipulated in the Qorānic text, reference was naturally made to the *Sunna*, to the custom of the Prophet. An example or decision of the Master was sought, excepting in those cases where the '*Khaṣā'iṣ*' of the Prophet, his strictly personal privileges, had placed him, as, for example, in the matter of polygamy, above the common law. Sometimes even a pious fiction did not hesitate to predicate what he would have decided in face of new situations.

SUNNA OF THE 'COMPANIONS'. Thousands of believers had obtained the signal favour of visiting and consulting the Prophet. This privilege gained for them the coveted title of '*Ṣaḥābī*', or Companions. In default of examples from the Prophet, posterity seeks to learn the attitude, conduct and sayings of these witnesses. The agreement of the 'Companions', duly attested, is considered infallible, since the Qorān (**48**, 18) has proclaimed them the object of 'the Divine pleasure'. Tradition never questions that the Master trained them to serve after him as guides to the Islāmic community, to play the part of religious instructors and educators. It assumes that, fully conscious of this delicate mission, they spent their time in observing, in photographing, as it were, 'the splendid pattern'; afterwards diligently noting down the smallest results of their observation in order to transmit them to posterity. To the '*Ṣaḥābī*' are sometimes added their descendants or immediate successors, hence called '*tābi'ī*', or followers. It is assumed that the first care of these followers was to collect the impressions of the 'Companions' and their recollections of the heroic age.

What this early generation had professed in matters of belief helped to fix precisely the rule of faith. What they had practised became in the eyes of their successors the model of a religious life. Beliefs and practices were called upon to supplement the deficiencies and solve the enigmas of the Qorānic text. It was established that they provided its living and authorized commentary. According to this historic conception, then, it was especially at Medina that the Prophet passed the most decisive years of his career in the midst of a *nubes testium,* the multitude of watching 'Companions'.

This is why Medina, the capital of Muḥammad and the first caliphs, was to become '*dār as-Sunna*', the home and centre of the *Sunna.* The first forty years were destined to rank as the golden age of Islām. In their turn, 'the followers of the followers', that is, the Muslims of the first century, would strive to transmit, first orally, and then in written collections, all that they knew or imagined that they knew about the words, the decisions, the outlook and even the silences of the Prophet. The authentic *Sunna* of the Prophet was nothing more than the customs practised in his presence by the whole body of the 'Companions', and carefully recorded by their successors. Henceforward it was to obtain the force of law, ranking with the Qorān and the 'custom of the Prophet'.

THE ḤADĪTH. This mass of meticulous notes and observations, collected with more zeal than discretion in the first century, was to give birth in the following century to a specific discipline, that of the *ḥadīth,* which was destined to have a prodigious development. The *ḥadīth,* literally narrative, is an act or saying attributed to the Prophet or to his 'Companions' by which it is sought to justify and confirm the *Sunna.* Thus the latter is anterior in point of time to the *ḥadīth.* Recourse must also be had to the *ḥadīth* in order to create a non-existent *Sunna* or to settle a current of ideas. Examples will be quoted below. But in order to avoid the suspicion of innovation, this expedient is described as ' resuscitating or reviving the *Sunna* '.

Each *ḥadīth* consists essentially of two parts, the *isnād* and the *matn*. The *matn* represents the basis, the actual text of the *ḥadīth*, which it most scrupulously reproduced. The *isnād* unwinds the chain of authorities which precede and introduce the *matn*, the uninterrupted succession of guarantors through whose channel the *ḥadīth* reaches the last transmitter or *muḥaddith*. Here is an example : ' A has told us (*ḥaddatha*) according to B, and the latter according to C, who had it from D, etc., that which follows.' Then comes the ' *matn* ' of the *ḥadīth*.

The science dealing with these *ḥadīth*, the collected volumes of which form an enormous library, likewise bears the name of *ḥadīth*. This science stoops to the most picturesque and realistic details. For the instruction of believers the *ḥadīth* tells us how Muḥammad performed his prayers and ablutions, how he ate, fasted, dressed and behaved in the home and with his contemporaries. From it we learn his favourite dishes, his wardrobe and the arrangement of his rooms. Here the Master is supposed to reply in advance to those difficulties of dogma, discipline and politics, which were to arise later. He enumerates by name the towns and countries whose conquest was reserved for the arms of Islām. He condemns the heretics of the future, the Khārijites, the anti-determinists, etc. He proscribes dangerous doctrines. And by all these clear statements he determines the *Sunna* and completes the summary prescriptions of the Qorān. Explanatory and *interpretative* in form, the *ḥadīth* frequently legislates, but always while sheltering behind the person of the Prophet, whose teaching it is supposed to expound. In this imposing mass of information, hastily collected, and recalling in its meticulous detail the method of the Talmud from which its compilers were not slow to borrow extensively, not every part could claim the same degree of authenticity. On more than one point, first the zeal and then the prejudice of the collectors had overstepped the mark.

The parties which rose up in the midst of primitive Islām soon sought to utilize the method of the *ḥadīth* to further their political aims. Omayyads, 'Abbāsids and 'Alids are to be seen fighting and disputing, calling to their aid multitudes of *ḥadīth*. They are imitated by the dissident sects. Just as they have their heterodox *tafsīr*, so do they claim to possess their individual *Sunna*, which can also be traced back to the Prophet. As regards their '*khabar*' (plural *akhbār*), a synonym which they prefer to *ḥadīth*, the Shī'as admit into the *isnād* only the names of the 'Alids, the *imāms* and their partisans. Orthodox and dissidents vie with one another in zeal. Each party, each sect, each school strives to possess the traditions which are most favourable to its claims or to its doctrines. The *ḥadīth* is even made to subserve personal grudges. To revenge himself on a schoolmaster who has chastised his child, a *muḥaddith* will invent traditions depreciating pedagogues. Others are invented against the police.

Some even took long journeys, became globe-trotters, '*raḥḥāl jawwāl*', in search of unedited *ḥadīth*; for the transmission must be oral. 'Go, even into China, to seek knowledge' (of the *ḥadīth*); thus enjoins a maxim attributed to the Prophet which Suyūṭī declares apocryphal. Some *muḥaddith* boasted of knowing by heart a hundred thousand *ḥadīth*, or even a million, others of having sacrificed a fortune of seven hundred thousand dirhams in acquiring them. Of variations alone, '*qirā'āt*', of the Qorān, a traditionalist has collected ten thousand. There are stories of masters of the *ḥadīth* in whose hands one might 'count ten thousand inkstands used to record their readings'.[1]

Soon the tenacious memory of the 'Companions' and the 'followers' could no longer suffice to feed this passion or enrich the literature of the *ḥadīth*. Every source was tapped, secular history and Biblical religions were ransacked. The '*qāṣṣ*', popular preachers, distinguished themselves in this pious sport. It is amongst such people that Muḥammad is credited with the aphorism: 'If you meet with a lofty utterance, do not hesitate to attribute it to me. I must have said it.' It is, therefore, not surprising to find among the collections of *ḥadīth* Biblical plagiarisms and quotations from the Gospels, including the Lord's Prayer, all hardly disguised. We may mention the parable of the workmen hired at the eleventh hour, applied to Muslims, and the dictum: 'Let not thy left hand know what thy right hand doeth.'

CRITICISM. These excesses were bound to provoke reaction. This is plainly visible from the third century A.H., i.e. the ninth century A.D., a period of stabilization for Muslim orthodoxy. Under pressure of *ijmā'*, the need for unity and systematic regulation began to be felt. There was a sort of gathering up of doctrines, a first classification. This was the movement destined to give birth to the collection of the 'Six Books' and the constitution of the four canonical rites. The unlimited liberty allowed in the search for *ḥadīth*, and

[1] Dhahabī, *Tazkirat al-ḥuffāẓ*, I, 355; II, 18, 110, 137. A traditionist reduced to the figure of 500,000 a collection of 1,500,000 *ḥadīth*; *Ibid.*, II, 125. Out of 500,000 *ḥadīth*, the celebrated Abū Dāūd (see later, p. 78) retains no more than 4,800 in his *Sunan*; *Ibid.*, II, 170.

the unreflecting enthusiasm which directed it, threatened to compromise the *Sunna*. To reduce it to order, the idea was conceived of creating 'the science (*'ilm*) of the *ḥadīth*', sometimes simply called 'the science', *'ilm*. It was to devote itself to examining the credibility and authenticity of the traditions, and to succeed in unmasking the '*Mauḍū'āt*', the apocrypha, a field of criticism in which later on an Ibn al-Jauzī (599 A.H.) was to distinguish himself.

This method is prudent and innocuous to a degree. far removed from that suggested to the mind by the term criticism. It avoids finding fault with the substance of the traditions, namely, the text of the *matn*. One would need to be a Mu'tazilite to denounce in them certain assertions of a character too strongly anthropomorphic. No question of internal criticism can therefore arise. The 'science of the *ḥadīth*' only employs external criteria. It shuts its eyes to the anachronisms and impossibilities, logical or historical, of the *matn*. When the *isnād* is formally unassailable, the *ḥadīth* itself must be declared '*ṣaḥīḥ*', *sound*. On the other hand the *isnād* is submitted to the most meticulous investigation. Is it not the 'foot' upon which tradition rests, 'the bond of the *hadīth*' which enables the parts of the *matn* to hold together?

But the *isnād* is composed exclusively of proper names. It is, then, important to prove the historical reality of these names; next, to become acquainted with the past of the '*rijāl*', men or attestors, quoted in the *isnād*. This operation is called in technical language '*ma'rifat ar-rijāl*'—the 'knowledge of the men'. And since everything depends on the consideration which these witnesses merit, it is necessary to fix, to apportion exactly their intellectual and moral value, another operation entitled '*jarḥ wa ta'dīl*'—*lesion and justification*.

These advance works rendered possible the construction of a complete ladder of qualificatives indicating the extent to which the attestors may be trusted. These qualificatives may only be conceded after mature consideration, if the witness is morally and intellectually above suspicion; if he neither professes nor propagates heterodox or dangerous opinions; if he is generally reputed truthful, and capable of giving evidence, and is entitled to do so in the courts of law. Should every point of the examination be in his favour he is declared '*thiqa*', worthy of confidence; '*mutqin*', accurate; '*'adl*', truthful, etc. Less laudatory are the following qualificatives: '*la bā's bihi*', nothing to be objected against him, or else 'not a liar', etc. In a lower category are the witnesses called 'fluent in the *ḥadīth*'; lower still are the *feeble*, '*ḍa'īf*'. Finally, there are the 'liars' and those 'whose *ḥadīth* is rejected'.

Even this inquisition did not appear adequate. The *isnād* postulates an uninterrupted and oral transmission. In Islām oral testimony alone is recognized. Necessity, however, sometimes forces the acceptance of a written transmission, and one may even go so far as to recognize the *ijāza*. This is the 'licence' issued by a master to transcribe and transmit his collected *ḥadīth*. These are concessions made after the first three centuries. As regards the previous period it remains to be proved that breaks in continuity or lapses of time have not slipped in between the links of the *isnād*, that the attestors met or might have met, or at any rate that they were contemporaries. This is an exceedingly difficult matter to check, and often in the end nothing more than an approximate statement can be made. It must be added that unscrupulous forgers have sought to frustrate criticism, to fill up the gaps in the *isnād*, by introducing names at hazard, or, as they were designated, *unknown persons*, '*majhūl*'. The presence of these intruders is sufficient to render the *ḥadīth* suspect.

It is certain that all these precautions taken together did at least enable Muslim criticism to weed out thousands of apocryphal traditions and draw attention to what it called 'the disorders of the *ḥadīth*'. The great Bukhārī had recourse to it, with the result that he retained in his collection not more than about ten thousand traditions out of the three hundred thousand which he had at first gathered up. Of this total, he declared two hundred thousand to be entirely apocryphal (Dhahabī, II, 135). But when all is said this unilateral criticism confines itself to settling the degree of credibility of the attestors and the possibility of their meeting. Beyond this, it leaves in suspense the very essence of the debate, namely, the judgment to be passed on the value of the tradition, that is to say, the *matn*. This method ended by establishing absolutely unassailable chains of the *isnād* in conformity with the rules laid down by 'the knowledge of the men'. The forgers hastened to attach these genuine *isnād* to apocryphal *ḥadīth*, a proceeding of which the works dedicated to the *Mauḍū'āt* complain unceasingly.

Recourse to internal criticism would have cut short this abuse. We may quote as an example 'Allah's cock the crowing of which in Paradise gives the signal to the cocks on earth to announce the hour of prayer'. The authors who denounce the apocryphal character of this tradition are usually satisfied with pointing out the weaknesses of its *isnād* and the slight worth of the attestors who are mentioned in it. We may likewise recall the Shī'a legend of the miracle of Joshua, repeated by Muḥammad on behalf of 'Alī. While recognizing the flaws in the *isnād*, Suyūṭī, in the end, seeks to save the *ḥadīth* by this quotation from Shāfi'ī:

'Muḥammad has performed miracles the same as those of the prophets of old and even greater.'

PRINCIPAL COLLECTIONS. The oldest date from our ninth century. This period saw the beginning of a systematic classification of the material which was to constitute the collections of *ḥadīth*. The theory and technology of the *ḥadīth* date from the following century. That also was the time when the auxiliary disciplines which came to be attached to them appeared: biographies and 'classes' of the attestors, philological exegesis of the *gharīb*, rare words met with in the *ḥadīth*, etc. All these collections have been drawn up in accordance with the principles of a purely formal criticism. They are indistinguishable from one another except in their varying degrees of strictness, in the composition of the *isnād*. Fundamentally, the *matn* remains manifestly unchanged, the same verses and narratives reappearing, sometimes preceded by new *isnād* and embellished by variants which are always picturesque and often suggestive. The principal difference lies in the grouping of the traditions adopted by the authors of the '*Musnad*', or of the '*Muṣannaf*'.

THE MUSNAD have arranged them in accordance with the *isnād*; whence their name of *Musnad*. There the *ḥadīth* is placed under the name of the attestor last quoted in the chain of the *isnād*. It is the *personal* order. Thus we find arranged under the name of 'Ayesha or Fāṭima all the narratives whose transmission can finally be traced back to the widow or the daughter of the Prophet; or again, under the heading of Abū Horaira, the hundreds of *ḥadīth* which we owe to this loquacious Companion. One of the oldest and the typical *Musnad* is the compilation in six quarto volumes, the work of the celebrated Aḥmad ibn Ḥanbal. This collection of 2,885 pages of closely-written text comprises about 30,000 *ḥadīth* traceable to 700 'Companions'.

THE MUṢANNAF or *Digest* adopt a less artificial method and display an anxiety to improve the arrangement. Abandoning the strictly personal principle which presided over the composition of the *Musnad*, the *Muṣannaf* arrange all the traditions according to subject-matter, e.g. prayer, pilgrimage, holy war, etc., without troubling to discover if they date back to Abū Bakr, to 'Omar or to others. This is the arrangement adopted by the disciple of Ibn Ḥanbal, namely, Bukhārī (†870), whose prestige was destined to make it the accepted method.

THE 'SIX BOOKS'. The compilation of *ḥadīth*, collected by Bukhārī, is called '*al-Jāmi'aṣ-Ṣaḥīḥ*', the *Authentic Collection*. The author has only included those traditions which a scrutiny of the *isnād* has permitted him to regard as perfectly 'sound', that is to say, non-suspect. He no more than others ever dreams of applying the rules of internal criticism to the *matn* before giving it entry to the pages of his '*Ṣaḥīḥ*'. The headings (*tarjuma*) of the paragraphs discreetly suggest how to use the narratives, often, too, the doctrinal opinion which they may serve to support. Bukhārī sometimes adds a very concise commentary to the *ḥadīth*. This annotation is not found in the collection of Muslim (†874), a contemporary of Bukhārī, which bears the same title and is compiled on the same method.

As regards the *ḥadīth*, Muslim and Bukhārī are regarded as classical authors; they are the 'two Sheikhs' *par excellence*. No better title could be found to indicate the high esteem in which their compilations, which are commonly called the 'two *Ṣaḥīḥ*', are held. Thus it would be very ill-advised to contest the traditions collected by them and the worth of the attestors named in their *isnād*. As to the latter, this mention is equivalent to the hall-mark of indisputable morality. *Magister dixit.* Both men appear to have pursued a practical aim. They divided their work into paragraphs (*abwāb*), as though they had had in mind the '*faqīh*', canonists, who would later come to them for *ḥadīth* to support their legal conclusions. It sometimes happens that they reproduce textually, without any variation, the same *matn*, or narrative, but preceded by a new *isnād*. It is, indeed, agreed that a tradition gains in authenticity if it derives from several parallel and supposedly independent sources or ways, '*ṭarīq*', pl. '*ṭuruq*'.

After Bukhārī and Muslim four great collections of traditions are known. They are commonly called '*Sunan*', or collections of *Sunna*, that is, of *ḥadīth* coming to the support of the *Sunna*. In a lesser degree they too are accepted as traditional authorities. With the two first-mentioned they form the collection of the 'Six Books'. They are the collections of Abū Dāūd (†888), Tirmidhī (†892), Nasā'ī (†915) and of Ibn Māja (†886) to which are sometimes added the 'Sunan' of Dārimī (†869). Tirmidhī was at once the disciple of Ibn Ḥanbal, Bukhārī and Abū Dāūd. While preserving the scheme of the 'two *Ṣaḥīḥ*', the 'four *Sunan*' are distinguished from them by a greater zeal in compiling the *ḥadīth* which serve to elucidate the practice of the *Sunna* and of the canonical law. They put aside the narratives whose interest is more expressly doctrinal or merely historical like the details of the Prophet's *Sīra*, which the 'two great *Sheikhs*' were careful to preserve. On the other hand, the 'four *Sunan*' are more accommodating about the value of the *isnād*, without becoming more exacting as to the substance of the *matn*. Thus they do not hesitate, Ibn Māja especially, to admit doubtful attestors whenever their insufficiency or improbity is not established by general agreement. Nasā'i goes into the very smallest details of religious practice. Tirmidhī often points out the canonical rite for which the *ḥadīth* that he reproduces may serve.

The inclusion of the '*Sunan*' of Ibn Māja among the 'Six Books', or the 'Six Divans', as they are also called, encountered opposition in the beginning. He was reproached for his 'weakness' in the *isnād*. Agreement on this point was not reached until the seventh century A.H. But in this collection of the *Six*, in which the *Musnad* of Ibn Ḥanbal, likewise highly esteemed, has not been able to gain admission, the believers unhesitatingly declare their preference for the 'two *Ṣaḥīḥ*', especially for that of Bukhārī. His collection has become the object of exceptional veneration. It is used in taking an oath, an honour generally reserved for the Qorān. In public calamities, such as plague, drought, etc., it is carried in solemn procession. A number of reciters divide up the sections of the *Ṣaḥīḥ* so as to give a complete public reading of them in one day, and this collection is supposed to preserve from shipwreck and fire. The author is buried near Samarqand, where his tomb has become the object of a pilgrimage.

The success of the 'Six Books' is explained by the fact that they came at the right time, at the moment when Qorānic religion was about to take definite shape, to become traditional Islām; on the eve of the day when 'the door of *ijtihād*, or independent research, was to be closed'. The method adopted by the compilers, the classification of matter in books, chapters and paragraphs, under clear rubrics, answered to the needs of the teaching and of the doctrinal currents which appeared in the bosom of the 'four canonical schools'. Their concern for orthodoxy could not but be generally appreciated—they excluded the strictly Shī'a *ḥadīth*, even Nasā'ī, personally favourable to

'Alī. Not less esteemed was the moderation of their opinions. It was this liberalism which made them retain in their collections the *ḥadīth* running counter to the doctrines which they themselves preferred. They record impartially the traditions for and against, or, to use the accepted terms, the *abrogated* (*mansūkh*) and the *abrogating* (*nāsikh*) *ḥadīth*. For this theory of abrogation is applied to the *Sunna* as well as to the Qorān, where it surprises us more. Thus the Prophet is said to have refused at first to pray over the coffins of Muslims who had died insolvent. But other *ḥadīth* testify on his part to the contrary practice, which has been adopted by the *Sunna*. The Prophet at first forbade a husband to beat his wife ; then he revoked this prohibition on condition that the correction be inflicted for a just reason and free from brutality.

After the success of the ' Six Books ', every tradition desirous of securing public favour had to conform to the method observed by Bukhārī, Muslim and their associates, especially by the two first-named. With the end of the fourth century A.H. the era of commentaries, manuals and compendiums opens in the ' science of the *ḥadīth* '. The fourth century A.H. sees the appearance of a few new compilations, such as that of Dārquṭnī (385 A.H.). The subject-matter remains the same and the method also. The terminology and predicates conceded to the attestors of the *isnād* are more precisely stated than before.

Among the summaries of manuals of the fifth century A.H., we should note that of Baghawī (†1117 or 1122), ' *Maṣābīḥ as-sunna* ', ' Torches of the *Sunna* '. The author, one of those who obtained the honorific title of ' reviver of the *Sunna* ', summarized and arranged the traditions under three heads, corresponding to their degree of credibility. First, the ' *Ṣaḥiḥ* ', *sound*, all borrowed from the classical ' two *Ṣaḥiḥ* '.

Next the *fair* ('*ḥasan*') traditions, mainly compiled from the 'four *Sunan*'. The last place is reserved for unusual or rare (*gharīb*) *ḥadīths*. These are considered to be the most weakly attested of any, because they have been transmitted by only one '*ṭarīq*', in other words, by a single chain of *isnād*. These three qualificatives, with the classifications which they entail, sum up in a fairly accurate manner the whole work of Muslim criticism on the material of the *ḥadīth*. The activity displayed by this criticism during a thousand years brings us back, in the last resort, to the corpus of the 'Six Books'.

Lastly, we must refer to a special class, that of the *ḥadīth* called '*qudsī*', *sacred*, or '*ilāhī*', *divine*. They are supposed to preserve the text of aphorisms and sayings attributed directly to Allah. On these grounds they enjoy a quite special consideration. While clearly distinguishing them from the other *ḥadīth*, called '*nabawī*', or *prophetic*, and collected by Bukhārī, his emulators and successors, tradition has not considered itself authorized, as one would have had a right to expect, to incorporate them in the text of the Qorān. Anyone contesting their authenticity would not thereby incur the stigma of infidelity. The collections which include them may be touched without the previous performance of ablutions which is required in the case of the Qorān, but they may not be used in ritual prayer, a privilege reserved for the Qorānic verses.

V

JURISPRUDENCE AND THE LAW OF ISLĀM

ORIGIN. The expansion of Islām beyond the borders of Arabia, the foundation and organization of the Caliphate brought about the formulation of the law, *fiqh*, literally 'wisdom', the (*juris*) *prudentia* of the Romans. As with the latter, but in a much narrower sense, the *fiqh* is *rerum divinarum atque humanarum notitia*, the knowledge and definition of institutions and laws both divine and human. Islām is essentially a legal religion; nothing is left to the believer's free will or initiative. Thus the *fiqh* embraces all the obligations that the Qorānic Law (*Sharī'a* or *Shar'*) imposes on the Muslim in his triple capacity of believer, of man and of citizen of a theocracy. The Qorān has played the part of a 'discourse on universal history'. It has taught him the mystery of the religious destinies of human societies (*v.* p. 55).

Now the *Sharī'a*, setting up as the interpreter of revelation, lays down for him the family code, penal and public law, his relations with non-Muslims; it regulates, in short, his religious, political and social life, reserving to itself the right to superintend its multiple manifestations and to direct its complicated rhythm.

Thus the '*faqīh*', the '*ālim* (plur. '*ulamā*, whence our 'ulema) or scholars, engaged in this study are not so much professional jurisconsults as theologians and moralists. On more than one point the *fiqh* has come under the influence of foreign legislations, amongst others that of the Romano-Byzantine Law, which was in force in Syria, when the Muslims settled there. The fiction of the *ḥadīth* allows all material borrowed from foreign sources to be attributed to the Prophet and to the *Great Companions*, and this borrowed material was, moreover, so completely assimilated that Islāmic jurisprudence produces an impression of unity and even of originality.

THE 'ROOTS' OF 'FIQH'. In theory the *fiqh* is as a whole and in all its parts a revealed law. To this conception it owes its rigid and immutable character. It draws its life from the two *roots*, 'usūl', of revelation, the Qorān and the *Sunna*.

Practice has nevertheless rendered inevitable the widening of this theoretical concept.

Just as the *Sunna* had come to complete and explain the Qorān, so experience compelled Muslims to recognize that the *fiqh* could not dispense with the operations of logic. It was admitted that it had become lawful to settle new cases by applying to them the rules laid down to meet analogous circumstances. It is thus that '*qiyās*' or *analogy* became a new *root* of the law. A fourth is called '*ijmā'*', or *universal consent*. This will be dealt with later.

Finally, in the absence of any '*naṣṣ*' or text in the Qorān or the *Sunna*, of any antecedent recognized by *ijmā'*, the creators of the *fiqh* were obliged to have recourse to the light of '*ra'y*', or liberty of opinion. But it was tacitly understood that such recourse would be exceptional and would not render '*ra'y*' worthy to be considered as a fifth *root*.

EARLY SCHOOLS. It is the predominance, more or less apparent, of traditional or speculative elements in the *fiqh*, the real or fictitious importance accorded to each one of the ' four roots ',—which explain the birth of the juridical schools '*Madhhab*', *rite,* or guidance (not *sect,* as the word is sometimes translated). In the beginning each man sought his own path and there reigned a rich variety of opinions. Those who were too lightly suspected of attachment to '*ra'y*', to the detriment of the Qorān and the *Sunna,* had at first to struggle for a place. It was not so much a question of principles as of winning over the multitude and securing the favour of authority, the dispenser of posts in the magistracy. One after the other we see the disappearance of these early schools, those of the Syrian Auzā'ī (774) and the celebrated historian and exegetist, Ṭabarī (*v.* p. 44). Such will also be the fate of the Zāhirites, a school founded by Dāūd ibn 'Alī (883) which long numbered adherents in Spain and in the Maghrib. They are called Ẓāhirites because among the ' roots ' of the *fiqh* they recognize only the Qorān and the *Sunna,* which they interpret according to the '*Ẓāhir*', i.e. the *apparent* and servilely literal sense. They reject with the utmost energy all speculative elements, but have recourse to them by devious routes. The Qorān (**17**, 24) forbids children to insult their parents, whence all the schools conclude that they are forbidden to strike them. According to the Ẓāhirites, the question does not arise ; it is '*mafhūm*', implied.

ORTHODOX SCHOOLS. From the seventh century A.H. onwards the struggles subsided and it was agreed to recognize four schools, all considered equally orthodox. They owed their regional diffusion to somewhat secondary circumstances ; less to the value of their teaching than to the prestige of their founder ; next, to the influence exercised by the most eminent of their disciples—such as the Qāḍi Abū Yūsuf amongst the Ḥanifites, and finally, to the grace and intervention of the sovereign who befriended them in their immediate neighbourhood. The geographer Maqdisī observes very justly that the Syrian school of Auzā'ī, which formerly spread as far as Andalusia, owed its gradual disappearance to its geographical repartition outside the routes followed by the pilgrims to Mekka.

The school of the Imām Shāfi'ī (819) predominated at first under the 'Abbāsids, to whom the founder was related, up to the time when the influence of Abū Yūsuf, a disciple of Abū Ḥanīfa, disputed its pre-eminence in Irāq. From Irāq the Shāfi'ītes spread along the Persian Gulf, into southern Arabia, eastern Africa, the Indian Archipelago ; Palestine, the Ḥejāz and Lower Egypt. Cairo possesses the tomb of the founder as well as the celebrated mosque Al-Azhar, whence Shāfi'īte teaching is disseminated.

The school of the Imām Mālik Ibn Anas (795) was founded at Medina, the cradle of primitive tradition, '*dār as-Sunna*' (*v.* p. 69). It therefore claimed to have remained the repository of pure orthodoxy, and in its decisions, to go back to the *Sunna*, followed by the Prophet and his first Companions. Formerly predominant in Andalusia where it supplanted the Auzā'ites, it prevails at the present time in the Maghrib, in western Africa, in the Sudan, in the whole of northern Africa with the exception of Lower Egypt, and lastly, in the Arab districts bordering on the Persian Gulf. The Turkish territories, those detached from the old Ottoman Empire, where only the Ḥanifite rite was recognized as official, those of Central Asia and the continent of India, followed the school of Imām Abū Hanīfa (767). Almost half of Islām in the world to-day professes the Ḥanifite *fiqh*. The Shāfi'īte school comes next in number of adherents.

That of the Imām Aḥmad ibn Ḥanbal (855), author of the Musnad or collection of traditions (*v.* p. 76), has almost disappeared. It was only from the sixth century A.H. onwards that after struggles, sometimes sanguinary, the Ḥanbalites succeeded in gaining recognition as a juridical school. Prior to this they had only been regarded as traditionists and it does not appear that their founder had any other aspiration. This school, very combative in tendency, represented the extreme right of orthodox intransigence. It adheres to the letter of the *ḥadīth* and the Qorān after the manner of the Ẓāhirites, but with a less exaggerated determination. Among the four schools none manifests a greater hostility towards *Ṣūfism*. It minimizes the extension of *ijmā'* and *qiyās* and is violently opposed to the dogma of Ash'arī (p. 57), which represents a compromise between the theories of the Ḥanbalites and Mu'tazilites. This school counted numerous adherents in Syria and Mesopotamia, where the Seljūks worked actively to spread the Ḥanifite *fiqh*. Ibn Taimiyya and his disciples brought about, as it were, a revival in Syria in the fourteenth century.

The influence of the Ottomans, continuing the reaction inaugurated by the Seljūks, dealt it a serious blow, from which the school of Abū Ḥanīfa benefited. This latter, born in the busy cosmopolitan atmosphere of Irāq, showed itself more open to casuistry, and therefore to speculative methods, than its rivals. In the middle of the eighteenth century the Wahhābi reform again brought Ibn Ḥanbal's system into vigorous existence in the centre of Arabia and exaggerated its hostility to every innovation.

METHODS. The school of Abū Ḥanīfa has been credited with understanding better than its rivals the need for reserving an adequate place for '*ra'y*', liberty of opinion, and also reproached with lessening thereby the rôle of the *Sunna*. Couched in these terms, praise and blame are equally unmerited. It is certain that the Irāqian school early encountered the opposition of the school of Medina, whose head Mālik conceived it his duty to vindicate the imprescriptible rights of the prophetic *Sunna*. The Ḥanbalites showed themselves even more implacable. They only allowed '*ra'y*' in desperate cases, in the absence of any Qorānic stipulation or traditional antecedent, and were thus obliged to welcome the most vulnerable *ḥadīth*. When one peruses the writings of their most representative polemicists, Ibn Jauzī (†1200) and Ibn Taimiyya, one thinks involuntarily of the scribes in the Gospel, for like these, they see salvation only in servile adherence to 'the tradition of the Ancients'.

The school of Shāfi'ī professed to intervene, to reconcile these disagreements and find the golden mean between the Ḥanīfites and their adversaries. They did at least succeed in determining with greater exactitude than before the respective value of the 'four roots' in fixing precisely the rôle accruing to '*qiyās*', or analogy, and, in this way, preventing possible abuse of logical deduction. Apart from these reservations, the tendencies of these schools and their methods present divergences more apparent than real. None of them can dispense with reason. The points on which they split frequently come down to differing classifications and decisions on minor matters, any of which can be admitted with a clear conscience.

Their agreement duly declared establishes general law or *ijmā'*. Their divergences are binding only on the followers of the rite. Every Muslim must belong to one of the four orthodox schools and conduct himself in accordance with the *fiqh* of that school. But he is not tied to it for life; he is permitted to pass from one to another. In the bosom of the same family, father and son may belong to different schools, just as in a special case jurists have the right to appeal to the decisions of a school other than their own. In the same way, the Christian theologian may range himself *ad libitum* on the side of Thomists, Molinists, Augustinians, Scotists, Probabilists or Equi-probabilists.

The better to understand the tendencies of the four schools let us take a concrete question very much discussed in recent times, especially since the bold innovations of the Kemalists: Is it licit to translate the Qorān? All the schools are in agreement on the ritual and liturgical use of the Qorān, and Shāfi'ī teaches that the formulæ of the *ṣalāt* must be recited in Arabic,—nothing less will do. 'Every believer will, then, be doing a meritorious work in perfecting himself in that tongue, the vehicle of the last prophetic revelation.'

Abū Ḥanīfa, himself of Iranian origin, allows, however, an exception in favour of the foreigner who is incapable of pronouncing the formulæ of prayer in Arabic. But is it lawful to teach the Qorān to non-Muslims—a question entailing the translation of the sacred text? Abū Ḥanīfa sees no difficulty in it. He relies on the *ḥadīth* and this time finds himself in apparent agreement with the doctrine of the Ḥanbalite school. Shāfi'ī sets forth the *pros* and *cons*. Mālik alone is resolutely hostile. His attitude is no less uncompromising when the question of a complete translation of the Qorān arises. As before, Shāfi'ī evinces hesitation and does not take a clear decision. Ḥanīfites and Ḥanbalites approve of an interlinear version, such as exists in Persian, Urdu, Malay, etc., or one in which the Qorānic text in Arabic faces the translation.

DIFFERENCES. There would appear to be no settled agreement on the strict obligation of circumcision. Certain collections of the *fiqh* refrain from mentioning it or only mention it in passing, and allow this practice, which some have insisted on regarding as the symbol of initiation into Islām, to be postponed until the age of fifteen.

Let us recall the discussions relating to the modalities in use in the performance of devotions. Which formulæ should be pronounced in a loud or in a low voice (*dhikr khafī*)? The Shāfi'ītes, in opposition to the Ḥanīfites, favour manifest recitation spoken aloud, '*dhikr-jahrī*'. Ought the arms to hang down during prayer? How high should they be raised when uttering the *takbīr*, '*Allah Akbar*', God is Great? What should be the position of the hands during prayer, above or below the navel? Does prayer remain valid if a woman takes her place by the side of a man or in the midst of the faithful? Here Abū Ḥanīfa takes an anti-feminist decision. With regard to '*zakāt al-fiṭr*', alms to be distributed at the end of Ramaḍan, the Shāfi'ītes consider it as '*farḍ*', a rigorous duty, the Ḥanīfites as '*wājib*', less strictly obligatory, and the Mālikites as '*sunna*', custom.

What becomes of prisoners taken in the Holy War? Abū Ḥanīfa condemns them to death or slavery. Shāfi'ī, however, allows them to be liberated on payment of ransom, or even without. On the other hand, Abū Ḥanīfa allows marriage with a Scripturary woman; an authorization contested by Shāfi'ī, on the ground that the Scripturaries, having 'altered the text of the Bible', must have lost the right to be treated as Scripturaries. Among the four schools, that of the Ḥanbalites shows itself, all things considered, the least tolerant towards non-Muslims.

How and when should fasts, omitted during Ramaḍan, be compensated? Ought the repentant renegade to make up the prayers and fasts that he has missed during his apostasy? Shāfi'ī and Abū Ḥanīfa, in opposition to the other schools, refuse to be entangled in such complicated calculations. Shall a foundling be considered a Muslim? Yes, reply all the heads of the schools, apart from Abū Ḥanīfa, who replies in the negative, if the discovery is made in a place inhabited by non-Muslims. According to the same authority a Muslim heretic, before being condemned, must be invited to repent (*istitāba*). This procedure is not required amongst the Mālikites. Mālik and Shāfi'ī condemn the apostate to death without regard to sex. In the case of a woman, Abū Ḥanīfa contents himself with solitary confinement. According to Mālik, blood money for a murdered tributary amounts to the half of the sum to be paid for a Muslim; according to Shāfi'ī to a third only. Abū Ḥanīfa, much more humane, disallows these distinctions, and exacts payment of the full price. In Arabia the heathen have only a choice between Islām and death. As to the other heathen, the schools are divided: may they be allowed to pay tribute, to contract marriages with Muslims? etc.

Failures in respect for the Prophet are punishable. In the case of a Scripturary, Abū Ḥanīfa is fairly lenient; the other schools demand severe punishments, and even death. Abū Ḥanīfa permits the execution of a Muslim who has murdered a tributary, but this is completely rejected by all the other schools. According to Mālik and Abū Ḥanīfa, the borrower of an article may lend it to others without asking the owner; but permission is indispensable in the opinion of Shāfi'ī. With regard to the legal duration of gestation, Mālik, who of the four *Imāms* held the most extreme views on this question, allowed it to last as long as four years, and according to this system, a child born three years after its father's death can claim its inheritance in law! On the subject of lawful or unlawful food, on the use, for example, of horseflesh, the schools are divided; Mālik alone authorizes the flesh of beasts of prey.

Casuistry. These and other questions have given rise to a rich literature in which the *'ulemā* give full scope to their subtlety. It is exercised on fictitious or imaginary cases with the greatest seriousness. What right can an ancestor in the fifth degree establish over the inheritance of a descendant in the same degree, deceased without issue? Do marriages with the *jinn* involve consequences affecting the law of succession? By what *ḥiyal* can one get out of difficulties, circumvent a legal obligation, a sacred oath, a troublesome stipulation of the '*Sharī'a*'? It is a complete science in which the school of Abū Ḥanīfa has displayed the inexhaustible fecundity of its inventive genius. These artifices, '*ḥiyal*', form a special branch of the practical *fiqh*, held in much honour by the Irāqi school, and special treatises have been devoted to it, even among the Shāfi'ītes who at first declared themselves hostile. These collections of quibbles, subterfuges and evasions that the jurisconsult recommends to his client have introduced a whole tradition of hypocritical laxity into the Sunni law: they permit believers to respect the letter in order the better to betray the spirit.

By a suitable application of the rules of supple hermeneutics certain *imperatives* in the Qorān can be transformed into simple *optatives*; that is to say, strict duties into works of supererogation. With the same facility the inverse operation is accomplished. 'Take in marriage, of the women who please you, two, three, or four,' says the Qorān (**4**, 3). An authorization, a concession, to all appearances, but some ingenious canonists have discovered in it a command and the explicit condemnation of celibacy. This is the triumph of casuistry. It permits of discovering in the text of the Qorān and also in the inner meaning of a *ḥadīth* decisions appropriate to the most unexpected circumstances and of adapting them to the needs of the moment. Muslim reformists and modernists are skilful to take full advantage of it.

MODERN PRACTICE. The *fiqh*, as we have already remarked (p. 83), is deemed to have sprung from Qorānic revelation, and owes to this conception its immutable character. It is not for man to modify the decisions of revelation. Moreover, this rigidity has always obstructed its plenary application except in certain matters: the personal statute and property in mortmain (*waqf*). Even in those countries governed by Muslim rulers the state has never refrained from laying down a complete code of independent secular law (*Qānūn*, *Mejellé*, etc.). This is how the *fiqh* has become a speculative science, concerned with an ideal law and a purely academic state of society, divorced from the realities of modern life.

With as much seriousness and diligence as a Māwardī, the theorist of power in Islām (1058), would have brought to the task, the *fiqh* continues to study a Muslim State which no longer exists. It describes in minute detail its component parts and the working of its machinery. It discourses on the administration and use of the imaginary revenues of this State. It starts with the postulate of a world-wide Caliphate, destined to make the universe bend under the law of Islām. It determines the rules of international law and the laws of war, together with the system of government to be applied to the tributaries of Islām. Its conception of commercial law and of civil contracts clashes with the organization of financial credit and with the economic relations established between modern peoples. It expatiates upon a penal law wherein the Qorān (**2**, 175) has maintained the Beduin principles of '*qiṣaṣ*', an eye for an eye. To the victims and their relatives, it leaves the choice between pardon and a pecuniary settlement, *diya*, and the decision of the injured party deprives the State of all power to punish violation of social law. In the case of certain offences the State likewise finds itself compelled to abide by the '*ḥudūd Allah*', penalties laid down by the Qorān (*v.* p. 64).

As in the case of the *Sunna* and *Tafsīr*, the dissident sects also possess their special *fiqh*. The principal points on which it differs from the jurisprudence of the Sunnis will be discussed in the chapter on sects.

IJMĀ'. The Prophet has said: 'My people will never agree in an error.' The dictum 'disagreement is a mercy from God' is likewise attributed to him. The meaning seems to be that the diversity of interpretations among the learned should set the conscience of the Faithful at rest by leaving them the choice of a decision. These two sayings are destined to explain the variety of the orthodox schools and also the origin of *ijmā'*.

It would seem that the honour of having outlined the first formula of *ijmā'* rests with Mālik, founder of the Medinese school. He thought he had found in it a weapon against Abū Ḥanīfa, whom he accused of having trifled with the *Sunna*. The theory, enlarged by the Imām Shāfi'ī, permits of an immediate decision in an ever-increasing number of cases, where the three other *roots* of *fiqh* led to no solution. *Ijmā'* was not long in exceeding the narrow limits within which it was intended to be confined, and it was thus that the deductions drawn from *Qiyās* had to be made homologous by the *consensus*. Soon the same thing happens to the *Sunna*: this also was subjected to a check, based upon the agreement of believers. The task of defining and then discovering this agreement still remained.

Who were to be its witnesses, its authorized interpreters? The absence of an ecclesiastical hierarchy has never permitted a clear understanding on this question. The 'Companions' of the Prophet and their immediate successors were at once suggested. As the first disciples, they were supposed to have been directly trained by the Master (*v.* p. 68), and all had lived in the era that has been considered the golden age of Islām. Such, one conceives, must have been the definition adopted by the Imām Mālik, the defender of the Medinese *Sunna*. It was destined to win the support of numerous Ḥanbalites and later that of the Wahhābis. The Ẓāhirites only acknowledged the *ijmā'* of the Companions. It was, however, necessary to broaden this concept in order not to close the door on the solution of new difficulties.

'The *'ulemā* are the heirs of the prophets', thus Muḥammad is supposed to have spoken. To them falls 'the mission of binding and loosing'. Are they not 'the learned men to whom is known the interpretation of Qorānic revelation'? (**3**, 5). It was, then, decided to define *ijmā'* as the agreement between the teachers and *'ulemā* of a certain period. What one generation of legislators had taught was considered by the following generation to have received the stamp of *ijmā'*. This teaching is supposed to transmit in its entirety the tradition of the 'pious ancestors' (*as-salaf-aṣ-ṣāliḥ*) and to be elastic enough to answer fully all the needs of later times.

A general consultation is not required and the organization of Islām would render it impossible. It is sufficient that the decision of a group of *'ulemā* meets with the tacit approval of their colleagues. The masses have nothing to do with these questions. In Islām the real heretics are those who refuse to submit to *ijmā'*. The Orthodox rightly call themselves not only 'people of the *Sunna*', but also 'people of *jamā'a*', that is, subscribing to the decisions of *ijmā'*. Thus understood, *ijmā'* in its fluidity and elasticity replaces the intervention of the infallible *consensus Ecclesiae* and ensures to a great extent the doctrinal agreement of the community. It tolerates, being unable to prevent it, a certain evolution of the *Sharī'a* ; but knows when to intervene at the right moment to prevent the abuses of unrestricted liberty. It is, generally speaking, the result of a compromise between extreme doctrines and follows upon the sometimes bloody struggles prolonged by the intolerance of the Ḥanbalites. The agreement is never complete, even within the limits of a school of jurisprudence. These divergences do not impair the *catholicity* of the Islāmic system ; *ijmā'* assumes responsibility for them all, and ensures to them its own character of infallibility.

It is *ijmā'* that has secured the admission of the vulgate text of the Qorān as well as its *Tafsīr*, or authorized exegesis. The 'Six books' of *ḥadīth* and the four juridical schools owe their official recognition far more to *ijmā'* than to the excellence of their method and the prestige of their authors and founders. Moral mysticism or orthodox *Ṣūfism* was to benefit, but much more tardily, by the same authorization. For this success, in spite of the opposition of the Ḥanbalites, *Sūfism* is indebted to the personal influence of Ghazālī, who had become one of the 'revivers of religion' (*muḥiy ad-dīn*) by his struggles against the abuses of philosophic and juristic speculation. *Ijmā'* leaves the door open to the entry of new formulæ and opinions, combated at first as dangerous innovations (*bid'a*). Then, as resistance dies down, they are partially admitted by the orthodox schools and finally confirmed by *ijmā'*, from which they obtain at least a sort of passport, a *tolerari potest*.

We may instance the cult of the Prophet, the festivals ordained in his honour, such as that of the *maulid*, birth, the belief in his miracles, a belief contradicted by the Qorān (*v.* p. 51), the existence and intercession of the saints (*walī, awliyā*)—primitive Islām recognized the quality of saintliness only in the prophets—the veneration of their tombs. . . . All these innovations are opposed in principle to the spirit of Qorānic monotheism. This latter acknowledges no intermediary between Allah and the believers. Ignoring the opposition of the Ḥanbalites, *ijmā'* has legitimized intermediaries by bringing to their support the consecration of Islām throughout the world, the approbation attested by popular custom and the silence of the teachers. It conferred on the Ottoman Caliphs the validation of their title and dispensed them from the necessity of belonging to the Quraish, a condition which *ijmā'* had first pronounced necessary. It finished by making lawful the use of tobacco and the lithographic reproduction of copies of the Qorān, the printing of which is still a subject of scruple to timid believers. The same organ of validation will doubtless soon pronounce in favour of the pictorial and photographic representation of living beings.

Ijmā' is a spontaneous phenomenon, born of the need for uniformity, a manifestation of what may be called the *instinct* of a believing people. We have seen how after many gropings Islām has agreed upon a formula elastic enough to be accepted, and of which 'the closing of *ijtihād*' assures the efficacy. Some Orientalists have thought that this elasticity could be utilized to adapt the *Sharī'a* to modern needs. 'What *ijmā'* has laid down, another *ijmā'* can modify.' Such is also the reasoning of Muslim modernists, whose claims would outrage the *'ulemā* who elaborated the theory of *ijmā'*. Doctrinal agreement settles nothing. It can neither be created nor organized as a whole; nothing can be done except to note its existence. It deals with the past not with the future, and when the doctors chance to invoke it this is solely to justify and legalize innovations, to link them laboriously to the '*Sunna* of the pious ancestors' and not to contest the perpetuity of tradition. It therefore seems rash to attempt to regard *ijmā'* as an ultimate means of introducing reforms to the *Sharī'a*.

THE LIVING AUTHORITY. Theory asserts that the *Sharī'a* derives directly from the Qorān and the prophetic tradition, and logic demands that the first duty of the Faithful should be to apply themselves to the study of these two 'roots' of Islāmic doctrine. This is not the case, even with the most independent minds such as the Ẓāhirite ibn Ḥazm (†1064) and the Ḥanbalite ibn Taimiyya, who claims to be guided by the Qorān and *Sunna* alone. In practice it is neither the letter of the *Sūras* nor the contents of the *Sunna*, but their interpretation by the living authority, residing in the person of the '*ulemā*, which serves as criterion for the settlement of litigious questions.

It has been agreed that from the fourth century A.H. 'the door of *ijtihād* is shut'. Since then, all the learned and Faithful have been reduced to *taqlīd*, unreserved submission to the decisions of one or other of the orthodox schools. The end of the third century A.H. coincides with the setting up of these schools and the compilation of the 'Six Books', with the crystallization of traditional dogma which was soon to accept the theodicy of Ash'arī (*v.* p. 57). These three centuries had permitted Islām to borrow from without the elements essential to its doctrinal and juridical evolution, merely disguising these borrowings under the authority of the Prophet. It was agreed to admit that all the great problems had been discussed and fully elucidated in the teaching of the orthodox schools.

IJTIHĀD, or, to be more precise, 'absolute' (*muṭlaq*) *ijtihād*, is the critical study, the independent discussion of the ' roots ' of the Qorānic revelation in their relation to dogma and discipline. It is the right to ignore the ready-made opinions of the schools and of the old masters, the four great Imāms, Mālik, Shāfi'ī, etc., to form and enunciate an interpretation based immediately on the text of the Qorān and the contents of the *Sunna*, without regard for exegesis and traditional glosses. The people of the first three centuries are supposed to have exhausted the right to go back to the sources and since then nothing has authorized the revision of their pronouncements, hallowed by centuries of *ijmā'*. There remains no other resource but the *relative ijtihād*; namely, the endeavour to explain the interpretations peculiar to each school, to rejuvenate them at need and to discover for them new applications.

It is on the decisions of the old masters, classified under special rubrics and collected in manuals, that the *'ulemā*, professors of the *fiqh*, expend their energy. Thus circumscribed, their teaching is limited to commentaries on the collections in use amongst the divers rites. There can be no question of going back to the ' roots ' of the law, that is to say, the Qorān and the *Sunna*, which these manuals have replaced. It is on secondary points, where the editors of the school compendiums find themselves in disagreement, that a professor is allowed to make his own choice and express a personal opinion, but even this is usually confined to an attempt to reconcile the divergent solutions. These commentaries end by being substituted for the manuals which preceded them. They give rise to other glosses and become the source of fresh compilations which, in their turn, rank as school texts.

Public teaching consists, then, in the *reading* of one of these texts which the professor accompanies by short philological and juridical explanations, drawn from the best commentaries of his predecessors. This shows within what narrow limits first 'relative' *ijtihād*, then the theory of *taqlīd*, the obligation to hold strictly to the opinions of one school, enclose doctrinal evolution, the progress of Islāmic speculation. The 'closing of *ijtihād*' could not fail to excite the protests of Muslim modernists. They see in it 'a crime committed against Islām by the *'ulemā* under the cloak of religion'. Others more moderate declare that no one has the right gratuitously to exalt the authority of human teachers at the expense of the Qorān and the *Sunna*.

No Councils. Nowhere have the weaknesses of the theory of *ijmā'* and *taqlīd* been more stressed than among the Shī'as. They have proclaimed the complete incapacity of human reasoning to arrive at absolute certainty in matters of dogma. For the *taqlīd* of the Sunnis these dissidents have substituted their own *taqlīd*. To the vacillating and variable concept of *ijmā'* they oppose an official and permanent organ of certitude which is nothing more or less than the judgment of the *infallible Imām*. This descendant of 'Ali possesses the sublime and hidden meaning (*ta'wīl*) of the Qorān, transmitted to him by his ancestors who had it from the Prophet's son-in-law. The Shi'a doctors are called '*mujtahid*'. They regard themselves as the interpreters and organs of the 'Alid Imām and, in this capacity, share in his infallibility. In the Shī'a there can thus be no question of schools or diversity of opinion. It recognizes nothing but the principle of authority.

The Sunnis are unable to admit the prerogatives of this hypothetical personage. Neither is *ijmā'* with them, as it is in the Christian church, the result of synodal assemblies and of decisions taken in council. Islām lacks a hierarchy charged to watch officially over the trust of Qorānic revelation. Never during the thirteen centuries of the Hijra has the idea of publicly consulting the Faithful on controversial questions occurred. Must this not be taken to indicate that a discussion of this kind is repugnant to the constitution of Islām? Its realization would have clashed with the independence and reciprocal autonomy of the orthodox schools. Since decisions taken in common would necessarily be based on the doctrine of one or other of these schools, they would have no binding value for the adherents of the other *madhhab*. Neither have the *'ulemā* living in the same country and belonging to the same school ever thought of deliberating together, since no one can claim the privilege of 'absolute' *ijtihād*. When those of the university of Al-Azhar, at Cairo, pronounce a collective opinion on a question concerning all Islām, they realize, or if need be they are reminded, that they only speak in the name of the Shāfi'ītes. The project lately advanced of a congress, representative of all Islam, to settle the problem of the Caliphate, is therefore an innovation fraught with grave consequences.

Islām exists on the postulate that the Qorān and the *Sunna* contain a reply to everything. What is the use of meeting for discussion when one possesses the treasure of the orthodox *tafsīr* and the decisions of the great *imāms*? The body of the *fāqih* and that of the *'ulemā* are charged to 'bind and loose', upon them devolves the mission of replacing the *vox populi*. It was, then, laid down in principle that the *via media* of the authorized *'ulemā*, i.e. their explicit teaching or even their mere silence (*taqrīr*), should be accepted as the rule, that the matters established by their doctrinal consent, by an agreement *quasi*-universal, could not be brought under discussion again.

It was upon this *ijmā'* of the orthodox teachers that in the eighteenth century the movement of the Wahhābis, with its claim to restore the purity of primitive Islām, was wrecked. On questions of detail, as the polemics of the Wahhābi precursor, Ibn Taimiyya, have shown, the innovators of Central Arabia may have been right. Their mistake was in wishing to confine *ijmā'* within too narrow chronological limits, in denying all later adaptation, in shutting the door on doctrinal and disciplinary evolution necessitated by the world-wide expansion of Islām. In the same way the Greek Church in the East claims to admit only the definitions of the first seven ecumenical councils. To subscribe to the claims of the puritan Wahhābis would have been tantamount to a tacit admission that the Muslim community had been united in error for more than a thousand years.

THE 'ULEMĀ, we have said, are regarded as the authorized interpreters of the *consensus*. It is to them that the simple Faithful turn, when in doubt, for the solution of cases of conscience or the definition of controversial points of doctrine. The written answers which they obtain are founded on Qorānic texts, on the *Sunna*, the doctrine of the four Schools, and, lastly, on *ijmā'*. These answers constitute a *fatwā*, or decision. For the believer the *fatwā* is as good as the arguments upon which the conclusion is based. The authors of these *fatwās*, when they are officially charged to give such solutions, are called *muftis*, literally givers of *fatwās*; they occupy a place apart in the body of *'ulemā*. In Turkey the 'ulemā are called *khoja*, in Persia and in India *mulla* (*maulā*), or master.

In the time of the Ottoman Empire, the supreme head of the *'ulemā* and *muftis* bore the title of Sheikh-al-Islām. He performed for Islām the functions of a Minister of Cults. From the religious and doctrinal point of view, his authority surpassed that of the Sultan-Caliph. But he was nominated by the latter and could be deprived of his office at will,—a precaution which safeguarded the ruler from any whim of independence.

THE QĀḌI, likewise chosen from among the *'ulemā*, is the titular head of a judicature or magistracy. We have already noted (*v.* p. 92) the existence of a kind of legal dualism in several Muslim countries and the attempts to modernize parts of the *fiqh*. It is thus that side by side with the Sheikh-al-Islām, to whom in theory the Qāḍis are answerable, the Ottoman Empire possessed a Ministry of Justice. Republican Turkey has completely overthrown and laicized the old Muslim jurisprudence. The Egyptian government, too, has revised certain points of the personal statute.

As to the Qāḍi, his judgments are based exclusively on canonical law or *Sharī'a* and profess to ignore the modifications introduced by the civil power. The matters which come within his jurisdiction are those for which the Qorān has enacted special laws, e.g. the personal statute, successions, pious foundations (*waqf*). In criminal matters (*v.* p. 64) and all other questions referred to him for examination by the civil authority, he applies the '*ḥudūd Allah*'. His tribunal admits oral testimony alone ; that of a non-Muslim is excluded. Muslim governments have always sought to restrict the jurisdiction of the Qāḍi, especially in criminal matters. They reserve to themselves the right not only of executing, but also of confirming the sentences passed by the canonical tribunals. The Qāḍi is at once judge and notary, and his province sometimes extends to the sphere of civil justice. He legalizes deeds, and by reason of this can be called on to intervene in the drawing up of bills of sale and also in marriage contracts. Nevertheless, his presence is not required to establish the validity of the matrimonial bond. He is the guardian of orphans, the supervisor and sometimes also the administrator of property which is *waqf*.

No Clergy. Islām possesses neither clergy nor, properly speaking, a liturgy. The *Ṣūfīs* alone in their meetings of *dhikr* organize something approximating to liturgical ceremonies. These comprise, with songs, and dances, the recitation of litanies, peculiar to each *Ṣūfī* fraternity. Orthodoxy looks askance at these manifestations, and displays as little enthusiasm for the illumination of the mosques and minarets on certain feast-days,—processions in times of plague, the celebration of the *maulid* and other ceremonies which come to break the monotony of the official cult.

The Muslim Friday has nothing in common with the Jewish Sabbath or Christian Sunday. As we have seen (*v.* p. 60), it entails no obligation of a weekly rest ; the Faithful are merely obliged to attend public noonday prayer. What, apart from its publicity, distinguishes this prayer from all others is the *khuṭba* or sermon, always in Arabic, which precedes it. The *Imām*, charged with delivering it from the *minbar* or pulpit, is called *khaṭīb* or preacher. Since there must be a congregation of at least forty of the Faithful (*v.* p. 59) for the Friday public devotions, the *khaṭīb* only functions in the principal mosques or *jāmiʿ*, to the exclusion of the *masjid*, or secondary mosques.

The use of the *khuṭba* has not succeeded in creating in Islām a literature which recalls the eloquence of the Christian divines. Its style is formal and cramped from recourse to assonance or *sajʿ*. The expositions and exhortations of which it is composed do not go beyond generalities and are often borrowed from earlier collections, especially in those regions where Arabic is no more than a dead language.

The principal interest lies in that part of the *khuṭba* which it has been sought to compare with our *Domine salvum fac*, with this difference, that it bears, much more than does the Christian liturgy, the character of a manifestation of political loyalty. I refer to the invocations in which divine blessings are called down on the sovereign of the country, on the princes and all Muslims. In the history of Islām, the prerogative of '*sikka*', or coinage, and also the right to the *khuṭba*, have always been looked upon as the external symbols of political independence and sovereignty. To omit mention of the ruler in the *khuṭba* was tantamount to a declaration deposing him. Therein lies the whole secret of the importance which the divers Muslim governments have never ceased to attach to it.

Here is an extract from the *khuṭba* in use in the Ḥejāz in the time of King Ḥusain ibn 'Alī prior to his claim to the Caliphate. This specimen likewise shows the degree to which political claims may appear in a *khuṭba*: 'O God! protect Thy servant, the son of Thy servant, guardian of Thy town in its firm security and of the city of his ancestor, the Lord of Prophets (Muḥammad), Sherīf and Amīr of Mekka, King of the Arab countries, our Lord and Master, the Sherīf Ḥusain! . . . Let all the Muslim rulers prosper; destroy the impious and the heretics and whoever devises evil against Thy faithful believers, from the East unto the West.'

In theory the Caliph is regarded as the head of all Islām. By virtue of this his name should figure in the *khuṭba*. Circumstances do not always permit the fulfilment of this duty, and that is why use of the 'tacit' or 'implicit' *khuṭba* has sprung up. Without pronouncing any name and as though there were a 'vacancy in the see', the *khaṭīb*, before mentioning the local sovereign, contents himself with praying for 'the Caliph of the Muslims'. This formula is less innocuous than would appear. It is the homage paid to a political supremacy, for the Caliphate carries with it no spiritual or strictly religious prerogative.

In Morocco nothing stands in the way of the 'explicit'

khuṭba in the name of the Sultan, who is at once Caliph and sovereign of the country. Another country using the explicit *khuṭba* is Egypt (in the name of King Fuad). Irāq and the regions subject to the Hāshimite Sherīfs pronounced it in the name of their father, the ex-King Ḥusain. In Afghanistan and the Wahhābi territory, after the name of the reigning sovereign they merely mention *in globo* ' the other Muslim Amīrs '. Republican Turkey has frankly cut out all allusion to the Caliphate in the *khuṭba*. In Tunis, in India, in Syro-Palestine and the Egyptian Sudan, this omission is said to be ' provisional ' until the meeting of the prospective Muslim congress.

In the absence of a liturgy and of religious ceremonies the existence of a body of clergy specially ordained to direct divine service would be purposeless. As for the spiritual care of souls, orthodoxy does not admit that it is necessary. It protests against the direction exercised by the *Ṣūfī* Sheikhs over their novices and disciples, which practice appears to the orthodox a gratuitous insult to the boundless efficacy of the *Sharī'a* and the *Sunna* of the Prophet. Knowing nothing of the sacraments and the Christian dogma of atonement, Islām has no place for a ministry, as sole and hierarchical medium of spiritual grace.

This latter conception, as well as the necessity for an ecclesiastical hierarchy, appears to Islām irreconcilable with the imprescriptible rights and absolute dominion of Allah over His creatures. The Qorān (9, 31, *cf.* v. 34) reproaches the Jews and Christians with having ' taken their rabbis and monks for lords '. This is really the rôle that the Shi'a reserves for its 'infallible and impeccable ' *Imāms*, the putative sources of blessings and of enlightening grace. There is no place in the Islāmic system for confession. Forgiveness of sins is obtained automatically by the canonical punishments, '*ḥudūd Allah*', stipulated in the Qorān in cases of specific transgressions: adultery, larceny, drunkenness, etc., in a word, by faith and the repentance of the guilty. The profession of faith, '*shahāda*', preserves the sinner from the eternal punishment of hell (*v.* p. 52). Ghazālī counsels sinners to exercise examination of conscience, contrition and firm resolution, and finally, to confess their sins before Allah.

The ministers, devoted to the service of the mosques, have no need, then, of any special training. It is enough for them to know their obligations and be capable of fulfilling them; for example, to have an adequate knowledge of Arabic. Certain subordinate functionaries whose duty it is to utter from the minaret the summons to daily prayers, or, to be more exact, to announce them, are called muezzins (*mu'adhdhin*). Sheikhs or Imāms are appointed to certain mosques or religious orders, and the heads of the *Ṣūfī* fraternities are likewise called Sheikhs. No position confers on its holder the exclusive right to lead at prayer, a right which is democratically shared among all the Faithful. This leadership may be taken by no matter what believer, if he is a good Muslim and is sufficiently acquainted with the modalities of worship. Thus, circumcision can be performed by the first barber who comes along.

Qāḍis and Imāms sometimes preside at marriages. They act in their capacity of privileged witnesses or by virtue of delegation from the civil authority with a view to legalizing the matrimonial contract, and not on the ground of any right inherent in their office, which is devoid of all spiritual character. The Qāḍi only intervenes *ex officio* when the bride has no relative (*walī*) to represent her. She may not marry a non-Muslim (Qorān **2**, 220). In the case of a man it is lawful to take a wife of a Scripturary persuasion; a concession which has been contested by certain schools (*v.* p. 89). The essence of Islāmic marriage, in which no ritual blessing occurs, consists in the exchange of a promise between the contracting parties sanctioned by the presence of two witnesses and by the payment of a dowry (*mahr, ṣadāq*) to the wife. So we come once more to the conclusion that there exists no Church in Islām, no sacerdotal hierarchy and no central See acting at once as director and preserver.

THE CALIPHATE. It is on behalf of the Caliphate that ingenious Orientalists have attempted to claim this centralizing mission. Instead of asking what Islām thinks in the matter, they have begun by assimilating the structure of the Muslim world to that of Christianity, and of the Ottoman Caliphate to the Roman Pontificate. This assimilation led them logically to endow the former with jurisdiction and spiritual supremacy over all Islām.

It was reserved to certain European statesmen to give consistency to this fantastic conception, to the extent of introducing it in the redaction of international treaties of which the first in date was that of Kutchuk-Kainardji (1774). In order to render acceptable to Muslim opinion the cession imposed on Turkey of provinces populated by Muslims, it occurred to European diplomats to distinguish between the dual authority of the Sultan, the spiritual and the temporal. All troubles would be avoided, the scruples of the believers would be quieted if in the provinces detached from the Sultanate the spiritual power of the Caliph should continue to be maintained, in token of which he would appoint the heads of the Islāmic magistracy there and his name would be mentioned in the Friday *khuṭba*. That is the myth which enabled the former Sultan 'Abdulḥamīd to organize his pan-Islāmic agitation and to pose as the official protector of all Islām.

It would have been difficult to invent a theory more directly contrary to the teaching of Islām and also to the interests of Europe, which countenanced it to its cost. Never has Sunni orthodoxy confused the Caliph with a Christian hierarch, Pope or Patriarch. Far from attributing to him spiritual prerogatives, it even denies him all doctrinal authority, including the power, conceded to the lowliest of the *'ulemā*, of giving a *fatwā*. The problem of the Caliphate has caused the gravest schisms in the bosom of Islām. Certain Muslim authorities, having allowed themselves to be too powerfully impressed by the memory of these disagreements, have yielded to the temptation to speak of the Caliphate as they would of a matter of dogma. But for them, too, the Caliph 'always has been and still is nothing more than the advance sentinel, watching at the door of Islām' (Dr. Perron), not a Pontiff, but the lay defender of the *Sharī'a*. They regard him as the mandatory of the community, whose duty it is to maintain intact the rules prescribed by the Qorān and, by its sanction, to recall the Faithful publicly to the respect due to the Canon Law. Thus the Czar in the old organization of the Russian Church and the King of England in the Anglican Church.

'The hidden' and infallible Imām of the Shī'as is no more than a caricature of this concept, inspired by a profound sense of unity. The Sunni Caliph has no legislative power at all; this is vested in the *Sharī'a* in the same way as the judicial power in the body of *'ulemā*. He is *Vicar* of the Prophet, but in temporal matters alone. Having only an executive power, he has to maintain the cohesion of Islām within and to secure its defence and expansion without. In the absence of spiritual weapons he can only assume this rôle by recourse to the sword, and the *fiqh*, in reserving to him the principal mission of the *jehād* (*v.* p. 62), has decided that he must take the offensive if need be ;—it could not compel him to be the passive guardian of a trust which he would be powerless to defend. This is what damns in advance all attempts of Muslim reformists and modernists to establish a Caliphate without a full command of sovereign authority.

In these days the most moderate among the orthodox Muslims see in the Caliphate the unique and permanent instrument of validation for canonical institutions: prayer, sentences of the courts, etc. They forget to tell us what judgments should be passed on the validity of prayers offered during the anarchical periods when Islām knew no Caliph at all and others when it numbered several. After first of all stripping the Caliph of Stambul of the Sultanate, the Kemalists of Angora simply decreed the suppression of the Caliphate.

The most recent thesis, also the most radical, has been developed by the Egyptian Qāḍi, 'Alī 'Abdarrāziq, in his book *Islām and the Bases of Sovereignty*, '*Al-islām wa uṣūl al-ḥukm*' (Cairo, 1925, several editions). These are its leading ideas : The Muslim religion is to cut itself off completely from every form of government, leaving this question to the free choice of the believers. Unknown to the Qorān, which has not made the slightest allusion to it, the Caliphate has no foundation at all in Islāmic dogma. It is the manuals of the *fiqh* that have created ambiguity on the subject. The *Sharī'a*, which is exclusively religious legislation, does not imply any necessary connexion with political sovereignty. The canonical tribunals cannot claim any religious competence ; the Qāḍis are wholly indistinguishable from the civil judges. Muḥammad's mission was purely religious and never aimed at founding any kind of government, and Islām, therefore, offers nothing but a spiritual legislation, a rule of faith and a moral discipline, without any sort of relation to an external power charged with the duty of ensuring its execution.

All these propositions have been condemned by the supreme council of *'ulemā* at the university of Al-Azhar, Cairo. The agitation round the problem of the Caliphate continues, and in order to resolve it, a proposal has been made to call together a world-congress of Islām.

VI

ASCETICISM AND MYSTICISM OF ISLĀM

THE *Sharī'a* does not legislate for the *conscience*. A social discipline, a sort of higher law, it confines its ambition to gathering all the faithful round the rites and observances of the Islāmic community, without troubling to enter into the details of their inner life. Fidelity to the *Sharī'a* is nevertheless supposed to be the way of spiritual perfection. To doubt this would be to question its character of revealed legislation. It is difficult to imagine a more precise antinomy than exists between this conception and that which gave birth to *Ṣūfism*.

THE QORĀN AND ASCETICISM. Undoubtedly, the mystical sense 'cannot be the sole prerogative of a race, a language, a nation' (Massignon). The Qorān purports to be nothing more than the redaction, for the use of the Arabs, of the great revelation which gave birth to the monotheistic religions. Several of its verses are merely transcriptions and reminiscences from the Scriptures altered in precisely the same degree as its prophetic legends. Many of them inculcate vigorously the fear of God and of His judgments, which is at the base of all sane asceticism. Other Qorānic passages stress the value of intention in the moral and religious life.

These texts, considered by the Believer as inspired and duly recited and meditated on by him, might end in attempts at 'interiorization', and gradually raise him, as we shall see in the case of Ghazālī, to a condition of mental prayer. But as a whole the Qorān appears little adapted to stir the inward and truly spiritual emotions. It knows nothing of the downfall of human nature and nowhere does it declare war on the old man in order to put on the new. The necessity for this struggle, axiomatic in Christian asceticism, and no less the dogma of the original fall, seem to Muslim orthodoxy *illusions of the devil*, '*talbīs iblīs*'. This lack of inner life, the predominance of the juridic element in official Islām, could not satisfy all consciences, nor, above all, suit the Muslim neophytes, deserters from earlier monotheisms. From their former religious education they had retained the memory of another ideal, as it were a nostalgia for spiritual perfection and ascent. These finer spirits were not long in finding themselves cramped within a rigid dogmatism devoid of liturgical splendour; a religion of warriors and shepherds, suited to the patriarchal society of Arabia before the Hijra. The outward formalism of the *Sharī'a*, the legislation meticulously elaborated by the orthodox schools, took no account of the spiritual 'sensibility and tenderness' that the Qorān has praised (**57**, 27) in Christians. 'In what way,' asks Ghazālī, 'do discussions on divorce and on buying and selling prepare the believer for the beyond?'

The ruthless Ḥanbalite polemicist, Ibn Taimiyya, goes so far as to contest the very principle of 'the virtue of poverty', invoked by the *Ṣūfīs* as an important condition of spiritual perfection. He finds no mention of it in the Qorān. This collection only speaks of '*zuhd*', which does not imply actual surrender of worldly goods but only mental detachment from them. In the 'poverty' of the *Ṣūfīs* Ibn Taimiyya will see nothing but a most blameworthy imitation of Christianity. Like him, the interpreters of strict orthodoxy admit only the observance of the legal prescriptions. Outside of this path, marked out by 'the pious ancestors', they recognize neither moral ascent nor religious progress. It is remarkable that the oldest sects, the Khārijites, and all the factions of *imāmism*, are definitely opposed to *Ṣūfism*. The same hostility may be observed among the Wahhābis, who profess to restore primitive Islām. Does this agreement not indicate that in Islām mysticism is a foreign importation?

In a hundred places the Qorān sets up as an ideal trust in God, absolute submission to the will of Him whom it proclaims the Merciful. On the other hand, its monotheism has placed Allah very high, far removed from weak humanity. It proscribes the Gospel appellation of 'Father which art in Heaven'. Between the Creator and His creature it admits no possibility of reciprocity. Love implies the idea of giving and receiving. The Sunni theodicy, therefore, distrusts and regards as meaningless the concept of 'the love of God' and still more that of *union*—'*wiṣāl*'—with Him. The vocable '*maḥabba*', marking the consummation of love and of divine union, appears odious in its eyes. It will admit therein nothing but a physical attraction and tolerates only those words that imply desire, appetite—such as '*shauq*'. In face of the denegations of the *'ulemā*, Ghazālī was forced to prove at length the possibility of the divine love whose effects he studied in the faithful soul.

Thus between God and man there is no direct and regular communication. Every effort to lessen the distance which separates them appears tainted by '*shirk*', a move in the direction of polytheism. The soul, in its struggle to gain salvation, cannot rely on the aid of any intermediary. In the most idealized portraits of the *Sīra* and the *ḥadīth* Muḥammad is never shown except as the instrument of revelation. Even then he did not receive the trust direct, but through the ministrations of an angel.

Ṣūfism. In opposition to such rigid theories, some Believers, like Ḥasan al-Baṣrī (†728) and Ibrahīm ibn Adham (†777), felt the need to lessen this distance. They sought to approach the Divinity more nearly by means other than fidelity to external practices and the path of legal justice. These Faithful aspired to a personal and more intense experience of the religious truths which should aid the gradual ascent of the soul to God. These tendencies, ill-satisfied in official Islām, gave birth to the mystical discipline, '*taṣawwuf*', or *Ṣūfism*.

This term derives from '*Ṣūf*', wool, because the earlier *Ṣūfīs* affected a dress of serge or woollen stuff in imitation of the Christian monks. Synonymous with *Ṣūfī* is the word '*faqīr*', poor, and the Persian *dervīsh*, meaning a beggar. Both allude to the detachment from the world professed by the mystics. In north-west Africa, they are more generally called marabouṭs, from '*murābiṭ*', an ascetic living in a '*ribāṭ*'. This name was given to the small forts erected along the frontiers, as well as to the outskirts of the urban centres where the first *Ṣūfī* adepts, lovers of solitude, settled for choice.

Christian Influence. The Qorān (**5**, 85) extols the humility of the monks. It praises (**57**, 27) monasticism, '*rahbāniyya*', a mode of life which they have 'spontaneously embraced so that they may win the favour of Allah'. This is a veiled allusion to the path of the Gospel precepts of which no other echo is to be found in the Qorān. The *Sūras* commend the practice of prayer and even of night prayer, no doubt in imitation of the nocturnal offices in use in Christian monasteries. Mingled with the eschatological conceptions which characterize the beginnings of the Mekkan period are to be found ascetic reflections on the vanity of worldly possessions and the fitness of weaning the heart from them.

Without ever going as far as *si vis perfectus esse*, or counsels of voluntary poverty, these observations, which always preserve a rhetorical tone, grow gradually milder until they disappear completely after the Hijra. Islām then accentuates its political and conquering character. If previously it had extolled the social duty of sharing with the poor and needy of the community, at Medina it proclaims the necessity of sacrificing worldly possessions for the Holy War. Unlike the Gospel, the Qorān nowhere distinguishes between the way of commandment and that of counsel. Christianity has an unquestionable influence on the beginnings of *Ṣūfism*, which claims nothing less than to introduce into Islām the way of counsel. It may be divined in the name of '*rāhib*', monk, given to the early Muslim ascetics, and also in the tendency of certain amongst them to profess to walk in the footsteps of Christ and even to place Him, in His dual capacity of ascetic and prophet, above Muḥammad.

Ṣūfism had its birth in Syria and Egypt, the cradles and primitive seats of monachism. It borrowed a part of its technical vocabulary from the Syriac language. In the second century of the Hijra we find no trace of organization amongst Muslim ascetics. They live in isolation without any common bonds or doctrine. Theory did not make its appearance until the following century. Satisfied with having found the path of perfection for themselves, and with showing the road to those who came to consult them, they were far more concerned with good works than with theories.

Various names are applied to them by the general

public. They are the '*qurrā*', reciters, devoted to preserving the text of the Qorān and of teaching it to the ignorant masses; also the '*bakkā'ūn*', weepers, and the '*quṣṣāṣ*', popular preachers. Among the last-mentioned, a certain number are attached to the staff of armies in the field. There they discharge functions remotely resembling those of almoners. They appeal to the emotions by eschatological descriptions and arguments. They are responsible for the introduction into the collections of the *ḥadīth* of narratives tinged with asceticism.

Out of their nameless crowd there arise in the third century A.H. certain personalities: Anṭākī (†835), Bishr al-Ḥāfī (†841), Muḥāsibī (†857), Sarī as-Saqaṭī (†870), Tirmidhī (†895), amongst whom can be traced a first outline of mystical doctrine. With their contemporary, Abū Yazīd Bisṭāmī (†875), this doctrine is already degenerating into pantheism; a peril averted by the prudence of Junaid (†911), one of the masters of Ḥallāj. From the fourth century of the Hijra onwards traces of a common life and legislation can be found among the *Ṣūfīs*; as in the case of those Muslim hermits encountered by the Syrian geographer, Maqdisī in Syria in the mountains of Lebanon and Jaulān.

'Allah wisheth you ease, but wishes not your discomfort,' proclaims the Qorān (**2**, 181; **22**, 77). 'Eat, enjoy,' he says again (*passim*), 'the good things that Allah has bestowed on you.' In return for their docility to the Prophet, he promises to believers 'victory over the enemy as well as the *spolia opima*' (Qorān **48**, 18, 19). *Ṣūfism* proclaimed its preference for the narrow way; it marked a reaction against the materialistic and worldly trend which men claimed to justify by these verses and, with the aid of the *ḥadīth*, by the Prophet's example and practice. 'Follow my *Sunna*' (tradition), he is reputed to have said,

'I drink, I eat, I marry.' All these *ḥadīth* are far from being authentic. Several have been spread abroad by the opponents of *Ṣūfism* to quiet the conscience of the worldly and also as a counterblast to the exaggerated traits of austerity that the '*quṣṣāṣ*' have introduced into the portrait of the Prophet. As noted above (p. 71), the schools continue to fight among themselves with the aid of multitudes of traditions. For example, in order to discredit *Ṣūfism*, certain traditionists portray Muḥammad as loathing woollen garments.

It is particularly evident from the last *ḥadīth* quoted that these laxist maxims aimed above all things at the exclusion of monastic celibacy. 'We will have no monachism in Islām—its monachism is the Holy War.' 'Celibates are brothers of the Devil.' 'Two prostrations by a married Muslim are worth more than seventy by a celibate.' Against these anticipated protestations, attributed to Muḥammad, the fact remains that *Ṣūfism* began by borrowing from Christian mysticism a number of practices to which it found no parallel in its own surroundings, practices designed to sweeten the liturgical relations of the soul with God: recollection, solitary meditations, prolonged vigils, recitation of Qorānic passages, and of litanies, *dhikr*. It did not hesitate to borrow other elements of asceticism, hardly compatible with the spirit of Islām, such as the necessity for a '*murshid*, Sheikh', or spiritual director.

'This world is not a permanent abiding-place. Penitence and no less the memory of our sins should wean us from it. We should bewail them, and expiate them by fasting, prayer and surrender of our worldly goods to the poor.' In imitation of the Christian ascetics, the fear of the Judgment and of the account to be rendered, *the gift of tears*—tears that the ancient Arabs regarded as a weakness unworthy of man—became the signs, the distinctive *charismas* of the great mystics or *Ṣūfīs*, those at least that are claimed by their biographies. All are called '*bakkā'ūn*', weepers. *Ṣūfism* extols the love of Allah, a love emotional and tender, not merely dictated by gratitude and desire to please the Supreme Good, as it was imagined by Ghazālī, ever dominated by speculation even in the outpourings of his mysticism. The '*ulemā* for their part admit only the love of submission, '*ṭā'a*', of resignation, '*ṣabr*', to the divine commands, where the *servant*, '*abd*, retains nothing but the sense of his own weakness. For this conception, which vigorously excludes the idea of son, the *Ṣūfīs* seek to substitute the equivalent of the Gospel *vos dixi amicos.* Their new ideal of spiritual life was destined to make proselytes in the Muslim world. It conquered certain theological circles which were lamenting the worldliness and formalism into which official Islām tended more and more to lapse.

Influence of Ghazālī (†1111). Ghazālī became the most illustrious and congenial exponent of this tendency. His prestige contributed powerfully to procure the approbation of *ijmā'* for the principles whence sprang *taṣṣawwuf*, the practice of which soon degenerated in the *Ṣūfī* fraternities. Theologian, jurist and philosopher, Ghazālī, after passing through all the experiences of ascetic life, sought to face in all its amplitude the problem of mysticism as it confronts Muslim orthodoxy. His thesis, a loyal attempt at conciliation between the *Sharī'a* and *Ṣūfism*, presents undeniable affinities with the theories of Christian asceticism. These two characteristics constitute its incontestable originality.

Like the Christian ascetics, Ghazālī supposes the existence of the three paths: purgative, illumination and union. The practice of the first enables the soul to cast off its imperfections. Then opens before it the mystic road, at the end of which it will reach the *stages*, ' *maqāmāt* ', of perfection and union with God. Ghazālī places, then, at the beginning of his mystical pedagogy, the necessity for repentance in order to attain the most absolute purity of heart. Mystical illumination depends on this condition. This illumination (*ilhām*) procures on the eternal truths a more absolute certainty than that obtained by the discursive workings of philosophic or theological speculation. Ghazālī distinguishes between mortal sins, ' *kabā'ir* ', and ' little ' or venial sins. If he avoids all strict classification, it is because he does not find the texts of the Qorān or *Sunna*—his two leading authorities—sufficiently explicit on the subject of a penitential canon.

He unhesitatingly recommends the rendering of the manifestation of conscience to the ' Sheikh ' or director. The disciple must submit himself to such penances and trials as his spiritual father may judge fit to impose for the healing of his moral infirmities. In this opening of conscience which comprises the avowal of faults, nothing is really lacking except sacerdotal absolution to recall, point by point, the sacramental confession in use among Christians. Ghazālī recommends and describes the daily examination of conscience with a precision unsurpassed by St. Ignatius Loyola. Directly he rises, the faithful must take care to form his intention, to make his firm resolution for the day and to provide against occasions of fall. When night comes he must subject himself to a detailed examination, ' *muḥāsaba* ', of the acts of the day. Ghazālī advises the use of a note-book, ' *jarīda* ' ; this will enable him to write down and compare the results of each particular examination. If he finds himself at fault, the ascetic must inflict penance on himself ; he ' will chide his soul', drawing inspiration from supernatural themes, such as may provoke contrition for his faults.

According to Ghazālī the spiritual life finds its most substantial food in meditation, '*tafakkur*'. To it are applied the three powers of the soul: memory, intelligence, will. This exercise begins with what the Christian ascetics have called 'the composition of place'. The text of the Qorān and the *ḥadīth* furnished the material. It is the meditator's business to fit it to the state of his soul. He must avoid losing himself in theological or merely pious speculations. The essential is to arrive at practical resolutions and to 'derive benefit' from them. Novices should begin by meditating on the ultimate aims and on the virtues to be acquired. As to contemplation on the divine perfections, this should be reserved for the most advanced. Ghazālī cautiously advises them not to choose the divine essence as a subject for contemplation if they wish to avoid illusions and even doubts concerning the faith. Let them be content to discover its reflection in created things. Ghazālī has likewise dealt with the subject of ecstasy. He regards it as a gratuitous charisma; he exhorts the faithful, however, to prepare for it by mental orisons, fasting, silence, retreat, and even by music or a spiritual concert, *samā'*; a more delicate expedient to which we shall have occasion to return. He admits the reality of the soul's mystic communion with God. But contrary to the pantheistic reveries of certain *Ṣūfīs*, he strenuously denies that the personality of the enraptured mystic can be annihilated to the point of absorption in that of God. He gives warning that certain abnormal phenomena, following on the mystical trance, *wajd*, are not necessarily a proof of moral perfection, just as he frankly admits that he, personally, has not reached the state of illuminative ecstasy, a fact which he attributes to the arid influence of his early philosophical studies.

In order to demonstrate fully the influence of Christianity on the evolution of this theory of mysticism it is necessary to emphasize the constant appeals made by the author to Christ and the authority of the Gospels. It is evident that he has been at pains to consult them; he habitually quotes from the text in use among the Christians, while the other *Ṣūfīs* appear to have known only the *logia* and the pseudo-evangelical sayings, preserved in the *ḥadīth*. It was his familiarity with Christian mysticism which doubtless inspired the avowal that 'Christianity would be the absolute expression of truth were it not for its dogma of the Trinity and its denial of the divine mission of Muḥammad'.

This was more than enough to win for him the undying hatred of an Ibn Taimiyya and the Ḥanbalites. The Wahhābis have put his books on the Index. Their hostility has not prevented Islām from regarding Ghazālī as one of those '*mujaddid*', *revivers* of religion, who appear at the dawn of every century. In him they recognize the authority of an 'absolute *mujtahid*' (*v.* p. 109). This is a tribute paid to his profound knowledge of the Islāmic sciences, as well as to his unremitting care for orthodoxy and his fidelity to legal observances, which he succeeded in reconciling with aspirations towards a more intense inner life.

Other Influences. From the second century A.H., when the movement of external conquest began to slow down, the intellectual centres of Islām came into contact with the Aramaic peoples. It was these people, both Christian and Jewish, who revealed Greek philosophy to them, or, more exactly, initiated them into oriental philosophic syncretism. Muslim asceticism borrowed from it Neo-platonic, Gnostic and even Manichæan themes. Later, when *Ṣūfism* penetrated into Central Asia, subjects of Buddhist origin as well as practices in favour among the Indian Yogis were added to these borrowings. Amongst others we may note *fanā*. This is the annihilation of the self, the *passing away* of human personality ending in *baqā*, *continuance* or *abiding* in Allah. With the orthodox Ghazālī, *fanā*, the concomitant of ecstasy, causes organic anæsthesia in the subject and suspends momentarily the exercise of free-will.

The first interpretation goes much further. The unity of God—thus argue its partisans—implies the absorption of the creature. The latter cannot exist outside His Essence; otherwise it would constitute a principle eternally distinct, a veritable divinity opposed to the divinity. The *Ṣūfīs* claim to support this doctrine by the Qorān (**54**, 49). In place of the inoffensive reading of the Vulgate text, '*Innā kulla shai*', they read, by altering a simple vowel, '*Innā kullu shai*', and translate without hesitation, 'We (Allah) are everything'! This is monism. *Ittiḥād*, *unification*, goes beyond the negative stage of *fanā*. It aspires to compass the disappearance of *dualism*, *ithnā'iniyya*, maintained by Ghazālī in mystic communion. It seeks to realize the actual union of the soul with God. The *Ṣūfī* claims to reach this stage by complete abstraction, by methodical training in the practices of ecstatic *Ṣūfism*. Thus Moses on Mount Sinai—this comparison had become familiar to *Ṣūfīs*—'in thinking of the Unique Being was so unified, simplified, and separated from created things, that God could no longer reveal Himself to him excepting in the perfect isolation of His simple Unity. It is then that the phenomenon of *shaṭḥ*, interchange of rôles, interversion of personalities, occurs.

The most extraordinary case is that of Abū Yazīd

Bisṭāmī, which ended in incredible excesses of arrogant exaltation. Thus in prayer he actually addressed the following words to Allah: 'Thou obeyest me more than I obey Thee.' One day, hearing the call of the muezzin, *Allah Akbar*, he exclaimed: 'I am still greater.' The most notorious of these bursts of arrogance was his counterpart of '*Subḥān Allah*'. It began by '*Subḥāni*: Praise be to Me! How great is My glory!' Bisṭāmī must have said it, explain the *Ṣūfīs*, in a state of ecstatic intoxication. An Ibn Taimiyya dares not call this intoxication culpable while at the same time he shows himself pitiless in the case of Ḥallāj. He and the *Ṣūfīs* seek to justify Bisṭāmī by affirming that he uttered these sayings when abstracted from the perception of self and perceiving in himself nothing but God.

Certain *Ṣūfīs*—we may mention the celebrated Ḥallāj—end by substituting themselves for God, by speaking in the first person, in the place of Allah. Ḥallāj one day cries: 'I am the Truth!' Here is the explanation given by the *Ṣūfīs*: 'Such words come from the mouth of the enraptured mystic when he perceives that he has completely realized *tauḥīd* or unity, that he is impregnated by it.' We find ourselves once more in the presence of the phenomenon *shaṭḥ*, the interversion of personalities occurring in the course of mystical union. God concedes His part to the ecstatic soul which becomes His mouthpiece; the latter can do no other than speak in the first person, or rather it is God speaking, as it were, by his mouth. Thus the gnostic Gospels make Christ say: *ἐγὼ σὺ καὶ σὺ ἐγώ* (S. Epiphanus Heresies, **26**, 3).

Deviations, Esoterism. There exists an orthodox Muslim *Ṣūfīsm*, the aims of which are revivification by the spirit of a loyally practised religion and detachment from the world. This asceticism, at once respectful in its attitude towards the *Sharī'a* and hostile to all pantheistic and monistic infiltration, hostile to '*ḥulūl*', *infusion*, or to any other mode of annihilation of individuality, was that which Ghazālī wishes to popularize. But, as has been shown by quotations, *Ṣūfism*, not even excepting that of Ghazālī, slips easily into esoterism. Moreover, he has refrained from telling us absolutely all his religious experiences. The temperate nature of this mysticism unfits it for the masses as much as does its esoterism.

It is this character conjoined with his Christian borrowings and his claim to 'spiritualize' the *Sharī'a* which draw down upon him the violent opposition of the Ḥanbilites. What *Ṣūfism* has always lacked is the supervision of a duly authorized hierarchy. Its intervention would have—as in the case of Catholicism —'captured the stream and canalized it before it became a muddy torrent. It would have imposed the rigorous control of moral rule, refusing to encourage a sterile ecstasy which would not become a means of perfection' (Maurice Barrès). Left to itself, the *Ṣūfī* system was logically bound to end in those excesses which were to bring upon it the just strictures of orthodox Islām.

The latter is, in the eyes of *Ṣūfism*, the 'religion of the limbs' or of 'outward appearances', *mobṣarāt*, as the *Ṣūfīs* say. It appears to them very inferior to the 'religion of the heart' or of the 'inner consciousness' (*baṣā'ir*). They proclaim loudly the superiority of the *ma'rifa*, the gnosis or divine Wisdom, over *'ilm*, acquired or discursive knowledge, to wit, that of the *'ulemā*, who concern themselves with nothing but the 'outside', or external lawfulness. The *Ṣūfīs* are the 'initiates'. Having reached the stage of *ittiḥād*, the ascetic endosmosis of the divine Essence, the *Ṣūfī* considers himself exempt from the practice of external works. He sees in them only allegories, symbols, in other words, *means*, '*wasā'iṭ*' essentially transient in character. They must yield place to the practices of mysticism, to spontaneous and not 'mercenary' works, as they summarily designate the practices of the legal religion. Thence it is only a step to declare their uselessness, '*isqāṭ al-wasā'iṭ*', the *abolition* of the *means* or external rites, once the end is attained. Ecstatic *ṣūfism* has taken it. It has descried in the external rites obstacles retarding the spiritual ascent of the soul.

Confident that they have reached the stage of mystic union, some *Ṣūfīs* have spoken in the very name of Allah. Some of these dicta have been admitted into the collection of '*ḥadīth qudsī* (*v.* p. 81). Starting from the hypothesis that *direct* mystic union transcends *mediatory* revelation granted to the prophets, they have imagined they could assume equal rank with the latter. Only the most outspoken have ventured to claim, what many of their brethren thought silently, precedence over the prophets. 'My standard,' cries Bisṭāmī, 'is broader than that of Muḥammad.' Ibn al-'Arabī (1249) asserts, 'We have plunged into the Ocean, while the prophets have remained on the shore.' There is, therefore, no cause for astonishment if, unlike orthodox doctrine, *Ṣūfism* is inclined to proclaim the pre-eminence of the *walīs*, namely, the *saints*, ascetics and mystics, over the prophets.

It did at least succeed in founding, and then in popularizing, the cult of the *walīs*, as well as the belief in their miracles, '*karāmāt*', or rather, wonders, prodigies. The orthodox '*aqīda*' recognize only in the prophets the gift of *mu'jizāt*, or miracles, properly so-called. This last word finds no place in the vocabulary of the Qorān, which uses only the terms '*aya*', sign, and '*borhān*', proof. It seems that the choice of the word '*mu'jiza*' must be connected with the theory of the '*i'jāz*' of the Qorān (*v.* p. 55).

Certain adepts, more consistent or more audacious than Junaid (†909)—one of the earliest theorists of orthodox *Ṣūfism*—have gone further still, and have even extended their scorn of the practices of the *Sharī'a* to embrace conventional morality and the interdictions decreed by the laws of the Qorān. These forerunners of Rasputinism affirm that instead of struggling against dissolute proclivities it is better to indulge them, in order to experience their vanity and to break away from them the more easily. It is the attitude adopted by the *Malāmātiyya*, literally the blameworthy, a sect resembling the cynics. They professed to humiliate themselves, to trample pride underfoot by committing the most unpardonable excesses, thereby manifesting their independence of public opinion and human judgment. It will not therefore be surprising to encounter among the *Ṣūfīs* complete agnostics, proclaiming the equality and uselessness of all professed religions who have reached the most complete doctrinal indifference. At least their aphorisms, taken literally, seem to justify such an attitude.

Ghazālī attached, as we have seen (*v.* p. 119), great value to mystic illumination, without prejudice, however, to the arguments of faith and reason. 'Woe,' cries Ibn al-'Arabī, the celebrated Spanish monist and pantheistic mystic, 'woe to him who bases his convictions on syllogisms, for they are always open to attack. The true faith is the intuitive faith, that of the heart, which is above contradiction.' Ibn al-'Arabī visualizes all creation as emanating from God and the mystic union as evolution in a contrary direction, at the end of which 'we again become' God. 'Since God is everywhere,' he argues, 'to attach oneself to a particular

Credo, chosen at the expense of all others, is to deprive oneself of a part of the true divine Essence.' It is from this agnostic immanentism that *Ṣūfism* has borrowed its general attitude of tolerance towards heterodoxy. Ibn al-'Arabī is an exception ; at least, in his correspondence with the Muslim rulers he calls upon them to revive in all its vigour the oppressive legislation against the unfaithful falsely attributed to the Caliph 'Omar I and dating from the 'Abbāsid Caliphs.

THE INQUISITION AND THE ṢŪFĪS. It is this same Ibn al-'Arabī who achieved the definite rupture between mysticism and the enlightening influence which it might have exercised on society by the salutary example of a life withdrawn from the world and consecrated to prayer. Exaggerating the discretion observed by the orthodox ascetics, such as Junaid and Ghazālī, he reduces *Ṣūfism* to a science which must not be divulged, but reserved for circles of initiates, ' supernatural opium dens ' (Massignon). Ibn al-'Arabī casts aside humble meditation as well as the discipline of the examination of conscience and gives himself up to the sway of his delirious imagination. The divine Essence reveals itself to him in the form of the vocable ' *Hū* ', Him, ' in the centre of a luminous geometrical design of dazzling whiteness, the whole standing out against a red background.' Yet again in his *Futūḥat makkiyya* (I, 8 ; II, 591) he relates solemnly how, one night, he contracted a mystical union ' with all the stars of the firmament ', followed by another ' marriage with the letters of the Alphabet '.

These extravagances show why this Andalusian has been diversely judged by Muslim opinion. Without realizing his incapacity to direct the current of mysticism, orthodoxy understood at least the need to watch the heterodox tendencies developed by *Ṣūfism*. The latter, sheltering behind the screen of esoterism, affected an outward respect for the Qorānic religion and text. It interpreted this collection allegorically (p. 45) and borrowed therefrom a part of its special vocabulary. The Inquisition, established by the 'Abbāsids to keep a watch on the secret sects with Manichæan or 'Alid tendencies, found its attention drawn to the groups of mystics which were beginning to multiply. The moment was judged opportune for a resort to decisive measures.

After a famous lawsuit, the most celebrated of the *Ṣūfī* adepts, Ḥallāj (*v.* p. 123), was condemned to capital punishment; flogged, mutilated, hung upon a gibbet and finally decapitated after his death (922). His corpse was burned. A Javanese rival of Ḥallāj got off more lightly. This *Ṣūfī* had adopted as profession of faith the formula 'I am Allah!' His fellow-mystics proposed to demand the death-sentence on this audacious blasphemer, but when the sentence was announced to him the judges thought they recognized by unmistakable signs that the accused *Sheikh* was in the right. He was only found guilty of having proclaimed 'a truth' which was too sublime for earthly minds, and which he should have kept to himself.

These facts show how real was the need of Muslim authorities to keep a watchful eye on the behaviour and the doctrine of the mystical fraternities. The Mamlūks of Egypt, in order to keep them under closer observation, were at pains to nominate in Cairo a chief *Sheikh* of *Ṣūfīs*. In the certificate of investiture issued to this chief the following injunction may be read: 'He shall take care that no one under his jurisdiction admits *ittiḥad* or *ḥulūl*, the infusion into man of the divine nature, nor presumes to believe that it is possible to approach God otherwise than along the path marked out by the prophets.'

Ibn al-'Arabī had lived for a long time in Egypt and

in Syria under the Ayyūbites. He must have recruited adherents in Syria, he who declared that country 'the best of Allah's lands, the one preferred by His servants'. Was the sentence of the Mamlūk government aimed against his monist doctrine? We do not know. But besides pantheism it condemned the very principle of *Ṣūfism* by proposing to confine it within the narrow limits of the *Sharī'a*. Not everything in the new paths opened up by *Ṣūfism* was deserving of reprobation. It had shown the inadequacy of a religious practice, which had become set in the mould of formalism and casuistic excesses; it had insisted on the necessity for an inner life where love of God and detachment from the world should find a place.

THE ṢŪFĪ FRATERNITIES. They are called '*ṭarīqa*' (pl. *ṭuruq*). The word signifies 'path', an ethical system, and may have been borrowed from the Qorān (**46**, 29, and *passim*). The organization of the *Ṣūfī* fraternities shows a distant analogy with that of the religious orders as well as with the cure of souls which had devolved on the Christian clergy. I refer to the voluntary subordination established between the master *Sheikh* and the *murīd* or novice aspiring to be admitted into the congregation. Ghazālī advised the manifestation of conscience (p. 119). The Bekṭāshis go much further, and are alleged even to make confession to their superiors and to receive from them absolution for their faults.

The *Ṣūfī* candidate must conduct himself towards his master *perinde ac cadaver*, or, as the *Ṣūfī* writings say, 'like the corpse in the hands of the washer'. It is impressed on him that 'obedience is the first religious observance'. The *Sheikh* can therefore order him to omit certain practices of external religion, if the welfare of his soul demands it. This is the one and only feeble trace of spiritual authority that is to be discovered in Islām, this religion governed by laymen, by lawyers. The authority which the *Sheikhs* assumed over the decisions of the *'ulemā* could not but outrage the pharisaism of the latter, to whom the *Ṣūfīs* made the obvious retort: 'Go and practise yourselves one tenth of the duties that you impose upon believers!'

No one was more alive than Ghazālī to the lack of understanding and to the spiritual inadequacy of these titular guides of Islām. But in his respect for the *Sharī'a*, and his conviction of the need to combat the illuminism and pantheism which, since Bisṭāmī, lay in wait for the adherents of *Ṣūfism*, he tried to establish his ethical mysticism, a kind of *via media*. *Ijmā'* gave to this attempt an approval limited by the abstention of the whole body of Ḥanbalites. Practising what he preached, Ghazālī adopted the retired life of the *Ṣūfīs*. He remained faithful to external practices, but strove to exalt them by the spirit, 'to pierce the outer shell in order to reach the hidden kernel'. 'It is the heart', he asserts, borrowing the language of the *Ṣūfīs*, 'which approaches Allah, not the fleshly heart but a spiritual gift, thanks to which we can grasp the divine mysteries which escape the bodily senses.'

The foundation of these large fraternities goes back to our twelfth century when collective hermitages also grew more numerous. In the nineteenth century, principally in Africa, the fraternities displayed great external activity. The manifestations of this activity, hostile to the progress of European colonization, have helped Islāmic propaganda in the dark Continent. The fraternities have all tried to increase the number of their adherents and to create a sort of third order by the admission of affiliated members. These are the *brothers* or '*Ikhwān*' (vulgarly *Khuān*). They are subject to the guidance of the *Sheikh* or *muqaddam*, and receive their instructions from him. They collect the offerings of followers and also the often substantial revenues from the foundations attached to the fraternity.

Each one of these fraternities has forged an *isnād* of admission, a *chain*, *silsila* of mysterious links of evidence by means of which they claim to trace their spiritual genealogy back to the Companions of the Prophet. In these we find the names of the earliest, or what are reputed the earliest, ascetics of primitive Islām: Abū'd-Dardā and even Abū Dharr. The Shī'a has transformed that fierce Ṣaḥābī Beduin into an ascetic as a reward for his hostility to the Omayyads. The *Ṣūfīs* have also taken possession of the most popular saint in Iraq, Ḥasan al-Baṣrī (728). In the history of *Ṣūfism* the name of Al-Khiḍr occupies a place apart. He is a mysterious personage who shows many of the combined traits of Elias in the Bible and of St. George. The Qorān (**18**, 64–81) presents him as superior to the prophets since he became the guide charged with directing Moses. Many *Ṣūfīs*, Bisṭāmī, Ibn al-'Arabī, etc., claim to have been in direct communication with him. These dispense with all artificial *isnād*, and derive their mystical initiation from Al-Khiḍr, without intermediary.

THE 'DHIKR'. The fraternities possess their *zāwia*, called also '*ribāṭ, khānqā, tekké*', etc. They are not so much monasteries as meeting-places, consecrated to the performance of liturgical exercises in common. These collective exercises are usually known by the name of *dhikr*, literally 'mention'. The *dhikr* consisted at first of a recital in chorus of Qorānic passages followed by a recollection or meditation on the texts that had just been heard. Before long these meetings degenerated, following the course of the fraternities. The promoters sought to develop the purely emotional side, to appeal to the feelings to the detriment of the inner spirit. As in all things touching the mystic life, the *Ṣūfīs*, desirous of finding cover against the censure of the orthodox, refer to the Qorān where they claim to find the *dhikr*. Does not this book recommend the faithful 'to remember God with frequent remembrance' (*dhikran kathīran;* Qorān **33**, 41)? They recognize it in this beginning of a verse (**6**, 91): 'Say: Allah!' and dozens of similar ones all of which seem to proclaim the virtues of the divine name and of its simple ejaculation.

Ghazālī must likewise have drawn inspiration from these passages in his reflections on the divers modes of prayer. One of these methods of mental prayer is nothing more than the pronunciation, incessantly repeated, of the name of God. Alone in his cell, with veiled head, the contemplative *Ṣūfī* sets himself to utter without intermission the word *Allah*, concentrating thereon his whole attention. He must persevere in this repetition until tongue and lips can move no more and there subsists nothing but the impression of the word in the depths of the heart. Let him not stop here but renew his exercise until this sensory image fades from the heart and there remains the immaterial idea of the divine name so vivid that the spirit can no more depart from it.

The members of the fraternities also replace the name of Allah in their *dhikr* by the pronoun '*hū*', Him, in which, always according to the Qorān (**3**, 1), they include the most complete abstraction of the concept of the Divinity. To this mysterious monosyllable Ibn al-'Arabī has devoted a special monograph. Those present must concentrate their attention and regulate their inhalations and exhalations on the vocables uttered during the *dhikr*.

The principal theme consists in the intensive repetition, taken up in chorus by the whole congregation of *hū*, *hā*, *hi*, or *Allāhu*, *Allāha*, *Allāhi*. One *dhikr*, attributed to the celebrated mystic Ḥallāj, is thus, described by Sanūsī, the founder of the fraternity of Senussis. It consists in the repetition of the name of Allah, 'by suppressing the initial syllable *al* and by adding to the final *h* the three vowels, *a* towards the right, *i* towards the left and *o* towards the heart'. The ceremony of the *dhikr* has preserved of the early meetings of 'recollection' the psalmody of invocations in the language of the Qorān and of passages from the Qorān.

Sometimes to these is added the recitation of mystical poems in which the divine love is celebrated with a profusion of images and of realistic comparisons, borrowed from the language of profane love. There is nothing in this promiscuity to shock the spirituality of a Ghazālī. He concedes that the Qorān does not meet every circumstance nor all the diversity of moral situations and that familiarity with the sacred text ends by blunting the sensibility of the congregation. The effect of lyrical poetry, above all when music is added to heighten its impression, seems to him very different. Each fraternity possesses its special formulæ of *dhikr*, its litanies of names and divine attributes, its collections of Qorānic or mystico-lyrical texts. Their recitation modulated in cadence should be accompanied by inclination of the body and exercises of the limbs designed, like the whole programme of *dhikr*, to promote ecstatic phenomena.

MUSIC. The *Sunna* allows only the chanting of the Qorān; it strictly proscribes any other use of music, even in secular life. Ghazālī, as we have seen, declares himself in favour of the *samā'*, or spiritual concert, in the meetings of the *Ṣūfīs*. He seems, however, to have divined the dangers of this concession, since he advises the exclusion of strangers, whose presence might become a cause of distraction, and also of the '*murīd*', novices, on the ground of their incomplete education. A singer, '*qawwāl*', intones mystical hymns, with or without instrumental accompaniment. Seated in a circle motionless, with bent head and rigid limbs and respiration controlled, the officiants are careful not to disturb the congregation until, a *Ṣūfī* beside himself, manifests by cries, applause or dancing the beginning of ecstasy. The congregation must then join in his manifestations. Ghazālī availed himself of this phenomenon to infer the lawfulness of the *samā'*. If the ecstasy was long in coming, the '*qawwāl*' would pass to other pieces chosen from his lyrical and musical repertory. In authorizing this performance as other mystics had done, Ghazālī unconsciously prepares the way for the artificial working up of ecstasy in the meetings of *dhikr*. From the twelfth century onwards the fraternities enter upon this scandalous course and seek to control the mechanical production of abnormal phenomena, such as loss of the senses, which the brethren persist in confusing with '*shaṭḥ*' (p. 122). It is in 'shaṭḥ' that God is said to grant to the soul supernatural communications: the mystery of predestination, the revelation of the secret of all hearts, not to mention other miraculous manifestations, such as bilocation or intimate familiarity with Al-Khiḍr. To obtain these *charismas*, which he enumerates at length, Ghazālī lays down as a first condition that they must be deserved by the control of the lower appetites and by a humble submission to the will of God. These wise counsels were destined to pass unheeded.

When we consider the exhibitions organized by the howling and whirling dervishes, with the aid of stimulants and narcotics, we cannot but share the disgust of enlightened Muslims for the *dhikr* of the Rifā'is and the 'Isāwis, commonly called Aissauas. These hysterical exhibitions are, in the absence of an authorized direction and a strong moral discipline, the inevitable end of the mystic movement in the bosom of Islām.

Internal Organization. Admission into a *ṭarīqa* is preceded by a period of trial or noviciate, called *irāda*; whence the name *murīd* given to the *Ṣūfī* aspirant. The initiation of the candidate is effected by the bestowal of the *khirqa*, as well as of the *isnād* of admission (*v.* p. 131) by which the fraternity claims contact with the great saints of Islām. Received from the hands of the *Sheikh*, or director, the *khirqa* or habit of the fraternity represents the poverty and detachment from the world which the candidate is supposed to profess. Certain fraternities bestow the *khirqa* on women also, a practice violently opposed by the Ḥanbalite, Ibn al-Jauzī. Celibacy is exceptional, unless it be among the Bektāshis, who favour it. The married members—sometimes even polygamous—live with their families. The famous mystic Ibn al-'Arabī had long passed his sixtieth year when he contracted, at Damascus, a new union with a girl of eighteen. The same Ibn al-'Arabī, as a youth, received lessons from two Andalusian women mystics. For two years he lived as disciple and usher in a reed hut with Fāṭima, an ecstatic who died at the age of ninety-five.

As a general rule, an individual should belong only to one *ṭarīqa*. But since the institution of a third order, affiliation to more than one fraternity has passed as meritorious among the tertiaries. The founder of the Senussis had received initiation into several fraternities. The diffusion among Muslims of a kind of rosary first mentioned by Abū Nuwās (*circa* 808–813) is probably due to *Ṣūfī* influence.

Prior to the twelfth century every *Sheikh* trained

directly by his teaching and mode of life the disciples (*khuddām*) who congregated around him. Between master and disciples there existed only a bond of obedience, essentially temporary and strictly personal. The transmission of the habit or *khirqa* which later symbolized the engagement contracted with a particular brotherhood was unknown. This liberty of mystic education ceases with the appearance of the first '*ṭarīqa*'. These fraternities retain the name of their founders to whom they are attached by a kind of spiritual filiation and by the assumption of the habit. I shall enumerate the most important ones.

PRINCIPAL FRATERNITIES. (1) The 'Qādirīs', founded by 'Abdalqādir al-Gilānī (†1166). These are scattered throughout the whole Muslim world. Their founder, a very popular saint, belonged to the Ḥanbalite school whose hostility to *Ṣūfism* has been noted. (2) The 'Rifā'īs', founded by Aḥmad ar-Rifā'ī (†1175). (3) The 'Maulāwīs', commonly known as 'whirling Dervishes'. Their centre is at Qūnia (Anatolia), round the tomb of their founder, the celebrated mystic poet, Jalāladdīn ar-Rūmī (†1273). (4) The 'Shādhilīs', founded by Alī al-Shādhilī (†1256); a fraternity mainly African, with numerous sub-orders bearing special names: Madanīs, etc. The convulsionary 'Īsāwis or 'Isāwa seceded in the fifteenth century from the main body of the Shādhilīs. (5) The 'Badawīs', so called after Aḥmad al-Badawī (†1274), are an Egyptian fraternity whose centre is at Ṭanṭa (Lower Egypt). (6) The 'Naqshibandīs', founded by Bahā ad-dīn Naqshiband (1389). (7) In India the 'Shaṭṭārīs' (so called after Shaṭṭār (†1415) are to be found. (8) The 'Bektāshīs' seem to represent a sect rather than a mystic order.

Before the sixteenth century, they served as *Imāms* to the militia of the Janissaries, who protected them against the Ottoman inquisition. Their secret doctrine, still imperfectly known, relates them to the 'Alī-ilāhīs and other Shī'a extremists (see Chapter VII). The Bektāshis, as we have seen, admit celibacy. Regarded with disfavour by the Turkish government, deprived of their natural protectors since the destruction of the Janissaries, they flourish in Albania where they have embraced the Nationalist cause. (9) The 'Sanūsīs' or Senussis, founded in 1837 by the Algerian *Sheikh* As-Sanūsī (1857), are clearly distinguishable from the preceding *ṭarīqa*. They form a congregation-State whose centre is established in the desert oases of Cyrenaica. Their aims are as much political as religious, and resemble those of the Wahhābīs. They are as Zenophobe as the latter, and like them they dream of a return to primitive Islām, with this difference, that the better to attain it they resort to *Ṣūfism*, abhorred by the Wahhābīs.

As a general rule the headship of these fraternities is transmitted by heredity, or at least in such a way as to remain in the family of the founder. This thirst for supremacy, and also the greediness of the quarrels which spring up over the revenues of the order, agree very ill with the fundamental principles of *Ṣūfism*.

THEIR PRESENT POSITION. The cohesion between the *zāwias* and the members of a single order, scattered throughout the divers States, has always left much to be desired. The attempts to bring them under a kind of Grand-Master have encouraged scissions. Every government has been mistrustful of a powerfully centralized authority independent of official control. In Egypt, the Mamlūks not only kept a watch on the doctrines of the *Ṣūfīs* (p. 128) ; they also took sureties against their intervention in politics. The Ottoman Empire did not display any greater degree of confidence in them. The *ṭarīqa* have really flourished only amongst the intellectually backward and in regions where anarchy reigns.

In Albania, the number of Bektāshīs and of their affiliated members is considerable. Observation shows the same to be true in Morocco where, in spite of undeniable signs of dwindling, the *Khuans* are still very powerful. Certain estimates give the proportion of initiates and affiliated members at a tenth of the total population. One branch, separated from the Khalwatīs, *circa* 1770, that of the Raḥmānīs of Kabylia, numbered about thirty years ago 150,000 members, distributed among 170 *zāwias*. The Tijānīs of 'Ain Māḍi (Algeria), regarded as Francophiles, numbered at the same date 25,000 adherents and 32 *zāwias*.

Everywhere else the fraternities are declining. We have already seen the attitude adopted towards them by the Ḥanbalites, the Wahhābīs and Khārijites. No less hostility is shown by the Shī'a sects of all shades: Zaidites, Isma'īlis, Imāmites, etc. This enmity arises from the Shī'a dogma of the infallible Imām, the exclusive guide of the believers and the sole medium of all illuminative and sanctifying grace, whereas the *Ṣūfīs* claim to enter into direct communion with the Divinity.

The decline of mysticism is chiefly accentuated in those Muslim countries which are open to Western influences. The progressive centres with orthodox tendencies, or Salafiyya, as they call themselves, are no less hostile to it than are the followers of modernist principles who look upon the *Ṣūfīs* as vulgar charlatans. In these regions, semi-political secret societies tend to take the place of the old fraternities. Like the Bektāshis in Albania, they have everywhere taken up and exacerbated the claims of local nationalism. This was the case in Syria on the eve of the world war, and it was the lodges of *Union and Progress* which prepared the Young Turk movement and the advent of Ḳemalism. Freemasonry has profoundly penetrated the upper classes of Muslim society. The Turkish Republic of Anatolia has decreed the official suppression of all *Ṣūfī* fraternities and organizations.

VII

THE SECTS OF ISLĀM

THEIR NUMBER. Muḥammad said, 'My people will be divided into seventy-three sects, of which only one will be saved.' The early Muslim heresiologists, 'Abdalqāhir al-Baghdādī and Shahrastānī, to quote no others, were at very great pains to make up, in their enumeration of the sects sprung from Islām, the traditional number of seventy-two. They thought they could fall back on the opinions and systems lauded in the philosophico-theological schools, Mu'tazilites, Qadarites, Murjites, and others, and by means of this arithmetic had no difficulty in counting twenty Mu'tazilite and ten Murjite sects. It was sufficient for them to detail the divers solutions that these Islāmic logicians claim to have furnished to the problems of Qorānic theodicy: the eternal apple of discord between the Islāmic schoolmen, the question of their divine essence and attributes (*v.* p. 57), then that of the substance and the accidents in relation to the creative action of Allah ; the question of free-will and predestination ; the nature and definition of faith, the anthropomorphisms of the Qorān, etc.

This method has allowed them to place among the heresiarchs Al-Jāḥiẓ, a witty sceptic (*circa* 868), author of brilliant paradoxes, and later, the mystic, Ḥallāj (*v.* p. 123). We will not follow them into these subtle distinctions, nor will we discuss sects which are now extinct. We shall consider as distinct sects the groups that have separated from historic Islām as constituted from the fourth century A.H., on questions regarded as fundamental by the *Sunna* with the agreement of *ijmā'*. As though the better to affirm their autonomy, each of these groups has an organization independent of Sunni orthodoxy.

It is not, as in the Christian Church, doctrinal discussions, but political disagreements which have given birth to the schisms and heresies of Islām.

After Muḥammad, to whom should the leadership of the new community fall? The Qorānic text furnishes no reply to this question; if the Prophet considered the problem, he died without having attempted to solve it. His son-in-law, 'Alī, claimed the succession; but on three several occasions, the choice of the Muslim community, or of the group of electors supposed to represent it, negatived 'Alī's claims by setting aside his candidature. Nevertheless, it was stipulated that the Caliphate should be reserved to the Prophet's tribe, Quraish, and this definite rule recorded by the *Sharī'a* and the great collection of the *ḥadīth* merely made into law the practice followed during the first centuries of the Hijra, as is shown in the history of the Omayyad and 'Abbāsid Caliphs. The Khārijites, literally dissenters, very early rose up in armed opposition to the prerogative conferred on the Quraishites. They form the oldest Islāmic sect.

THE KHĀRIJITES proclaimed that leadership could not become the exclusive property of a particular family or tribe, that the Prophet's successor should be chosen by the votes of the Believers from among the worthiest, not excepting negroes. These representatives of the equality-loving instincts of the ancient and modern Beduins recognized none the less the legitimacy of the first two Caliphs. For the rest, the

Khārijites differ from the Sunnis or orthodox only in details, in the prescriptions of the *Sharī'a* and the observance of a more primitive ritual. Preceding in point of time the discussions raised by the learned schools, they did not come wholly under the influence of the Mu'tazilites. They refuse to admit that the Qorān is uncreated, and will not reserve for non-Muslims the eternal torments of hell. As regards Muslims, faith and the intercession of the Prophet are not sufficient to save them without good works. They prohibit the cult of the saints, local pilgrimages and *Ṣūfī* fraternities. The revolts of these democratic Muslims troubled the first three centuries of the Hijra and caused the shedding of rivers of blood.

To-day they are commonly called 'Ibāḍites' (or 'Abāḍites', a more prevalent pronunciation), after Ibn Ibāḍ, chief of the least extremist of the numerous sub-sects into which they are divided. Certain of them desire to exclude from the Qorān the curses uttered against Abū Lahab (**111,** 1) with the exception of the *Sūra* of Joseph. On this point of exegesis, they agree with certain Mu'tazilite commentators. They interpret literally the penalty of hand-cutting which the Qorān inflicts on thieves irrespective of the importance of the larceny committed. They admit, even against an Ibāḍite, the testimony of a heterodox witness.

They are to be met with in scattered groups, principally in the north of Africa, in the Mzāb (Algeria), in the neighbourhood of Ghardaya, in the island of Jerba, at Jebel Nefūsa (Tripolitania), and finally in the province of 'Omān (Arabia), whence they crossed to Zanzibar. In Algeria their opposition to the Sunnis has brought the Mzābites into friendly relations with the French government, especially since the latter has authorized them to be judged according to their own laws. The devotion of Syria to the cause of the Omayyads has always prevented Khārijism, a sect of the first century, from penetrating into this country.

THE SHĪ'AS. The thorny question of the prophetic *vicariate* was to provoke the birth of other scissions including that of the Shī'as, the most important of all by reason of its extent and ramifications. They derived their name from the word Shī'a, a party, as they were the 'partisans' of 'Alī, '*Shī'at 'Alī*'.

The political question which first gave rise to the conflict was reinforced later by doctrinal divergences, some of them exceedingly daring especially among the extremist factions of the Shī'a: belief in the survival of the Shī'a *Imām*, in his reappearance, in metempsychosis, and in the partial or total incarnation of the Divinity in the person of the 'Alids. 'Alī's ambitious and numerous descendants soon split up the Shī'a into a multitude of sects—computed at about seventy —each of which called down anathemas on the others.

All, except the modifications admitted by the Zaidites (*v.* below), deny that the Caliphate—or Imāmate as they call it—can be subject to election. They believe it to be reserved for the descendants of Fāṭima, daughter of the Prophet and wife of 'Alī, by virtue of an express stipulation of Muḥammad. Since 'Alī, every *Imām* has the right to nominate his successor from among his sons. The 'Alids form the caste of the *Sherīfs* or nobles, a title especially reserved for the direct descendants of Ḥasan, the eldest son of Fāṭima. That of *Seyyid*, lord, is the qualificative of the Ḥusainids; the line of Ḥusain, younger brother of Ḥasan. Excluded from power by the Omayyads, imprisoned or killed by the 'Abbāsids, lacking in political acumen, jealous and quarrelling fiercely among themselves over the title of *Imām*, they constituted an opposition party whose conspiracies and badly organized revolts fill the annals of the two first centuries of the Hijra.

The commemoration of the death of Ḥusain, Muḥammad's grandson, who fell in the mad escapade of Kerbelā (Oct. 10th, 680), forms one of their chief festivals. It is a feast of mourning, celebrated on the tenth of the month of Muḥarram ; a sort of Shī'a Holy Week, filled with dramatic performances (*ta'zia*) intended to commemorate the tragedy of Kerbelā. The fall of Ḥusain, a quite mediocre person, excites the Shī'as to the point of delirium. 'We shall continue to mourn him unto the very bosom of Paradise,' writes an Indian Shī'a. 'The heart of every true Shī'a is the living tomb of Ḥusain.' And in a book with the pretentious title *Husain in the Philosophy of History* (Lucknow, 1905) the same author calls his hero 'the primordial cause of existence'.

Among the Shī'as, even the most moderate, the cult of '*ahl al-bait*', 'The People of the Family', the title borne by the direct descendants of Muḥammad, is followed to the detriment of the veneration in which Islām holds its Prophet. Muḥammad is slightly eclipsed by 'Alī, just as 'Alī is somewhat thrown into the shade by Ḥusain. The pale hero of Kerbelā has completely supplanted his elder brother Ḥasan whom the Shī'as cannot quite forgive for making terms with Mu'āwiya, the first Omayyad Caliph. Ḥusain is deemed to have sacrificed himself voluntarily in order to reconcile God with humanity and thus effect, as it were, a redemption. Muḥammad, 'Alī and Ḥusain form a Shī'a trinity. The first-named represents revelation, 'Alī interpretation or the esoteric meaning (*ta'wīl*) of the Qorān, and Ḥusain redemption.

The tomb of Ḥusain at Kerbelā, and that of 'Alī at Najaf, are to the Shīa's objects of pilgrimage not less sacred than the holy cities of the Ḥejāz. Kāẓimain and Samarra (Irāq) are also numbered among their holy cities, to which, as well as to Kerbelā and Ṇejd, they like to convey the mortal remains of their dead. In these centres dwell the great *'ulemā*, or *mujtahid*, as they are called, whose authority has the force of law in the sect.

The ' Kitmān ' or ' Taqiyya '. The surveillance of the Omayyads and still more the bloody repression of the 'Abbāsids having reduced them to dissimulation and conspiracy, they invented the doctrine of '*kitmān*', or secrecy, which is characteristic among the tendencies of these sectarians. They also called it '*taqiyya*', prudence, a word borrowed from the Qorānic vocabulary (**3**, 27). All the Shī'a collections contain a special chapter entitled ' book of the *taqiyya* '.

The Ḥanifites themselves foresee and legitimize the case where to save self or relations and friends recourse is had to mental reservation. The Shī'a *taqiyya* goes far beyond this exception. A true Shi'a not only feels authorized, but obliged by conscience to hide his intimate feelings and still more his religious convictions. Among the enemies of his beliefs, he can speak and behave as though he were one of them. In acting thus, in bearing false witness or taking false oaths, when the interests of his sect demand it, he thinks he is obeying the command of the supreme or hidden *Imām*. The *Imām* of the Shī'as being, according to their conception, infallible, the adept acquires by dissembling the right to speak as would the *Imām* in the same circumstances, while believing inwardly as the *Imām* believes. It is unnecessary to point out the moral consequences of this doctrine, of this law of secrecy, which maintains and legalizes perpetual equivocation. With the exception of the Zaidites, all the sects which have sprung from the Shī'a have recourse to the *taqiyya*. It is practised with the utmost rigour by those Shī'a extremists who are organized in secret societies: Isma'īlīs, Noṣairīs, and Druses (*vide* below), especially the last two.

THE HIDDEN IMĀM. In place of the Sunni Caliph, a usurper in the eyes of the Shī'as, the chief of the latter takes the name of *Imām*. He must, as we have seen (p. 144), belong to the 'People of the Family' or 'of the House'. This expression is borrowed from the Qorān (**33**, 33). The context clearly shows that it denotes only the harem and the wives of the Prophet who were united under his roof at the time when the text was given out.

Traditional exegesis began by extending it first to his descendants and then to his kindred. This last extension was artfully made by the 'Abbāsids, who used it to prepare the way for their ascent to the Caliphate. The Shī'as consider it completely valueless for the purpose of deciding who is to hold the Caliphate, or sovereignty of Islām. In their eyes the *Imām* Caliph should be a direct descendant, not simply a relation of the Prophet. This entails reserving the dignity to the Fāṭimids, the children of Fāṭima and 'Alī, to the exclusion of the offspring of other marriages contracted by 'Alī, to the exclusion, above all, of the 'Abbāsids, the posterity of 'Abbās, the uncle of Muḥammad.

Persecution obliged them to disguise their religion, and since the decease of their twelfth *Imām*, who died without issue, the Shī'as, seeing themselves without a leader, invented a strange doctrine: that of the *ghaiba*, or absence, that is, the absence of the *Imām*. Since then, they constitute a 'hidden community'. It is directed by a mysterious *Imām*, himself immune from death. Be he known or unknown, the adepts are bound to swear fealty to him, as much as to Allah and the Prophet. This is the *walāya*, or allegiance to the *Imām*, which is superimposed on the 'five pillars of Islām ' and amongst the Shī'as is placed first in importance.

Unlike the Sunni Caliph, a temporal leader deprived of all authority in the matter of dogma, guardian merely of the *Sharī'a* and civil defender of Islām, the Shī'a *Imām* becomes its Pontiff and infallible teacher. He is not only Muḥammad's temporal successor, but also the inheritor of his dignity, from which he has received the super-eminent prerogatives of witness and interpreter of the revelation. He is in very sooth a religious and spiritual leader, with an even stronger title than that of the Pope in the Catholic Church, since to the privilege of infallibility, *'iṣma*, he adds the divine gift of impeccability. Thus he is the sole and permanent channel of all sanctifying prerogatives and illuminative inspirations.

In view of this, the Shī'a cannot, as we have seen, admit the principle of *Sūfism* and its methods of spiritual perfection, independent of the hidden *Imām* and exempt from his control. As for his exceptional prerogatives, the *Imām* is said to owe them to a portion of the divine knowledge and illumination which have descended into his soul. He himself, however, remains a merely human being, as were his 'Alid ancestors. The distance that separates the Shī'a *Imām* from the orthodox Caliph is obvious. He possesses the esoteric knowledge (*ta'wīl*) communicated by Muḥammad to 'Alī and transmitted to the *Imām*. This is a further reason for the hostility of the Shī'a to *Ṣūfism*. The *Imām* alone has the right to decide controversial questions. In his infallible authority, which admits neither the restriction nor the control of discussion, the Shī'as believe they have found something better than the agreement (*ijmā'*) of the community, an agreement necessarily incomplete, difficult to establish, and in the last resort open to error. The Shī'as do not fail to exploit these deficiencies in their polemics against the Sunnīs.

THE IMĀMITES OR TWELVERS. These are the points that might be called common to the divers factions into which the Shī'a divided at an early date. In the family of 'Alī unity always left much to be desired. Among his numerous descendants, the offspring, or otherwise, of his marriage with Fāṭima, and then among the 'Alids, genuine or so-called, the aspirants to the rôle of *Imām* continued to multiply and gave birth to new sects. The most widespread and the one which has remained nearest to the starting-point of the Shī'a is that of the ' Imāmites ' or ' Twelvers ', *ithna-'ashar-iyya.* They are called by the latter name because they acknowledge the existence of twelve *Imāms,* of which the list is appended ; it will be found to contain likewise the genealogy of the *Imāms* to which Zaidites and Ismā'īlīs trace the origin of their sect :

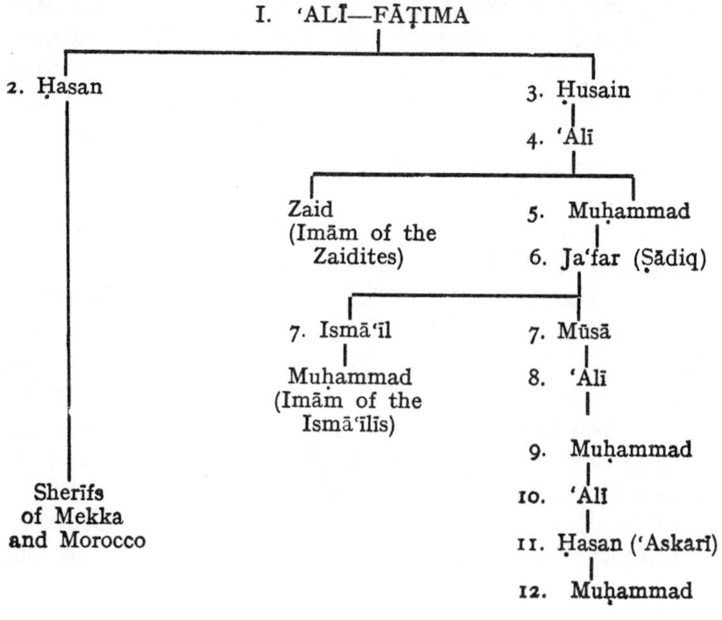

The twelfth and last in the line of these direct descendants from Fātima is a hypothetical Muhammad, surnamed 'Al-muntazar', or the expected, son of the eleventh *Imām,* Hasan, called Al-'Askarī. This Muḥammad, born in 873, is said to have disappeared early and in mysterious circumstances. This disappearance is the origin of the 'Shī'a' *ghaiba* (*v.* p. 144). Some say that he is dead, others that he has risen again. But all his partisans agree that he must reappear, when the hour strikes, in order to fulfil the mission assigned by tradition to the 'Mahdī', '*he who is guided aright*', to bring righteousness to a world filled with iniquity and to restore the golden age. It is he, 'the hidden *Imām*', the '*qā'im az-zamān*', the Master of the Hour. All the Shī'a factions believe in the return, in the second coming of a Fāṭimid *Imām,* an *Imām* deified by the extremists. Since the Ṣafavids (1501–1722), Twelvist *Imāmism* has become the State religion of Persia. The Persian sovereign, unlike the Caliph, the temporal Vicar of the Prophet, is regarded only as the provisional *locum tenens* of the hidden *Imām* until the reappearance of the latter.

IMĀMISM numbers about seven million adherents in Persia. To this figure must be added five million adepts scattered throughout British India and a million and a half in Irāq. The great majority of Persian Shī'as belong to the faction of the '*uṣūlī*', directed by the canonists or '*mujtahids*'. The minority —a million in number—have taken the name of 'Akhbārī', because, beside the Qorān, they only admit the 'Akhbār' or traditions. We shall speak later of the *Sheikhīs* (*v.* Bābism) and of the branch of the Imāmites called *Metoualis,* scattered throughout Syria.

THE MAHDĪ. The belief in an *Imām*-Mahdī and in his second coming forms the centre of the Shī'a creed.

Similar millenary traditions have penetrated into orthodox Islām, without gaining the same importance as in the Shī'a or becoming articles of faith. In their earliest form, these Sunni traditions refer to the second coming of 'Isā or Christ. Certain of them, born of the need of the masses to hope for a better future, consider the Mahdī as the religious and political restorer of Islām. Other *ḥadīth*, doubtless desirous of rendering their beliefs inoffensive to public law and order, present the Mahdī simply as the precursor of the end of the world and defer his reappearance to that date. It is the eschatological mission originally reserved to Christ whose part the Mahdī thus doubles.

The Mahdī of the Sunnis is an ill-defined personality, who, apart from his descent from Fāṭima, recalls but distantly the Shī'a *Imām* reappearing after centuries of 'absence'. He must bear the same name as his ancestor, the Prophet of Islām, Muḥammad ibn *'Abdullah*, a detail which certainly seems designed to rule out the candidature of the Shī'a *Imām*, Muḥammad ibn *Ḥasan*. The mission of restorer of Islām, assigned to the Mahdī, is nevertheless a disquieting matter. Despite its more moderate form, which has indeed enabled it to sink deeply into the popular mind, adventurers and political agitators have been able to exploit the Sunni doctrine right up to recent years (we may recall Muḥammad Aḥmad, the Mahdī of the Sudan) and to stir up revolution in Muslim countries by giving themselves out as the Mahdī.

Among the Shī'as, the *Imām*-Mahdī, notwithstanding his 'absence', is said to remain in constant communication, through the medium of his 'privileged ones', with his followers, who may not resist his commands. When, in October 1908, the Constitutional Party in Persia launched its appeal to the people, it pressed for 'consultation with the doctors of the Holy City of

Najaf'. Their decision affirmed that 'to oppose the Constitution was equivalent to drawing the sword against the *Imām of the Hour* (the Mahdī). May Allah grant us to witness his return!' Two years previously the opening of the first National Parliament had likewise taken place under the auspices 'and in the presence of the hidden *Imām*'. In the Constitution the second chapter was declared 'unalterable until the return of the *Imām*'!

DIVERGENCES BETWEEN THE SUNNIS AND SHĪ'AS. The main line of demarcation between the two parties is drawn by the fundamental dogma of the *Imām*-Mahdī. From the orthodox point of view this doctrine, which is at once political and religious, makes of the Shī'a a heresy and schism. The Shī'a *Imām*, hereditary chief of Islām, is '*ma'ṣūm*'; he enjoys the double prerogative of infallibility and impeccability Orthodox Islām recognizes these prerogatives only in the prophets who are immune from doctrinal error as well as from physical and moral imperfections which might be harmful to the success of their mission. In matters of dogma, the Shī'as adhere in the main to the theories of the Mu'tazilites. Their devotion consists entirely in the cult of the *Imāms*. All Persians bear the name of an *Imām*, often preceded by the words ''Abd, Gholām'—servant—or by a predicate referring to a prerogative of the *Imāms*.

Otherwise, in the matter of beliefs, rites and discipline the divergences between the Shī'a and the *Sunna* are hardly more marked than those separating the four juridical schools. Indeed, it has been proposed to count it as a fifth school, with the name accepted by the Sunnis of '*Ja'farī*' rite, an appellation derived from the sixth Shī'a *Imām* 'Ja'far aṣ-Ṣādiq' (*v.* p. 148), whom the Shī'as regarded as the author of the Imāmite *fiqh*. They cannot forgive the great

Bukhārī for having excluded him from the *isnād* of his '*Ṣaḥīḥ*'.

Among the Sunnis the new moon of Ramaḍan must be established empirically and attested by witnesses; the Shī'as admit its determination by astronomical calculation. They have introduced a slight variant in the *adhān* or call to daily prayers. In the funeral prayers they add a fifth *takbīr* to the four in use among the Sunnis. The latter take as their chosen title '*ahl as-Sunna*', people of the *Sunna*, or Sunnis, in order to mark their attachment to the *custom* and traditions of the Prophet.

From this it has been erroneously deduced that the Shī'as reject the *Sunna* and the *ḥadīth* which are supposed to establish it and that they do not recognize these as the second 'root', after the Qorān, of dogma and religious discipline. But they claim to possess their own *Sunna* and traditions or '*akhbār*', a word which they substitute for *ḥadīth*. These *akhbār*, which they consider as the only ones authorized, differ from the *ḥadīth* because the *isnād* admits only the testimony of the 'Alids, the *Imāms* and their partisans. These collections, scarcely less voluminous than those of the Sunnis, have been compiled and are interpreted with still less regard for internal criticism; the sole object is to support the privileges of the *Imām*, the Shī'a dogma of the *Imām*-Mahdī and the exclusive claims of the 'Alids to the Caliphate.

SHĪ'A EXEGESIS. They also believe that they find these claims in the Qorān, by means of *ta'wīl*, or allegorical interpretation. This elastic symbolism has furnished them with a rich exegetical literature which they trace back to the *Imāms*. *Ta'wīl* allows them to utilize and preserve the text of the official Qorān, while awaiting the hour when the hidden *Imām* shall come to reveal the original text to the world. The *ta'wīl* is often puerile; for example, in the Cow which is to be sacrificed (*Sūra* II, *v.* 63) they propose to recognize 'Ayesha, the mortal enemy of 'Alī. In effect they agree that they interpret the same Qorān as the orthodox, while affirming that it does not represent the first version. In places they assume the existence of variants, they slip in glosses, without, however, going so far as to keep these tamperings in the text used for religious ceremonies.

The absence of mention of 'Alī in the book of Allah embarrasses them greatly. But in the epithet *'Alī* which the 43rd *Sūra*, verse 3, applies to the Qorānic revelation, they recognize the name of Fāṭima's husband. Elsewhere, in place of *Ilyāsīn* (**37**, 130), the Qorānic name of the prophet Elias, they suggest reading "*Alī yā sīn* '. Obsessed by their Imāmite theories, they substitute for the word 'omma', nation, '*a'imma*', very similar in Arabic writing, which permits of their finding in the sacred text (Qorān **2**, 137; **3**, 106, etc.) an allusion to the *Imāms*. They discover yet another allusion—this time to the esoteric wisdom of the *Imāms*, in the verse 'Allah has taught the bees', meaning the 'Alids. 'The wholesome fluid produced by the bees' (**16**, 70) can be nothing other than the Qorān. It is to this bold exegesis that 'Alī owes his original sobriquet of Emir of the Bees conferred on him by the Shī'as, especially by the religious writings of the Noṣairīs. One last trait will complete the description of the '*tafsīr*' of the Shī'as. He found thee 'erring' (*ḍāllan*). Thus Allah addresses Muḥammad in the 93rd *Sūra*, *v.* 7. This verse refers to the polytheistic error, professed by the future Prophet, prior to his mission. A Shī'a interpreter found this a stumbling-block. Substituting the nominative for the accusative of the text, he has read '*ḍāllun*' in place of '*ḍāllan*'. This correction gives the meaning 'one gone astray has found thee', or has met thee, which appears to him to save the prestige of the Prophet, the ancestor of the *Imām.*

After the central theory of the *Imām*-Mahdī and the corollaries which proceed from it, the most serious point of discipline which separates Shī'as and Sunnis consists in *mut'a,* or temporary marriage. This union, which may be dissolved after a period stipulated between the parties, is severely condemned by the orthodox *fiqh,* which classes it with adultery.

THE METOUALIS. The Shī'as, with the exception of the Zaidites, are still further distinguished from the Sunnis by an attitude markedly more intolerant toward other religions. They differ also in interpreting literally this dictum of the Qorān (**9**, 28): 'The Infidel is unclean.' They infer from it that to touch him or merely to be in his company entails moral defilement, they refuse to eat or drink out of a utensil touched by one of the heterodox, to partake of food prepared by him, or to marry a Scripturary woman. They curse all the enemies of 'Alī, namely, all those among his contemporaries who did not take up his quarrel, without excepting even the most intimate friends of Muḥammad. This is an excess severely criticized by the orthodox *Sharī'a,* since the Qorān (**9**, 101) has canonized the whole company of 'Companions' of the Prophet by declaring them 'the object of Allah's favour'.

This savage intolerance can still be observed to-day among the Shī'as of Syria, known in that country by the name of *Metoualis,* an appellation derived from '*mutawāli*', a partisan, that is of 'Alī and the 'Alid *Imāms.* They are chiefly to be found in communities gathered in the territory of the Great Lebanon, where they number about 130,000, to which must be added 25,000 scattered over other parts of Syria. They reject the historical title of *Metoualis,* popularized by the early documents, and substitute for it the name of Shī'as or Ja'farites, after the juridical rite to which they adhere. They belong, like the Persians, to the sect of the Imāmites or Twelvers, but are neverthess Syrians by race.

THE ZAIDITES. Settled in the mountain groups of Yemen (Southern Arabia), they have founded an independent 'Alid Imāmate and rejoice in an organization which is in theory very democratic. They are the most moderate of the Imāmite factions and the nearest to the Sunnis. In place of the fifth *Imām* of the Twelvers, they acknowledge a certain Zaid, grandson of Ḥusain, himself the Prophet's grandson (see table, p. 148). This Zaid conceived it his duty to vindicate, by force of arms, the rights of the 'Alid family. He perished while fighting in Irāq against the troops of the Omayyad Caliph Hishām (740). The manner of his death brought him into prominence. His name has been borrowed without justification; since all through his lifetime he remained in perfect harmony with current orthodoxy. The Zaidites, none the less, consider him as the founder of their sect and of their particular legislation.

The Zaidites maintain the highest right of 'Alī to the Caliphate, less on account of his relationship to the Prophet than in virtue of the super-eminent qualities with which they endow him. But this does not cause them to contest the legitimacy of Muḥammad's two first successors. They refuse to curse them, they admit neither the esoteric science of the infallible 'Alid *Imāms* nor temporary marriage (*v.* p. 154), as do the Twelvers, nor temporary hell for the Muslim who has died impenitent and guilty of '*Kabā'ir*'. The *Imām*, a Ḥasanid or Ḥusainid, it matters little which, must be a man of action and assert his right. Thus it is clear that they do not adhere to the theory of the hidden *Imām* nor to the practice of *taqiyya*. All these characteristics produce in the Zaidites much more openness than is found in the Imāmites and the other Shī'a sects. They are hostile to *Ṣūfism* and the cult of the saints. But they hold resolutely to their political independence under an 'Alid *Imām*, chosen by election. More than one Muslim scholar finds in this attachment an insufficient reason for excluding them from '*jamā'a*', or the congregation of the orthodox.

On the whole the Zaidite opinions are in obvious agreement with what has been called 'laudable' or 'moderate' Shī'ism, *tashayyu' ḥasan*. This theory, held in the past by Sunnis of high standing, professes a discreet cult for 'the People of the House', that is to say, the Prophet's family, without falling into the exaggerations of the Shī'a. It reserves all its severity for the Omayyad Caliphs. The ancient dynasty of the Sherīfs of Mekka who belong to the line of Ḥasan (*v.* table, p. 148) at first adhered to the Zaidite confession.

The following sects sprung from Imāmism are strictly secret and *initiatory*, that is to say, admission is by way of initiation only. They have preserved the principles laid down by the Twelvers on the pre-eminence of the 'Alid *Imāms* to their most extreme conclusions. None has constituted a graver menace to the future of Islāmic orthodoxy than Ismā'īlism, a doctrine which continued to develop until by way of Carmathianism and Fāṭimidism it gave birth to Drusism.

The Ismā'īlīs take their name from Ismā'īl (762), son of the sixth *Imām* of the Twelvers, Ja'far aṣ-Ṣādiq (*v.* p. 148). In this Ismā'īl they end the line of 'visible *Imāms*'. But because he died before his father or was disowned by him, the other Shī'as disputed his right to the title of Imām. The Ismā'īlīs, more logical in their 'Alid legitimism, claim that his title must have passed to his son Muḥammad and they practically consider Ismā'īl and his son together as the seventh *Imām*. It is for this reason that they are also called 'Sab'iyya', or the *Seveners*.

They proclaim the necessity for a *ta'līm*, or teaching placed above human discussion, whence their sobriquet of '*Ta'līmiyya*'. They consider that this doctrine can only be dispensed by the *Imām*. As a natural corollary they exact from their partisans a blind adherence to the *ta'līm* of the Ismā'īlī *Imām*, whose character of infallibility and superhuman prerogatives they stress, even more forcibly than do the pure Imāmites. The Ismā'īlite *ta'līm* did not at first differ substantially from the '*ta'wīl*', or allegorism, in use among the Shī'as. Since the Carmathians, the last word of this teaching seems to have been that the divers religions are symbols for the use of the masses. For the initiated is reserved a philosophical and abstract doctrine, the science of '*bāṭin*', of the inner meaning, concealed in the verses of the Qorān. This exegetical method has gained for them a third title, that of 'Bāṭiniyya'.

In the midst of the disintegration of the Shī'a, when the claimants, almost all insignificant, multiplied and fought amongst themselves, the *Seveners* seemed destined to form an Imāmite sub-sect propagated by emissaries (*dā'i*, pl. *du'āt*) in the service of a new hidden *Imām*. They would have vegetated in obscurity but for the doctrinal adhesion of Carmathians, savage revolutionaries, whose career of violence drenched Syria and Mesopotamia in blood in the ninth to eleventh centuries. In its turn, Carmathian Ismā'īlism begot the Imāmism of the Fāṭimid Caliphs (909–1171). This dynasty, which was founded in the Maghrib by the adventurer 'Ubaidallah (909–934), and which gained control of Egypt and Syria, was able to modify the fierce energy of the Carmathians and turn it into channels where it might profitably be used for purposes of political domination.

Since its adoption by the Carmathians, Ismā'īlism had been transformed into a kind of carbonarism uniting all the malcontents, Arabs and Iranians, in order to lead them to the assault on the 'Abbāsid Caliphate. The principle of the 'Alid legitimism served to mask a complete programme of social revolution and democratic justice. They endowed these claims with the attraction of mystery and of scientific novelty, by exploiting the Platonic ideas current since the translation of the Greek philosophers. In religion, Carmathianism made use of a systematic catechism adapted to all religions, races and castes, by incessant recourse to gnostic cabbala, and reference to the *inner* meaning, ' *bāṭin* ', of the sacred Books.

The Carmathian leaders ended by ceasing to have any interest in 'Alidr legitimism and by working for their own ends. The Fāṭimids who claim descent from 'Alī and the seventh *Imām* were primarily concerned with dynastic interests, and reverted to Ismā'īlian Imāmism. Social reform faded into the background. Of its Carmathian *stage* it preserved nothing but its hermetic science, a secret organization concerned with propaganda and the grades of initiation, recalling the degrees of freemasonry.

We possess only in fragmentary form the original writings of the sect. Other sources of a later date fail to give us adequate information as to the evolution of the Ismā'īlian doctrine in its passage from Carmathianism to Fāṭimism and finally to ' *da'wa jadīda* ', Neo-Ismā'īlism or reform, inaugurated by the ' Assassins ' of Alamūt (1090) and those of Syria. Beside the *postulata,* borrowed from the most advanced factions of Imāmism, the most striking feature in the system of the *Seveners* is the part played by the number seven, maintained, in spite of the addition of Muḥammad to his father Ismā'īl, in the number of the *Imāms* and later in that of the degrees of initiation.

Ismā'īlite cosmogony seems to be gnostic in origin. God is without attributes and inaccessible. He has no communion with the universe except through seven degrees of emanation : God, Universal Reason (*'aql*), the Universal Soul, primitive Matter, Space, Time and the terrestrial World. God has created the lower world by Universal Reason and the Universal Soul. Time is divided into seven cycles, each corresponding to a manifestation of the divinity. Seven is likewise the number of the prophets or '*nāṭiq*', speakers. The list of these *speakers* begins with Adam and ends with Noah, Abraham, Moses, Jesus, Muḥammad, and, lastly, the Ismā'īlite *Imām.* The '*nāṭiq*' is the incarnation of Universal Reason. He is helped by the Universal Soul, also incarnate, and called *asās,* or base. These helpers or *bases* are again seven in number. Their mission consists in making manifest by the method of the *inner* meaning the esoteric doctrine of the *speaker.* Thus it is that Aaron has helped and completed Moses, and Simon-Peter Christ. 'Alī has given the allegorical and final interpretation of the Qorān or of the preaching of Muḥammad.

Finally, there are seven degrees of initiation, brought up to nine under the Fāṭimids. First, by insinuation and a series of insidious questions, then by systematic doubt (*tashkīk*), the adept is gradually brought to take an oath of blind submission to the *ta'līm* of the infallible and half-deified *Imām.* Arrived at the stage of *ta'sīs*, or *stabilization,* he then finds himself placed above all beliefs, and freed from all religious obligations. For these are nothing more than symbols : hell denotes ignorance ; paradise the state of the soul which has attained to perfect knowledge ; resurrection (*qiyāma*) is the manifestation of the Ismā'īlite *Imām*, of the '*qā'im az-zamān*', or the 'Master of the Hour'. It is this grade which has won for the Ismā'īlis the name of 'Ibāḥiyya', libertarians or nihilists, as well as causing them to be accused of immoral practices and licentious assemblies. Proof of these has never been forthcoming.

The great majority of adepts never go further than the third degree, where they deliver themselves over to the authority of the Ismā'īlite *Imām*. The missionaries and propagandists (*dā'i*) scarcely attain to the last but one. The political assassinations to which the *Seveners* owe their sinister reputation do not form a tenet of their *ta'līm*, or secret doctrine. It is 'propaganda by deed', one of the excesses ordered by the terrible Grand-Masters of Alamūt which Carmathian carbonarism had already put into practice.

Neo-Ismā'īlism or '*da'wa jadīda*', half schism, half reformed Fāṭimism, inaugurated by Ḥasan ibn Ṣabbāḥ (†1124), was in fact the religion of the partisans of the 'Sheikh al-Jabal', or 'The Old Man of the Mountain', nicknamed 'Assassins' (from the Arabic Ḥashshāshīn) because they were said to be addicted to *ḥashīsh* and other narcotics. In the time of the Crusades they terrorized Syria by their political assassinations. Their descendants, numerically much diminished and in any case quite harmless, still form a small group there (about 20,000) in the mountains between Ḥamā and Latakia, as well as in Salamiya, to the east of Ḥoms. They are equally widespread in Persia and Afghanistan.

Their chief centre is in India, where they take the title of Khoja or Maulā. There they form wealthy communities in which emigration to East Africa is popular. They are Nizāriyya, that is to say, partisans of the Imāmate of Nizār, eldest son of the Fāṭimid

Caliph Mustansir (1094). This Nizār had been ousted in favour of his younger brother, who became the Caliph Musta'lī (1094–1101). The Bōhoras or proto-Ismā'īlīs of India support the Imāmate of the latter. The Bōhoras are themselves divided into sub-sects of which the most numerous, that of Dāūdīs, numbers 130,000 adherents.

The present Chief of the Khojas is Sir Muḥammad Shāh ibn Aghā 'Alī, commonly called the Aghā Khān. This descendant of Ḥasan ibn Ṣabbāḥ, the first Grand-Master of Alamūt and initiator of Neo-Ismā'īlism, is counted as the forty-seventh *Imām*, going back to 'Alī, son-in-law of the Prophet. He is a great nobleman, fabulously rich, and very well known in high society in the West. The Khojas hand over to him a tenth of their revenue and a visit to this deified personage takes the place of the pilgrimage to Mekka.

A few representatives of Carmathian Ismā'īlism are still to be encountered in Arabia (in the country of Najrān) and in the province of Aḥsā (Arabia), an old Carmathian stronghold. The Ismā'īlī sects trouble no more about the other 'pillars of Islam' than they do about pilgrimage. Notwithstanding the dislike which the Sunnis and Shī'as vie with one another in showing towards them, it is remarkable that the leading Ismā'īlīs, and foremost the Aghā Khān, exhibit a lively feeling of Muslim solidarity of which they have given proofs in the recent crisis of the Caliphate.

THE DRUSES. The Sunni theologians have always been careful to maintain the distance separating God from His creatures. They show Him as communicating with them only by the summary revelation of indispensable laws and sanctions. The Shī'a sects, on the contrary, have sought to diminish this distance. They thought to achieve success by exalting, in various degrees, the pre-eminence of the 'Alid *Imāms*. Did the *Imāms* or Fāṭimid Caliphs share in the divine nature? The Ismā'īlite doctrine does not affirm it *ex professo*: but is content to insinuate it.

In an official letter, intended to recall the dissident Carmathians to their allegiance, the Fāṭimid Caliph, Al-Mu'izz (952–975), under whom the conquest of Egypt was completed, did not hesitate to proclaim the pre-existence of the *Imāms*, his ancestors. It was for their sake, he asserted, that the world had been created. 'They were the eternal world of Allah, His perfect names, His dazzling lights, His brilliant signs and the ineluctable decrees of the divine Fatum: the Universal Soul proceeding from the earthly Intellect, celestial wonders which had become tangible and visible.'

When the fanatical Fāṭimid, Ḥākim (996–1020), gave himself out as the final incarnation of the Divinity, he merely drew the ultimate conclusions from those premises, which are contained in germ in the system of Fāṭimid Ismā'īlism; he gave birth to Drusism.

The Druses do not dispute the inconsistencies and eccentricities of their hero, any more than the Christian doctors disavow 'the follies and the shame of the Cross'. The creators of the sect even insist on them with complacency, look them full in the face and experience no embarrassment in giving them an allegorical interpretation. All these oddities were intentional and symbolical. 'They must not be regarded as other than emblems whose object was to establish the unitarian doctrine' (S. de Sacy), that is, the doctrine of the Druse religion. Ḥākim allowed his hair to grow long because the hair is the emblem of the external practices of the Law. He affected woollen apparel, which is the symbol of *ta'wīl*, or the internal Law. He adopted as his steed an ass which represents (*sic*) the ' nāṭiq ' or *speakers* of the previous religions which he came to abolish.

Among the earliest and the most active propagandists of Drusism must be named Darazī, an intimate companion of the Caliph Hākim. Forced to leave Egypt in consequence of excess of zeal, Darazī spread the sect in the cazas of Syria where the presence of Ismā'īlī communities had prepared the soil for him. From Wādi't-taim, at the foot of Hermon, it spread into the Lebanon, then into Jabal Summāq and other mountainous districts in the region of Aleppo. Darazī entered into conflict with Ḥamza ibn 'Alī, the spokesman of Ḥākim and the real creator of the religious system of the Druses. He endeavoured to supplant his rival but went down in the struggle ; his name was given over to execration and himself condemned to death. His ministry must have been remarkably fruitful, since, in spite of these sorry memories, the Druses have inherited from Darazī their popular and historic name, which they themselves disown.

The Caliph Ḥākim perished mysteriously. His partisans refused to believe in his death. As his human form was only a semblance and ' the transparent veil of his divinity ', this death could only be a test intended to separate the Believers from among the hypocrites. Ḥākim was temporarily concealed in his divine Essence in order to reappear at the chosen moment, to give over to his Faithful the dominion of the world and to punish evil-doers. Until the time of his return, no other appearance or incarnation of the Divinity was expected.

To-day the Druses no longer exist except in Syria, where their wild spirit of independence has caused them to rise against successive governments in that country. Colonies of them occur in Southern Lebanon, Wādi'-t-taim and in the mountain of Ḥaurān, which is called after them 'Mountain of the Druses'. Their number slightly exceeds 100,000 adherents.

As this account implies, Drusism, the outcome of Fāṭimid Imāmism, is really nothing more than an Ismā'īlī sect, but a sect of extremists. Their early theories readily borrowed from the Ismā'īlīs the number seven in the enumeration of the *Imāms*, the 'speakers', the 'bases', etc. They observe, in accordance with this cabbalistic arithmetic, that Ḥākim allowed his hair to grow for seven years and only rode on asses. They have adopted the most audacious theories of Ismā'īlism, and confine themselves to adapting them indifferently to the postulate of the divinity of Ḥākim.

This postulate brought about the revision of the Ismā'īlī system. It was effected by Ḥamza ibn 'Alī, who arrogated to himself the lion's share in this work of recasting. The Fāṭimid Caliph having risen to the rank of God, it was necessary to hand on to another the title which had previously belonged to him. Ḥamza inherited it. The Druses have preserved the Ismā'īlī theories concerning the Universal Intelligence and Universal Soul, which they regard as the two chief ministers of the God Ḥākim. A third minister embodies the Word (*Kalima*), produced by the Soul through the Intelligence. The two last ministers are the 'Forerunner', *sābiq*', and the 'Follower', '*tāli*'.

These five ministers are alleged to have been incarnated in historical personages who played a prominent part in the foundation of Drusism. It is thus that, in Ḥākim's lifetime, Universal Intelligence was called Ḥamza ibn 'Alī. It is to Ḥamza that all living creatures owe their existence. He is the sole mediator between them and God, the channel of all supernatural knowledge. Further, we may mention the fifth minister, whom the Druse writings call Muqtanā and Bahā ad-dīn. He was one of their most active emissaries, and, perhaps, the most fertile controversialist in their religious literature. This latter, somewhat lacking in variety, habitually takes its polemical arguments from the Ismā'īlite arsenal.

During their short period of expansion, the Druses also adopted in outline the propagandist organization of the Ismā'īlīs, or rather they confined themselves to maintaining that of the Fāṭimids. The Druse emissaries were divided into three categories: the '*dā'i*' or missionaries, the '*ma'dhūn*' or licentiates, and the '*naqīb*' or watchers. These agents formed a class apart and all other men were commanded to offer them the most absolute submission. At the head of this quasi-clerical caste appeared the *dā'i*, or chiefs of mission, who commanded the members of the two other classes. The *licentiates* received the oaths and the signed promises of the adepts. The function of the '*naqīb*', also called '*mukāsir*', or *breakers*, is imperfectly known to us. This organization, possessed of a well-marked hierarchy—exceptional in Islām—was not destined to survive the period of expansion. One is entitled to wonder whether it was not exclusively designed for that period.

Druse propaganda appears to have gained adherents in all the centres where Ismā'īlīs were to be found in Egypt and Arabia, in Syria and India. It was likewise addressed to Christians. The whole movement stopped abruptly in consequence of the troubles caused by the Ḥamza-Darazī quarrel and by the death of Ḥākim. Since that date Drusism, in order to be more sure of preserving its secret, has retired jealously within itself. It has kept this attitude of mystery and isolation down to our own times. Not only has it ceased to use propaganda, but it obstinately refuses any proselytes who offer themselves. The death of Ḥākim, and the fall of the Fāṭimids, undoubtedly deprived it of the power to retain the adepts who had been won outside the borders of Syria.

The Druse dogma is summed up in 'the knowledge of God Our Lord, *maulānā*', that is to say, Ḥākim. Its theodicy, as is the case with all Shī'a sects, reflects the ideas of Mu'tazilism concerning the ineffable unity and simplicity of the Divine nature. 'God' (Ḥākim), says Ḥamza, 'is One, without attributes; He is alone, but not through limitation, too exalted to be defined. The tongue is mute, the reason confesses its incapacity adequately to express the unity of its Creator.' The Druses are so transported by these reasonings that they esteem themselves alone able to profess the '*tauḥīd*' or divine unity in all its strictness. That is why they call themselves 'Muwaḥḥidūn', or *Unitarians*. We have seen above how they try to bring about in Ḥākim the union of humanity with the divine nature. 'He has permitted us,' says Ḥamza again, 'to see the *veil* beneath which he is hidden and the *place* whence he has deigned to speak to us in order to be adored in tangible form; and all this through pure mercy and kindness to man.' It is this mystery, so argue their theorists, which constitutes 'the merit of the Druse faith and permits it to become a free acquiescence of the spirit'.

In the ethics of Drusism we encounter once more the number seven borrowed from Ismā'īlism. Accordingly, seven precepts are substituted for the 'five pillars' of Islām which Ḥamza had arbitrarily augmented by two through the addition of the Holy War and submission to authority. Druse unitarianism either overthrows the five pillars or contents itself with getting round them by allegorical interpretation. Thus to fast is to renounce previous religions. Ḥamza does not hesitate to pour ridicule on the pilgrimage to Mekka; Ḥākim when he reappears will destroy this city as well as Jerusalem.

The first duty of a Druse is truthfulness. This must be absolute and unrestricted between 'unitarian' adepts. With others they are authorized to resort with a clear conscience to the subterfuge of *taqiyya* (*v.* p. 145). This theory, common to the whole Shī'a, has nowhere been further developed than among the Druses. One of their religious books dispenses them from 'frankness with people plunged in ignorance and darkness'. Truthfulness is then reduced, says the same writing, to a mere duty of politeness, but entails no moral obligation towards non-Druses. This obligation only exists towards *Unitarians*. The latter, where a non-Druse is concerned, may deny everything: debts that have been incurred, trusts which have been received, participation in a crime—when avowal would compromise either themselves or a *Unitarian* or when they are in temporary financial difficulties. Except in these cases truth claims all its rights and candour becomes an obligation, in order, sententiously conclude the Druse moralists, 'not to destroy reciprocal commerce in the world'. It is this theory which has led them, as in freemasonry, to invent signs and passwords which permit them to recognize one another.

The second duty comprises the mutual help which Druses ought to render each other. The third, the fourth and the fifth enjoin the recognition of the religion of Ḥākim, the profession of the unity of 'Our Lord' and the renunciation of all other cults. These precepts compel them inwardly to embrace the Unitarian doctrine and cleave to it with heart and mind; but do they impose the public profession of this belief at all costs?

The actual teaching of the Druses, as well as their formulary, authorizes them not only to dissimulate their religion, as the doctrine of *taqiyya* recommends, but also to conform outwardly to the practices of the dominant cult. Among the Druses to take advantage of this authorization is to incur no discredit, neither does it amount to apostasy. One of their religious books forbids them 'to communicate the mystery of "Our Lord" (Ḥākim)', and the formulary adds that 'preaching is abolished and its door is shut', to the non-Druses, be it understood. The sixth and seventh rules enjoin 'to be satisfied with the works of Our Lord and obedient to His will'. The number of souls is considered as invariable; metempsychosis condemns them to pass successively into divers bodies and they are unceasingly and immediately reincarnated. There is, therefore, a constant balance between births and deaths.

This whole religious and moral code applies to initiates of both sexes, for women have an equal right to initiation. The proportion of women initiates has always remained extremely low.

To-day the Druses are divided into two categories: the spirituals, '*rūḥānī*', and the corporeals, '*jismānī*'. The first category comprises those initiated 'into the mystery of Our Lord'. The initiation is supposed to have, as it were, dematerialized them by uniting their limited intelligence with the Universal Intelligence. These 'spirituals' guard the treasure of doctrine, kept strictly secret. Among the 'spirituals' are distinguished the '*ra'īs*', or '*ra'īs ad-dīn*', or again '*sheikh al-'aql*', religious chiefs properly so-called, always few in number; then the '*āqil*' (pl. '*uqqāl*'), literally the wise, the general title given to the initiated. That of '*ajāwīd*' denotes the initiated of the second degree. For the women *spirituals* or initiates, there are likewise three degrees of initiation: (*a*) '*āqila*', (*b*) '*jawīda*', (*c*) '*rāqiya*'.

The category of 'corporeals' comprises the multitude of the profane, or non-initiated: the Emirs, then the '*jāhil*' (pl. *juhhāl*), literally the ignorant. The Emirs administer the temporal affairs of the Druse community, of which they constitute the secular arm. The *ignorant* are the soldiers. This duty is equally incumbent on the *spirituals* of every grade, not excepting the religious chiefs who, in time of war, go into battle democratically mingled, without distinction, in the ranks of the 'ignorant'. The Druse freemasonry does not possess even the embryo of a liturgy. It has no religious edifices, but contents itself with lodges or '*khalwa*', retreats, reserved for the initiates alone.

THE NOṢAIRĪS. Several of these sects had, as we have just seen, carried their fanatical veneration for 'Alī and his line to extremes. The Muslim heresiologists apply to them collectively the name '*gholāt*', fanatics, persons of exaggerated views. Some proclaimed 'Alī the equal or even the superior of Muḥammad. Consciously or not, the archangel Gabriel is said to have transmitted the Qorānic message to Muḥammad instead of to 'Alī so that the Imāmite faction of the 'Ghurābiyya' considered themselves justified in cursing the archangel. Other Shī'a groups admitted the infusion of the divine nature into 'Alī and the *Imāms*. Certain Ismā'īlī sub-sects had, in deifying 'Alī, paved the way for Drusism and the Neo-Ismā'īlism of the Khojas. Among the Ismā'īlī extremists, 'Alī, already the incarnation of the Universal Soul, the emanation of the Divine Essence and creator of the external world, rose one step in order to become God.

No one has advanced farther along this path than the Nosairīs, often called ' Anṣāriyya ', by reason of a verbal corruption unfortunately popularized by Western travellers which is liable to cause confusion with the Anṣār of Muḥammad (*v.* p. 28). In accordance with the request addressed by them to the French Mandate in Syria they are now called ' 'Alawites ', or ' 'Alawīs ', an amphibological name, since the latter form belongs, strictly speaking, to the 'Alids, that is to say, to the Sherīfs, or descendants of 'Alī.

The sect dates back to a certain Ibn Noṣair. He was a fanatical partisan of the eleventh 'Alid *Imām*, Ḥasan al-'Askarī (*v.* p. 149), who died in 873. His existence in Syria is referred to by Bāqilāni (†1012), Ibn Ḥazm (†1062) and by the Druse polemicists, Ḥamza ibn 'Alī (p. 164) and others. The religious system of the Noṣairīs forms a bizarre syncretism of Christian, pagan and Muslim elements, the latter borrowed from the most fanatical Shī'a theories and closely resembling Ismā'īlism, which appears to have influenced them. With the Noṣairīs, 'Alī became an incarnation pure and simple of the divinity. Another characteristic feature of their religion is the development given to the liturgy which in all the other factions of Islām has remained in the embryonic stage.

The first of their dogmas is that of a divine triad. It consists of a first cause called '*Ma'nā*' or *Idea*, and of two hypostases proceeding from the *Idea*. The two hypostases are called '*Ism*', or *name*, and '*Bāb*', or *door*. The *Idea* represents the archetypal divinity, the very Essence of God. These appellations ' derive from a very curious theory of the mechanism of knowledge, the genesis of ideas and initiation into truth ' (Massignon). The *Name*, called also *veil*, is the outward manifestation, the public revelation of the *Idea*. The *door* leads to it, and is a kind of Paraclete, whose part is to facilitate access to the hidden idea, to the mysteries of religion; for we are dealing with an esoteric and initiatory religion.

The three persons of the triad have clothed themselves in human flesh in each of the seven cycles—borrowed from the theories of the 'Seveners'—which divide the history of the world. The last of these manifestations or incarnations coincided with the period of the Hijra. It was composed of 'Alī, Muḥammad and Salmān al-Fārisī. Announced by Salmān, his precursor, 'Alī was enthroned by Muḥammad. As to Salmān, he is an obscure Companion of the Prophet, specially venerated by all the Shī'a sects, who look upon him as one of the chief partisans of 'Alī.

Although the persons of the divine triad are declared 'inseparable', the two last are not placed on a footing of equality with 'Alī. Rather are they presented as emanations of the archetypal divinity; that is, 'Alī. It is the last-named who created Muḥammad. The latter, in his turn, 'has created the Lord Salmān from the "light of his light"'. It is this very marked pre-eminence of 'Alī which enables the Noṣairīs to call themselves 'Muwaḥḥidūn', or Unitarians. The triad is denoted by the symbol '*'Ams*', formed by the letters *'ain, mīm, sīn*, the initials of the names of the three Noṣairī hypostases: 'Alī, Muḥammad, Salmān. The relations between the three divine persons constitute 'the mystery of 'Ams', the grand arcana revealed to the adepts in the services of initiation. Salmān has taken upon himself to create the 'Five Incomparables' (*aitām*). The list of these has been made up by choosing from among the 'Saḥābīs', or Companions of the Prophet, the strongest partisans of 'Alī. It is on these Incomparables that the creation of the world devolved.

So far all the Noṣairīs declare themselves in agreement. But in what external symbol does the divinity manifest itself in a permanent manner? Which among the natural phenomena is to be regarded as the habitation of the divine being and the tangible object of religious worship? The definition of this emblem gave birth to the four sects, into which they are divided: the Ḥaidarīs, Shamālīs, Kilāzīs and Ghaibīs.

Some seek the religious symbol either in the sun or the moon, or in the dim light which precedes the rising or setting of the sun. Others imagine they recognize it in the air or atmosphere. These divergences of opinion have won for the 'Shamālīs' the name of 'Shamsīs', or sun-worshippers; for the Kilāzīs that of 'Qamarīs', or worshippers of the moon. A new source of division was opened when the question arose of determining whether these natural phenomena are the symbol of 'Alī, Muḥammad or Salmān. These discussions have been food for subtle polemics among the Noṣairī theorists. We will do no more than allude to them.

The Noṣairīs believe in metempsychosis. The Milky Way is made up of the souls of the 'Unitarian' faithful, transformed into stars. The second *Sūra* of their Qorān is nothing but a prayer imploring, as a favour, escape from the lower degrees of metempsychosis, that is to say, from transmigration into the bodies of animals, a punishment which really constitutes the Noṣairī hell. They alone among the Muslim factions admit the Fall. In the beginning, these souls were all glittering stars and enjoyed the vision of 'Alī; but they delighted in the contemplation of their own excellence and to punish this pride 'Alī banished them to earth and imprisoned them in human bodies.

Like the Druses, they are divided into two classes: the multitude of the profane (*'āmma*) and the chosen few of the initiated (*khāṣṣa*). Initiation, presided over by a kind of godfather, or 'uncle', does not begin before the age of eighteen, and lasts for at least nine months. Women are never admitted to initiation. The Noṣairīs possess no edifices set apart for worship. Their country is, however, covered with '*qubbas*', or cupolas, which, erected on the summits of prominent hills, shelter the tombs of their saints. They are surrounded by venerable trees, which have themselves become the object of a superstitious worship. The religion of the profane multitude consists in visits to these tombs and sacrifices offered up there. The people have practically returned to the worship of the high places, *sub omni ligno frondoso* (Jeremiah **2**, 20). For the initiated, religion consists in the revelation of the sacred symbol '*'Ams*' and in the allegorical interpretation of the religious books.

Noṣairism, sprung from the Shī'a consecrated to the worship of 'Alī, has adopted several Shī'a festivals. The greatest is that of 'Ghadīr Khomm', which commemorates the anniversary of the day when, according to the Imāmate tradition, Muḥammad solemnly appointed 'Alī as his vicar. This theme could not satisfy the 'Alid fervour of the Noṣairīs, according to whom the Prophet declared that 'Alī was the '*Ma'nā*' or *Idea*, the very Essence of the divinity. They celebrate also the commemoration of Kerbelā (*v.* p. 144), but without the circumstances with which the Imāmites surround it.

Much more unexpected, in fact a peculiarity unique among the Muslim sects, is the adoption by the Noṣairīs of the great Christian festivals: Christmas (December 25, Old Style), New Year's Day, the Epiphany, or Baptism, '*Ghaṭṭās*' (of Christ), Palm Sunday, Easter and Whitsuntide. To these they add borrowings from the martyrology of the Eastern Churches: the festivals of St. Barbara, of St. John Chrysostom, and of St. Catherine. They also bear Christian names: Matthew, John (' Yūḥannā ', the Christian form substituted for the Muslim spelling *Yaḥyā*), Gabriel, Spiridion, Helen, Catherine, etc., a phenomenon without analogy in Islām.

The religious festivals are sometimes celebrated at night, the better to observe secrecy. Only the initiated are present and the meeting-place is a private house, belonging to one of the Faithful who undertakes to bear the expenses of the ceremony. The *Imām* or officiant is chosen from among the *Sheikh ad-dīn*, the counterpart of the '*Ra'īs al-'aql*' of the Druses (*v.* p. 168), who takes his place between two assistants or acolytes. In front of them are disposed candles, incense, fragrant plants and wine. One of the assistants censes the *Imām* and the nearest of those present. Then he hands the thurible to the second assistant, who passes along the ranks of the congregation in order to cense them. Some prayers (*quddās*) are recited over the cups of wine that have just been censed and those present exchange the kiss of peace. After further prayers, the *Imām* mixes a portion of his cup of wine with that of the acolyte, and at this signal all the congregation empty theirs and intone religious chants.

It would be difficult to ignore the analogy of this liturgy with Christian ceremonies. It becomes still more striking when considered in conjunction with a remark in the Noṣairī catechism. This collection openly mentions ' the consecration of the wine '; after which it adds: 'The greatest of God's mysteries is that of the body and blood of which Jesus has said: "This is my Body and my Blood; eat and drink of them, for they are life eternal." The wine is called '*Abd an-Nūr*, because in it God has revealed Himself.'

According to M. René Dussaud, the Noṣairīs present 'a remarkable example of a people passing immediately from paganism to Ismā'īlism'. Presumably they have never been Christians. We have, therefore, to explain this fact, completely isolated in the history of the variations of Islām, and to clear the adoption and the origin of borrowings preserving so clearly the stamp of Christianity; the use of wine, of candles, of incense, the kiss of peace; a liturgical language frankly Christian; and a whole collection of festivals and ceremonies, jealously eliminated from the religious practices of Islām, not excepting those sects furthest removed from Qorānic orthodoxy.

Religious secrecy is, if possible, observed still more strictly than among the Druses. Its violation entails the death penalty. They, like certain other sects, are allowed to conform outwardly to the dominant religion, and be Christians with Christians, Muslims with Muslims. 'We Noṣairīs,' they sometimes say, 'are the body and the other cults a garment. Now, the garment does not change the nature of the man but leaves him as he was. Thus we always remain Noṣairīs, although outwardly we may adopt the religious practices of our neighbours.'

Licentious practices and assemblies have been imputed to them as to their neighbours and bitter enemies, the Ismā'īlīs. The profound secrecy in which they enwrap their nocturnal ceremonies, and the liturgical use of wine, necessarily confirmed, especially in the eyes of the Muslims, these malicious reports. The French Mandate has put an end to the petty persecution to which they were subjected under Turkish rule. The Noṣairī liturgy replied by maledictions directed against Islām and prayers 'for the destruction of the Ottoman power'.

At the present time, the ''Alawites' participate in

the government of their mountains where they are in the majority and no longer hesitate to declare themselves openly. The women are not obliged to observe any religious practice ; they enjoy great freedom of movement and are not compelled to wear the veil. The men occasionally avail themselves of the Qorānic licence to marry four wives. They carry on no propaganda and admit no proselytes. Their religious literature—polemics and liturgical poetry—shows great intellectual poverty. Their principal sacred book, the '*Kitāb al-Majmū'* ', a pale copy of the Qorān, is divide into sixteen *Sūras*; another '*Majmū'* ', or collection, enumerates and expatiates on the liturgical festivals peculiar to the sect. They form a population of husbandmen scattered in Northern and Central Syria as well as in Turkish Cilicia, and number in all about 300,000 adepts.

THE 'ALĪ-ILĀHĪ. The origin of the Noṣairīs dates back to the beginning of the tenth century. Their religious system was completely formed when the first Druse missionaries arrived in Syria and attacked their doctrines. Allied to the Noṣairīs with whom they are often confused, even to the extent of being called by their name, is the much more modern sect—it cannot be earlier than the seventeenth century—of the 'Alī-ilāhī, or ' 'Alī-allāhī ', partisans of the God 'Alī. They are self-styled ' Ahl-i-Ḥaqq ', or *People of the Truth.*

They are scattered throughout Anatolia and Persia, in Turkestan and the South of Russia ; among the Kurdish clans in Northern Syria they number about fifteen thousand. They form compact groups in these diverse regions but seek to hide their identity by adapting themselves to the formal religious practices of their neighbours. The wide area over which they are dispersed, the fact that they are split up into various nationalities, Kurdish, Turco-Mongol, Persian, whose aspirations are mutually antagonistic, the mystery in which they are forced to enwrap themselves, the fact that their religious collections are drawn up in Turkish, Persian and Kurdish, make up a tangle of unfavourable circumstances which has prevented their attaining, like the Noṣairīs, a unity of doctrine and religious practices.

They are divided into numerous sects. Their liturgy recalls that of the Noṣairīs, and also includes a kind of ritual communion in which bread and wine occur. All are agreed concerning the divinity of 'Alī. They consider him as one of the *seven* incarnations of the divine essence, but they persist in looking for a final coming. Those in Anatolia, often called ''Alawīs' or ''Alawites', and popularly 'Qyzylbāsh', or red-heads, have points in common with the Bektāshis (*v.* p. 136) and their religious leaders maintain relations with these and with the Noṣairīs. The latter are apt to consider the 'Alī-ilāhī as one of their sub-sects, and this is one of the reasons which have driven the Noṣairīs of Syria to demand the official name of 'Alawīs.

The dogmatic concepts of these Anatolian 'Alawīs—the majority of whom are Kurdish—can be thus summed up: There is only one *Truth*, '*ḥaqq*', namely, 'Alī. It is, then, to 'Alī that all revelations can be traced; 'Alī who has spoken through the medium of all the prophets. All, Moses, Christ, Muḥammad, held their prophetic mission by the grace of 'Alī. It is, then, to 'Alī that the esoteric teaching of all the messengers from Heaven ultimately relates. The name of 'People of the Truth' professes to proclaim these doctrines.

It is unnecessary to add that these sects—Druses, Noṣairīs, 'Alī-ilāhīs—all sprung from the Ismā'īlian

Shī'a,—have no longer anything in common with Islām in spite of certain conventional observances behind which they seek to conceal their religious separatism. This is no doubt why their representatives have not been invited to the 'Congress of the Caliphate' (see below), to which other sects, Ibāḍites, Imāmites, Zaidites, and even the Ismā'īlīs, have been summoned.

VIII

REFORMISTS AND MODERNISTS

REACTION AND REFORM. One of the characteristic traits of Islām is its conservative spirit. It professes to be the cult of the *Sunna* and of the Tradition. Outside the path traced by the *Sunna* or custom of the Prophet and followed by the 'pious ancestors' (*as-salaf aṣ-ṣāliḥ*), it knows no salvation. Every innovation, '*bid'a*', every departure from the *Sunna* appears to it suspicious and synonymous with heresy. This is the principle proclaimed by the title of *Sunnis*, adopted by the orthodox, and of the more modern 'Salafiyya', namely, partisans and imitators of the ancestors.

But life pays no attention to abstract theories. In order to live, Islām has had to bow to the conditions governing all living organisms. It has unbent and adapted itself to surroundings and circumstances; it has admitted modifications and compromises. This evolution, which began a short time after the Prophet's death and in Medina itself, the 'cradle of the *Sunna*', has continued throughout the whole course of its history. *Ijmā'* has covered with its authority these innovations, fiercely resisted at first—as for example printing, authorized only by *fatwās* in 1729. In order to legalize them it has discovered the theory of laudable and salutary *bid'as*.

Its intervention has not disarmed opposition.

Zealots have never been lacking who made it their mission to revivify *custom*, '*ihyā as-sunna*', and declaimed without ceasing against the abuses introduced under cover of the *consensus*. Such was the attitude adopted by the Ẓāhirites or *literalists*. Next, it is among the Ḥanbalites that this reaction has always evoked the most persistent echo. No setback discourages them; they do not recoil even before the prestige of a Ghazālī. And yet orthodox opinion owed him a debt of gratitude for having laboured towards 'the restoration (*iḥyā*) of the religious sciences', by demonstrating the possible agreement between philosophy, theology and mysticism.

Ibn Taimiyya. The most singular among all these makers of protests is incontestably the Syrian polemicist Taqī ad-dīn, whose name has already been mentioned several times. His inordinate activity overflowed the whole domain of Islāmic discipline. A ruthless logician, Ibn Taimiyya declared himself against the speculative methods which the Ash'arites and Ghazālī had placed at the service of orthodoxy.

He refused to recognize the value of *ijmā'*, created by the laborious agreement of the *'ulemā*. He was an indefatigable detector of heresies, who passed his life in denouncing novelties and discovering heterodoxies. The bitter enemy of the mystical fraternities, Ibn Taimiyya, whom Dhahabī calls 'the standard of the ascetics', proscribed not only casuistry in jurisprudence, but the honours paid to the Prophet, the cult of the saints and of their tombs. He was an adherent of the Ḥanbalite school, and demanded the punishment of error by the most drastic penalties, often capital. His polemical pamphlets bore suggestive titles such as 'The unsheathed sword', '*Aṣ-ṣārim al-maslūl*'. His integrity cannot be called in question, but his mistake lay in refusal to tolerate any religious ideal save one—his own. This intemperate zeal, nourished by an incontestable erudition on the subject of the traditions, could not but disturb the conservatism of his contemporaries. The latter, according to Ibn Baṭṭūṭa, judged him 'to have a disordered brain', the victim of a mental derangement sometimes called *odium theologicum*.

Thus he spent the greater part of his stormy career in the prisons of the Muslim Inquisition at Cairo and Damascus—he died confined in the citadel of the latter town—without abating his intransigence or ever interrupting for a moment, even when in irons, his polemics both oral and written (1328). His disciple, the Damascene Ibn Qayyim al-Jauziyya, passed through the same trials and displayed the same lack of discretion in his polemical activities.

To both befell later the strange fate of being extolled and quoted alike by Wahhābis and modernists. The latter edit or re-edit the most long-forgotten pamphlets of the implacable Damascene controversialist, Ibn Taimiyya. They see no better way of showing their gratitude for the vigorous blows which he dealt to the superstitions introduced into Islām. Ibn Taimiyya 'was buried in the cemetery of the *Ṣūfīs*' at Damascus (Dhahabī). The sepulchre of the great adversary of the cult of tombs continues to receive the homage of pilgrims.

THE WAHHĀBIS. All the sects that we have studied in the previous chapter owe, as we have seen, their origin to a political dispute, the question of the Caliphate. In the eighteenth century, an Arab of Nejd proceeded to create a fresh dissidence. This innovator, called Muḥammad ibn 'Abdalwahhāb (1703–1791), was born at 'Oyaina, a small place in Nejd. It was his father, the Ḥanbalite *'ālim* 'Abdalwahhāb, who was to give his name to the Wahhābis, although he was far from approving his son's exaggerated Puritanism. Under his guidance, Muḥammad was initiated into the wisdom of Islām. His tendency to innovate, his rejection of certain observances of traditional Islām, were already manifest when he departed for the Ḥejāz. He studied for some time at Medina, and it was perhaps in this town that he was fired with enthusiasm for the writings of Ibn Taimiyya. However, he was outspoken in his criticism of the visits to the tomb of the Prophet and the ceremonies performed there. After a brief sojourn at Nejd he went to Baṣra, whence his views caused him to be expelled. He settled at last in his own country, and addressed himself, but without success, to several Arab chiefs with the object of winning them over to his doctrine. Towards 1745, he established relations with Muḥammad ibn Sa'ūd, Emir of Nejd (†1768), who became his stepson. Supported by the latter, he imposed on Nejd, partly by persuasion, partly by force, his creed, which became the State religion of Nejd and was thereafter propagated and maintained in that country by the secular arm.

The Wahhābi innovator took up all the themes of his master, Ibn Taimiyya. Like him, in order to restore Islām to the golden age of the Prophet and his Companions, he preached the return to the two 'sole' sources of revelation: the Qorān and the early *Sunna*. He proscribed all speculative glosses in theodicy, exegesis and the traditions. He accepted, after the manner of the Ẓāhirites, the literal meaning of the Qorān and the *ḥadīth*, their whole anthropomorphic mode of expression, without attempting to scrutinize the '*kaif*' or modality, without even considering the very discreet compromises admitted by the Ash'arites (*v.* p. 57). He condemns all the innovations by which Islām has attempted to adapt itself to changing conditions, the laxity introduced by the spirit of worldliness and forgetfulness of early austerity. Let mosques be restored to their condition in the time of the Prophet : without mosaics or gilding, as also without minarets. This is anti-modernism in all its rigour.

The Ottoman Sultans, such as Murād IV (1632–1640), had begun by forbidding tobacco and coffee until *fatwās* authorized their use. Ibn 'Abdalwahhāb refuses to recognize this legitimizing by *ijmā'*, and his condemnation includes music and the wearing of silken apparel and gold and silver jewellery by men. With the early tradition the puritan Wahhābis sanction *istisqā*, or prayers for rain in times of drought ; but they abhor to ask this same favour or any other at the tomb of a saint, not excepting that of the Prophet.

Without formally condemning visits to this last-named monument, they forbid that prayers should be offered there. They also prohibit public prayers in times of plague and other calamities. 'We proscribe', wrote Ibn Sa'ūd, Emir of Nejd, at the beginning of the nineteenth century, to the Pasha of Damascus, 'the erection of edifices on tombs, trust in the saints, prophets and martyrs ; next the fraternities of *faqīrs*, and Dervishes, in a word the rôle of intercessor attributed to creatures. We regard these beliefs and institutions as tainted with polytheism. We liken them to serious sins, such as drinking wine, swearing, except in the name of Allah, gaming . . . !'

From polemics, the Wahhābis soon passed to action. Their first onslaught was on the holy cities of the Shī'a, pillaging the rich sanctuaries at Najaf and Kerbela. Masters of Central Arabia, they seized Mekka and Medina in 1803 and 1804. There they forced the '*ulemā* and the population to countersign their own '*takfīr*', that is, to acknowledge officially that up to that date they had lived as infidels. Not content with demolishing the mausoleums and the cupolas erected on the tombs, they replaced the silken veils covering the Ka'ba with common stuffs. At Medina they plundered the accumulated treasures of the tomb of Muḥammad; but the local '*ulemā* had to send them *fatwās* justifying this audacity and alleging the use of the treasure in the interest of the Medinese population. For several years they plundered the Mekkan pilgrims and finally caused the cessation of the pilgrimage. It was necessary to subdue the iconoclasts of Nejd by force of arms. Owing to the decadence of the Ottoman Empire, the mission had to be entrusted to the powerful Egyptian Pasha, Mehemet-'Alī, who, with his sons, only accomplished it after a campaign lasting no less than quarter of a century.

IBN SA'ŪD. After that no more was heard of the Wahhābis. They divided into the Northern and Southern factions, headed by the two rival families of Ibn Sa'ūd and Ibn Rashīd, whose dissensions long stained the desert with blood. At the end of 1921, 'Abdal'azīz ibn Sa'ūd, the hereditary Emir of Southern Nejd, succeeded in vanquishing his adversary Ibn Rashīd, Emir of Shammar or Northern Nejd. He took his capital Ḥā'il and massacred the rest of the family. In conflict since 1918–1919 with Ḥusain ibn 'Alī, Grand Sherīf of Mekka and since 1916 King of the Ḥejāz, Ibn Sa'ūd took possession of Ṭāif and Mekka during the summer of 1924. A year of blockade delivered into his hands the port of Jeddah, the last refuge of King 'Alī, who had succeeded his father, the ex-King Ḥusain. This success brought the ephemeral Sherīfian dynasty of the Ḥejāz to an end.

Ibn Sa'ūd, who had previously taken the title of

Sultan, appeals to a world-congress of Islām to decide the future of the Ḥejāz. His victories have made him the most powerful sovereign in Arabia. His possessions extend to the borders of Irāq, Palestine, Syria, the Red Sea and the Persian Gulf. His striking personality has expressed itself in the creation of the 'Ikhwān', or *brethren*. They are a brotherhood of Wahhābi activists; the Englishman Philby calls it a 'new freemasonry'. They form the propagandist organization of the sect, the nucleus of Ibn Sa'ūd's army; picked soldiers in war-time, agriculturists in time of peace. Nejd numbers a score of agricultural colonies created by the Ikhwān.

Wahhābi proselytism has spread into the Arabian states bordering on Nejd, into Mesopotamia, 'Omān and Somalia. India has numerous groups classed under the various names of 'Salafīyya', 'Ahl al-ḥadīth', 'Farā'iḍiyya', etc., who without adhering completely to the doctrinal programme of the Wahhābis, all draw inspiration from their reformist tendencies. These Neo-Wahhābi communities aim at purging Islām from the contamination of Hindu polytheism.

The mistake of Wahhābism has been to deny, or at least to limit, arbitrarily the function of *ijmā'*. They have incurred the strictures of the Sunnis by their readiness to anathematize (*takfīr*) all the other Muslims, by the excesses of their sumptuary puritanism, no less than by their acts of violence against the persons of their adversaries, and the traditional monuments and institutions of Islām, excesses which only their partisans attempt to dispute. In strict law they do not, however, constitute a sect, still less a heresy properly so-called. They are the *ultras*, the *integretists*, of orthodox Islām. Disciples of Ibn Taimiyya, they form the extreme right wing of the Ḥanbalite school. Within the last few years they have, moreover, somewhat relaxed their early intolerance.

In the course of their recent occupation of the holy cities of the Ḥejāz, they have given proof of a relative moderation, appreciable, however, when compared with their attitude of a century ago. Some specially lofty cupolas and tombs were again razed to the ground. Certain sanctuaries were declared apocryphal and were cut off. But the treasure of Muḥammad's mausoleum was respected. The prohibition of coffee —the favourite beverage of the Wahhābi sovereign —has been revoked or has fallen into desuetude. Circumstances have forced them to make other concessions, no less significant. The King of Nejd has added to his title that of King of the Ḥejāz and does not believe that he has come to the end of his career and ascent to power. As he has appealed to the Muslim world, political considerations oblige him to treat Islāmic opinion with tact, and particularly the Islām of India, where he numbers his most influential partisans. On July 2, 1925, at the close of the annual pilgrimage, in the presence of the delegation of Indian *'ulemā*, he made the following declaration, every word of which deserves careful consideration:

'Before God and all Muslims I pledge myself to urge them to cleave to the old religion. My belief and my confession of faith are those of the *pious ancestors*; my rite (*madhhab*) is their rite. Whenever there is an explicit *Qorānic* verse or an authentic *ḥadīth* or a prescription dating back to the four first Caliphs or confirmed by the unanimous conduct of the Companions of the Prophet; when agreement between the four *Imāms*, founders of the juridical rites (*v.* p. 85), can be established, or agreement among their successors, the *'ulemā*, without departing from the Qorān and the *Sunna*, in all these cases I adopt no other belief but profess what our pious predecessors professed.'

It would be difficult to imagine a more astute formulary. Vexatious questions have been evaded. It is drawn up in a manner which, while insisting on doctrinal agreement, avoids defining the rôle which *ijmā'* is to play therein and determining the *terminus ad quem* of its chronological extension. Under these conditions Sunnis and Wahhābis could both lend it their support. Here is the explanation of the sudden change which has been effected in the orthodox camp. Hardly does a voice here and there recall the *fatwās* that formerly condemned the Wahhābis, under pressure, as is now admitted, of the Ottoman authorities. To-day Sunni writers readily undertake the vindication of their doctrine and represent them as a calumniated sect whose rehabilitation is a work of justice.

The Wahhābite sympathies of the Muslim intellectuals and modernists must necessarily be more unexpected. Their doctrinal scepticism seemed bound to separate them from such sincere believers as the innovators of Nejd, for whom progress consists essentially in a return to the most remote past. Leaving out of account the Neo-Wahhābi factions of India, the reformist school of the *Manār* (see p. 211) is entirely devoted to the Wahhābis. These sympathies were noisily expressed on the occasion of the recent events which revolutionized the political situation in the Ḥejāz. The modernists flatter themselves that in the Wahhābis they have found useful auxiliaries who will facilitate for them the reform of Islām. Furthermore, the two parties are at one on another point of their common programme, the desire to close the Arabian Peninsula to all foreign penetration. Which will carry the day? The laggards of Arabia, or those who propose to skip the intermediate stages in order to make up lost headway on the road of modern progress ?

AḤMADIYYA. A more recent reformist movement in Islām, dating from 1880, has resulted in the creation of a new sect, that of the 'Aḥmadiyya'. The founder from whom it takes its name, Mirzā Gholām Aḥmad (†1908), a native of Qādiān in the Punjāb (India), claimed to have discovered the veritable tomb of Christ, who he alleged had found refuge in India and died there. This *find* served as the starting-point of Aḥmadiyya.

Its three chief novelties are its Christology, its theory of the Mahdī and that of the *jehād*. It is this last which gives it an appearance of Islāmic reform. It arbitrarily revises not only the Christology of the Gospel but also that of the Qorān (*v.* p. 50). If this collection (**4**, 154, etc.) denies the Crucifixion, it affirms on the other hand that Christ is not dead, but that 'Allah in His omnipotence raised him up to dwell with Him, that all the Scripturaries shall believe in him, before his death, and that at the Day of Judgment he shall bear witness for all men'.

A *ḥadīth,* exploited by all aspirants to the title of Mahdī, announces the appearance of a restorer of Islām at the dawn of each new century. Gholām Aḥmad gave himself out as this reformer, appearing on the eve of the fourteenth century of the Hijra (1880 A.D. = 1299 A.H.). He combined the double mission of the Messiah and the Mahdī, whom he declared to be one and not two persons as the Sunnis suppose (*v.* p. 149). The Mahdī of the Aḥmadiyya has a horror of bloodshed. The Holy War must therefore be waged chiefly with spiritual weapons. But he hints at the use of more energetic methods should circumstances happen to change.

The sect numbers adherents chiefly in the Punjāb, variously estimated at seventy-five thousand to half a million. The latter figure is furnished by the Aḥmadiyya. They possess a few mosques in Europe (England, Germany). They edit periodicals and propagandist tracts. The sect aspires to become, as it were, a universal religion 'not only for the reform of Islām, but for the regeneration of the Hindus, the Muḥammadans and the Christians'. The Aḥmadiyya have met with no success in Muslim centres which have excommunicated them.

After the death of the founder, they divided into two distinctly opposite factions. The older, that of Qādiān, remains under the conduct of his son and continues his teaching. The second, whose centre is at Lahore, seeks to draw near to Sunni Islām without renouncing its activity amongst the Hindu sects. Its chief claim to originality consists in its spirit of proselytism. It has set on foot a missionary organization such as none of the other Muslim communities has ever possessed. This propagandism operates chiefly in the African colonies; we are indebted to it for the translations of the Qorān into English (condemned by order of the *'ulemā* of the Cairene University of Al-Azhar) and other languages: Urdu, Malay, etc. The chief of the primitive Aḥmadiyya, in his character of Mahdī, Messiah, Jesus returned to earth, aspires to the title of Caliph, the while professing himself the loyal subject of His Britannic Majesty. The adversaries of Aḥmadism accuse him of being in the service of English politics.

Bābism. If the Wahhābite reform is a reaction, a return to the past, that of Bābism was to bring about the creation of a new religion. In the over-excited atmosphere of Persian Imāmism, a religious dreamer, native of Eastern Arabia, the 'Sheikh' Aḥmad

Aḥsā'ī (1753–1826), had founded a new Shī'a school, that of the 'Sheikhīs'. It drew inspiration from pantheistic ideas and carried to the point of fanaticism the cult of the hidden *Imām*, whose imminent appearance it announced. The Sheikhīs, from the moment of their appearance, were violently combated and persecuted by the 'Twelvist' teachers. They probably number to-day two hundred and fifty thousand votaries. The Sheikhī centre was to be the cradle of Bābism, a cult borrowing from the Sheikhīs their extremist doctrines concerning the *Imāms* and the Mahdī as well as the Ismā'īlian theory of the Universal Intelligence (*v.* p. 159).

The founder of Bābism, the Seyyid (therefore a Ḥusainid, a descendant of the Prophet) 'Alī Muḥammad, born at Shirāz (Persia) in 1821, gave himself out as an emanation of this Intelligence. In him dwelt the mind of the Mahdī and of the prophets. *Bāb*, or Gate, is an eminently Shī'a title. In the Shī'a, 'Alī, and the *Imāms* after him, are the Gates of esoteric knowledge, of the inward and veiled meaning of religion. This Gate will be re-opened at the second coming of the hidden *Imām*. 'Alī Muḥammad began by adopting the title of Bāb, whence the name of his votaries. It was he who was the Gate of communication between the Faithful and the hidden *Imām*, in whose name he would proceed to the radical refashioning of Islām, or, to be more exact, of Imāmite Islām; for it is not proved that the outlook of the Bāb went beyond the horizon of the Shī'a.

The Bāb disparages its ritual and disciplinary practices. He pulls down the juridical edifice, laboriously erected by the Masters, in order to substitute his own conceptions. Against the Sunnis, Imāmism, with more virtuosity than success, had employed the tendencious process of *ta'wīl*, or allegorical interpretation. The Bāb in his turn adopts the allegorical method, and applies it not only to the text of the Qorān, but to the dogmas still held in common by the two great Islāmic factions: the Judgment, Paradise, Hell and the Resurrection.

He favours the equality of the sexes, abolishes the obligation of the veil for women, circumcision, ablutions, the theory of legal impurities, and that of the sumptuary laws. He allows interest on goods sold on the deferred-payment system. The number 19 corresponds to the number of Arabic letters which compose the complete formula of *Bismillah.* This number plays an important part in Bābism: annual fast of nineteen days; year divided into nineteen months; months into nineteen days; daily reading of nineteen verses from the '*Bayān*'.

The Bayān. Such is the name of the collection containing the Bābist reform. It is drawn up in the style of the Qorān, which has manifestly served as model to the Bāb, but its phraseology is bombastic and involved to the point of obscurity. This book is animated by a more liberal and modern inspiration; but the Bāb takes care not to represent it as the final word of revelation. Others, he asserts, will come after him to improve and complete it.

Such is, at least, the interpretation of the *Behāīsts.* But they had, as we shall see, an interest in presenting the Bāb as a simple precursor. It may be that, like the author of the Qorān with the theory of the *abrogating* and *abrogated* verses, the Bāb merely desired to reserve to himself the opportunity of revising his work and of announcing more explicitly his own advent. His adversaries left him no time for this; but before disappearing he declared himself to be the Mahdī and the *Imām* whom the Shī'as awaited.

Behāï'sm. In the month of July, 1850, the Bāb was executed by order of the Persian Government. After his death, one of his disciples, Behā Allah, the 'splendour of Allah', born in 1817, arrogated to himself the mission of revising thoroughly the works of the vanished master. Behā Allah's half-brother, known by the name of Ṣubḥ-i-Azal, 'the Morning of Eternity', clearly seems to have been nominated as the official successor of the Bāb and he desired to preserve the substance of the original Bābist doctrine. He was violently denounced by Behā Allah. Their rivalry degenerated into an open schism and ended in assassinations which decimated the ranks of the 'Azalīs', as the partisans of the minority of the proto-Bābists or continuators of the Bāb were called.

The Bāb had really only intended a reform of the Imāmite Shī'a, that of the 'Twelvers', such as an evolution of several centuries had made it. In order to bring this about, he had had recourse to well-worn expedients. He was content to utilize the principles laid down by the Shī'a sects: Imāmism, Milenarism, Sheikhism. Behā freed himself resolutely from this constraint. He founded a new religion, 'Behāï'sm', so called after him.

He announced himself as the emanation of the Divinity, the Apostle of the final revelation, no longer for the Shī'a or Islām alone, but for the whole of humanity. This claim led him to make a clean sweep of all the Imāmite conceptions preserved by the Bāb, who was no longer regarded as more than a simple precursor of Behāï'sm. He abolished the last ties—the liturgy and the ministers of the cult—which attached Bābism to Islām.

The new revelation is set forth in the '*Kitāb-i-aqdas*', or *the most holy Book*, another imitation of the Qorān, which Behā completed with a series of official missives addressed to the heads of governments. These lucubrations preach universal peace and brotherhood. Wars are condemned. The establishment of a universal tribunal is extolled, also the adoption of 'a universal language to be chosen or created, in order to put an end to the misunderstandings between nations, races and religions'. Monogamy is recommended, bigamy tolerated, but as the extreme concession in matrimonial legislation. Every man should pray where and when he chooses, so that there are to be no religious edifices! Mortification of the flesh is prohibited, and Behāï'sm recognizes no forbidden foods; 'everything is lawful except what is repugnant to the human intelligence'. The resources of the community consist in fines, and later in the tax of a nineteenth, levied once and for all on capital.

'ABBĀS-EFFENDI, the eldest son of Behā, born in 1844, succeeded his father, who died in 1892. He adopted the titles of "'Abd al-Behā", or *Servant of the Splendour*, and 'Ghoṣn A'ẓam', or *Supreme Branch*, shortened from 'Ghoṣn Allah al-A'ẓam'. He had already assumed the direction of the Behāïs during the lifetime of his father, who passed his days in prison or seclusion. 'Abbās, like his father, also came into conflict with his half-brother, Muḥammad 'Alī, called 'Al-Ghosn al-Akbar', or *Major Branch*.

Settled at Ḥaifa and Acre (Palestine), where he had been interned with his father, 'Abbās again emphasized the cosmopolitan, pacifist and humanitarian character of Behāï'sm and its aspiration to become a universal religion. 'Humanity is one . . . fanatical attachment to a religion, a race, a country, destroys this unity . . . men should free themselves from traditional beliefs and cleave only to the principles of divine religion.' He has found encouragement in this path, especially since the success of his propaganda in America.

The Behāï dissidents who have followed Muḥammad 'Alī are called ' Muwaḥḥidūn ', or *Unitarians*, and are excommunicated by the adherents of 'Abbās. There subsists no more than a modest group of Bābis who have remained faithful to the original doctrine of the Bāb. As for the ' Azalīs ' (*v.* p. 192) who were persecuted and decimated in Persia (1906–1912), they probably number about fifty thousand. These two factions represent the conservative or orthodox party in the movement inaugurated by Seyyid 'Alī Muḥammad. A conservative form of Behāï'sm is also adopted by the small group of adherents of Muḥammad 'Alī, the *Unitarians*. In effect, 'Abbās has created a new revelation, sprung directly from Behāï'sm ; a second religious avatar of Bābism in which 'Abbās figures as the Messiah and the son of God.

Syria numbers only a few hundred Behāïs, early emigrants from Persia who have settled round the centre Acre-Ḥaifa, which has the same attraction for the adherents of Behāï'sm as Mekka and Medina for Muslims. The adepts are chiefly distributed in Persia, where their number amounts to a total of eight hundred thousand to a million, on a rough estimate. In the crisis through which Persian Imāmism is passing, liberalism and Behāï'sm have been practically merged. Then, too, a considerable number of Behāïs of all sects finish by swelling the army of agnostics and the indifferent.

Arrived at the stage where 'Abbās-Effendī has left it, Behāï evolution with its borrowings from Biblical monotheism, from humanitarianism, pacifism and internationalism—demands the establishment of obligatory arbitration, a Parliament of Humanity

—this syncretism of Bābist origin no longer has anything in common with the Qorān. Its doctrinal originality is slight but it nevertheless claims 'to realize the highest ideal, to sum up the best tendencies of Christianity, Judaism, Buddhism, Islām, Freemasonry and Theosophy . . .'

On the other hand, its political importance as regards the future of the East is not to be despised, assuming that the statistics of the sect relating to the number of Behāïs can be trusted. The first European expert on the Bābist question, Mr. Edward Browne, asserts that 'the Power which, by winning over their supreme Pontiff at Acre, succeeded in utilizing their organization in Persia, would be able to secure an enormous influence in that country'.

In the United States there are some thousands of adherents, and Germany numbers several scattered groups of Behāïs. The introduction of Behāï'sm into America is due to the propaganda of Dr. Ibrahim George Khairallah, a Christian Lebanese, born at Bḥamdūn (1849) and one of the first pupils of the American College at Beyrout. After a visit paid to Acre in 1898, he was led to break with 'Abbās and declared himself in favour of Muḥammad 'Alī. But he did not succeed in carrying with him the majority of the American Behāïs. These religious dilettanti on the other side of the Atlantic, while they applaud from motives of snobbery the humanitarian theories of the Prophet of Acre, have been careful not to break with their protestant 'congregations' whose churches they continue to attend. Their number appears to have remained stationary.

In any case, the contribution of the American disciples enabled 'Abbās-Effendī to intensify his propaganda. He himself visited the United States in 1912. He died at Ḥaifa (November, 1921). The

British government had conferred a knighthood on him, and the English High Commissioner of Palestine was present at his funeral. 'Abbas left only daughters. His grandson, Shauqī Rabbānī, a student at Oxford, has been proclaimed his successor, but has not succeeded in rallying to his candidature the unanimous support of the Behāïs, followers of 'Abbās-Effendī.

THE PRESENT-DAY PROBLEM OF THE CALIPHATE. The Qorān knows nothing of the organization of the Caliphate. As for the early tradition, it is content to demand for its holder a Quraish origin. We have seen above (*v.* p. 107) the functions assigned to the Caliphate by Orthodox Islām, to fulfil a mission of centralization within and defence against dangers without; and to act as an organ of validation for canonical institutions.

Slowly elaborated by the jurists from the time of Māwardī (eleventh century), the theory of the attributions of the Caliphate had passed from the speculation of the schools into certain manuals of *fiqh* and into the *'aqā'id*, or catechisms. There it was sometimes characterized as being a 'required duty', *farḍ al-kifāya*, binding on the Muslim community as a whole; this is significant for it is applied by these manuals to the obligation of pilgrimage. It explains the mistake made by Westerners, including Orientalists, who have likened the Caliphate to the Papacy.

The Sultan 'Abdulḥamīd (1876–1908) took advantage of this instruction to intensify his pan-Islāmic activity. After his fall the Young Turks took up the theory, on which they based their demand that European diplomacy should recognize the 'spiritual power' of the Sultan-Caliph and as it were his right to supervise the whole Muslim world. The Great War marked a decline of these ideas and of the external prestige of the Caliphate. Its call to Muslims for the *jehād* found no answering echo. However, on the morrow of the Armistice, when the question of Turkey's disseverance arose, it was not the danger which menaced the Caliphate, but the nationalist ideal which roused the Turks of Anatolia. The Indian Muslims alone appealed to Islām and set up committees for 'the defence of the Caliphate'. Their chiefs proclaimed that on no consideration would they allow 'the Caliph to be Vaticanized'.

On the 1st of November, 1922, *the Grand National Assembly of Angora* by a simple decree deprived the Sultan-Caliph of Stambul of all temporal power. The Indian Muslims made no move. On the 3rd of March, 1924, the same Assembly with one stroke of the pen abolished the Ottoman Caliphate. Two days later, on March the 5th, King Ḥusain ibn 'Alī, Grand Sherīf of Mekka, proclaimed himself Caliph. The capture of Mekka by the Wahhābis (13th of October, 1924) brought about the fall of King Ḥusain and rendered vacant the office of Caliphate.

We would call attention to the feeble reaction of the Muslim world in face of the rude suppression of the Caliphate. It occurred to the 'Indian Committee for the Defence of the Caliphate' to demand explanations from Mustapha Kemal, President of the Turkish Republic, from whom they received this reply: 'The age-long dream cherished by Muslims that the Caliphate should be an Islāmic government including all Muslims, has never been capable of realization. It has become, on the contrary, a cause of dissension, of anarchy and of wars between the Believers. The interest of all, now more clearly understood, has brought to light this truth: that it is the duty of Muslims to possess separate governments. The true spiritual bond between them is the conviction that *all the Believers are brethren* ' (Qorān **49**, 10).

The merit of frankness in this reply is indisputable. It proclaims in plain language the bankruptcy of the traditional Caliphate and proposes to replace it by the bond of brotherhood between Muslim peoples. The idea will make its way. As to the protests of the Old Turks and the Kurds of Anatolia, they were stifled in blood. Of the two last Ottoman Caliphs, who were successively deposed, the first, Muḥammad VI, Waḥīd ad-dīn (1916–1922), abdicated in favour of King Ḥusain. His successor, 'Abdulmajīd (1922–1924), was discredited beforehand by accepting from an Assembly, without a mandate *ad hoc*, a Caliphate shorn of temporal power. He continues none the less to maintain his right to the Caliphate.

Under pretext of putting down the partisans of the fallen Caliphs, the Kemalists have decreed the suppression of all the fraternities, confiscated their property and closed their meeting-places. Outside Turkey hardly a voice has been raised—except that of a partisan of the King-Caliph Ḥusain—to proclaim ' the irregular state of an Islām deprived of a Caliph. What becomes of the Friday canonical devotions for all those who make their authorization by the *Imām* a condition of validity ? '

The Arab countries are divided between two tendencies : that of the Hāshimites of the Ḥejāz and that of the Wahhābis. These latter, in conformity with their democratic principles, had, until recently, paid no attention to the Caliphate. This is a disconcerting fact to discover among these puritans who are considered as the interpreters of Islām and the depositaries of its most ancient doctrine. If the Wahhābis have abandoned this exclusivism, if they have consented to mention the problem of the Caliphate in their programme, it is in consequence of pressure exerted by the powerful Indian Committees which supported them so effectually in their war against the Ḥāshimites. But they protest against the tendency which desires to assimilate the Caliphate to 'a spiritual function (*waẓīfa rūḥiyyā*), the monopoly of a race or of a group.'

NATIONALISM. In the majority of Muslim countries a recent phenomenon, the awakening of nationalism, has singularly damped enthusiasm for the organic reconstitution and unification of Islām—the mission which it was desired to assign to the Caliphate. Formerly each Believer considered himself as a citizen of Islām and his country as a province of the *omma*, the Islāmic nation. This sentiment is weakening, to the profound despair of the old conservatives. It is giving place to the theory of race, to the concept of ethical solidarity. The influence of blood and language are getting the upper hand again.

The Muslim nationalists, Turks, Arabs, Egyptians etc., are succumbing to the temptation to fall back on their immediate surroundings and historic past. They no longer consider the period prior to the Hijra as 'centuries of ignorance' (*jāhiliyya*) and barbarism. On this point they break resolutely with the historic traditions of Islām. The Muslim Turks and Turanians exhibit pride in their pagan forefathers, the Scythians, Attila and the Huns, Chingiz Khān and the Mongolians, Kubla Khān, the Mongolian conqueror of China. In the Persia of to-day the new generation strives to forget the Muslim past in order to think of the great ancestors of the pre-Hijra period: the Achæmenians, the Parthians, the Sassanids, the legendary heroes Rustem, Isfendyār, etc.

This evolution of ideas renders Islāmic opinion accessible to the suggestions of the Kemalists of

Anatolia, namely, that 'the interest of Muslims rightly understood is to have separate governments', each to promote its particular ideal and work peacefully towards the realization of national aspirations. M. L. Massignon draws attention to the 'elements particularly pernicious to Islām which are inherent in the extreme pursuit of the principle of nationality'. The Nationalists take no notice. Many are indifferent to the quarrel of the Caliphate or declare themselves, in principle, partisans of a plurality of local Caliphates: which is the negation of the traditional thesis.

There remain the reformists and the partisans of a democratic solution of the problem. This solution they find in a return to the '*shūrā*' of primitive Islām, the elective period of the first Caliphs. After the disappointments inflicted on them by the Kemalists, the Indian Committees have professed adhesion to this programme. It envisages the creation of a supreme Council of Islām, of which the Caliph would be no more than the delegated administrator. Opinions differ concerning the powers of this Council. Are its members to be re-elected annually or nominated for life? The most moderate would limit their scope to religious questions; the most advanced, under the influence of the Muslim Communists of Russia, suggest conferring on them dictatorial powers after the manner of the Muscovite Soviets. We have analysed above the radical thesis of the *'ālim* 'Abdarrāziq (*v.* p. 109).

A project intended to solve the crisis of the Caliphate, but which, however, runs the risks of complicating it, is the summoning of a sort of Council, or, if preferred, of a pan-Islāmic Congress.

PAN-ISLĀMIC CONGRESS. Islām, as we have seen, knows nothing of conciliar assemblies or synods. It might be added that its constitution does not permit councils, and it claims to fill their place by the completely spontaneous intervention of *ijmā'*. Are we to assume, then, that in the midst of present complications the operation of *ijmā'* has lost its former elasticity? Has the hour come to re-open wide 'the door of *ijtihād*'? There is no doubt that in the first centuries of the Hijra, the proposal of a conciliar meeting would have roused the suspicion of heresy, '*bid'a*'; and would, without fail, have been denounced as a Christian counterfeit. 'Adopt the reverse practices to those in force among the Scripturaries.' Thus says a *ḥadīth*, attributed to the Prophet. This dictum expresses admirably the sentiments of primitive Islām.

A Syrian *'ālim*, Sa'īd al-Karmī, Grand-Qāḍi in Transjordania, has not failed to make the most of this antinomy. He rightly observes that 'it is an innovation unheard of in the annals of Islām'. He confesses to have searched in vain to discover any legitimatism of it in Islāmic legislation. 'If a single precedent for it is known, how comes it that no one up to the present day has either remembered or thought of advancing it? Occasions have, nevertheless, not been wanting in recent times when the question has arisen of legalizing the recognition or deposition of the Sultans 'Abdul 'azīz, Murād, 'Abdulḥamīd, Reshād, Muḥammad VI, Waḥīd ad-dīn. In these circumstances was not religion at stake? Were there not at that time, in the bosom of Islām, persons charged with *binding and loosing* with whom counsel should have been taken? Was it fitting to leave the Caliphate, like a plaything, in the hands of the Young Turks? In these numberless successions of Sultan-Caliphs did anyone trouble ever to discuss whether the canonized stipulations had been observed? How is the silence of the *'ulemā* during that time to be interpreted?' These are the questions which the *'ālim* Sa'īd al-Karmī has addressed to his colleagues at Al-Azhar. All have remained unanswered.

In Turkey itself not all the believers approved of the deposition of Muḥammad VI nor of the arbitrary mutilation of the Ottoman Caliphate, voted by the *Grand National Assembly* of Angora. These conservatives do not consider the Caliphate assimilable to a constitutional monarchy. They find illegal, the dissociation of the Caliphate and Sultanate, in short, the transfer of the Caliphian powers to a body of persons. As for 'Abdulmajīd, the day following his fall, while claiming only the exercise of the canonical prerogatives of the Caliphate, he yet appealed to the decision of a Congress of Islām. He has been recognized as Caliph, in Egypt, in India and elsewhere. We have already seen that the Indian Committees for 'the Defence of the Caliphate' have also referred the solution of the problem to a Congress. But their adherence is dependent on a condition which goes substantially farther than the original dispute. They desire that the assembly shall first of all decree a number of urgent reforms, destined to bring about co-ordination amongst all followers of the creed.

The apprehension which this condition arouses among the Salafiyya can be readily understood. The latter, moderate reformists, at once conservative and progressive, accept on principle the Indian programme, or rather they resign themselves to it in order not to remain isolated in the midst of the general adhesion. But they feel dubious about the outcome of the pan-Islāmic Congress. They wonder whether the discussion will not end by increasing the confusion and what authority will have the strength to resist the pressure of the laity and the parties of the Left.

In order to put an end to the indecision, the Rector

of the University of Al-Azhar took upon himself to convoke the Congress at Cairo for the month of March, 1925. Immediately counter-projects arose and protests were multiplied. The initiative of the *'ulemā* of Al-Azhar was censured and their authority contested. 'Egypt', urged the objectors, 'does not enjoy political independence.' So they proposed going to sit in Turkey or Afghanistan. For his part, under pressure of his Indian partisans, the Wahhābi Sultan, Ibn Sa'ūd, launched an appeal inviting Muslims to meet at Mekka in order to settle the fate of the holy places of Islām. Is not their fate already settled, since Ibn Sa'ūd has proclaimed himself king of the Ḥejāz and refuses to evacuate the country? In the presence of so marked a disagreement the date of the Egyptian Congress has had to be postponed. In the confusion of proposals, of parties and committees, no agreement was reached either as to the programme or the future Congress, its members or its meeting-place.

A condition essential to success is to invest the meeting with an œcumenical character. How can this be done? On the very active 'Indian Committee of the Caliphate' are some notable Shī'as. Can they avoid summoning their co-religionists? Should they be joined by Zaidites, the least Shī'a among all the Imāmite sects? Their admission carries with it an obligation to give them the right to vote and to treat them on a footing of equality, in short, to give them the brevet of orthodoxy. In other words, it is breaking with the whole past of historic Islām.

The same questions arise in respect of the Kemalists of Anatolia, the Muslims of Russia and Central Asia, influenced by Bolshevism and won over to republican ideas. Will the Muslims of Morocco, the backward partisans of the two last Ottoman Sultans and those of King Ḥusain, be summoned? For them the problem of the Caliphate does not exist, or reduces itself to a return to the past. With the admission of the Kemalists and the Muslims belonging to the Soviet republics, the door is wide open to laic and even communist claims. These complications amply justify the absence of enthusiasm among the conservatives for the project of a pan-Islāmic Congress. Experience will show if and how it will succeed in adapting itself to the system of traditional Islām.

The attempt recently made at Cairo and at Mekka has not been encouraging. The pan-Islāmic Congress, after a delay of two years, was at last held at Cairo in the month of May, 1926, and was treated by Muslim opinion with complete indifference. It assembled about forty *'ulemā* and delegates, representing not countries but private associations. The great majority of the invitations issued remained unanswered. The congressists deliberated behind closed doors on the nature of the Caliphate and the qualities requisite in its holder. Finally, they testified to the breaking up of the old religious internationalism in Islām and the advent of nationalism with the creation of Muslim States, differing in their institutions and political tendencies, but all jealous of their independence.

This statement led them to declare that any practical solution in the matter of the Caliphate appeared to them premature. Meanwhile, they advise the creation of a pan-Islāmic organization. It would have a central commission, at Cairo, representing all countries, as well as national committees, acting as executive bodies. These local committees would also be charged with the task of solving religious problems until the meeting of a fresh pan-Muslim Congress at Cairo. The Sheikh Muḥammad Rashīd Riḍā bids Muslims not to lose heart. He calculates that it will take numerous congresses and 'several decades to set up again an institution overthrown by the assault of centuries'. Such appears also to be the conviction of the congressists who met at Mekka (June, 1926), since they saw fit to draw up the statutes of the future pan-Islāmic congresses which it is proposed to convoke annually at Mekka, on the occasion of the pilgrimage.

After the spectacle of two pan-Islāmic congresses functioning on parallel lines and affecting to ignore one another, it is easy to understand the bewilderment of the Muslims, who wonder anxiously whether the *conciliar* expedient will not open a new source of division in their midst.

Modernism. The attempts at reform just referred to have led to the formation of separate sects or even new religions, such as Behāï'sm. It remains to point out the currents of modernist opinion which disturb Islām and particularly the world of Sunni orthodoxy, where they have caused an internal crisis which, in the opinion of the review *Al-Manār*, threatens to become 'more baneful than the offensive of the Crusades. These latter sounded the rallying call amongst Muslims. The modernist crisis, a struggle of ideas and principles, brings dissension into their ranks and raises them up one against another. The sport of their enemies, they rend each other with their own hands.'

In the Islāmic East, modernism owes its birth to contact with European civilization, which taught Muslims how backward they were, chiefly in the domain of technique and the natural sciences. Nothing had prepared them for this brusque revelation, and among the intellectuals the humiliation inflicted on their self-esteem shook the boundless confidence which, until then, they had reposed in traditional knowledge. They threw the responsibility on to 'the closing of *ijtihād* ' (*v.* p. 97) and thought of nothing but making up the lost headway, convinced that the one thing needful was to learn from Europe. Hence the following topic appears amongst those debated in Muslim periodicals : ' What are the causes of the decline (*inḥiṭāṭ*) of Islām and how is it to be remedied ? ' The usual reply is : ' By the diffusion of modern knowledge.'

' I cannot believe ', writes a Muslim intellectual, ' that God has shut the door of progress in the face of His people, elected to attain to the greatest heights that man can reach. I refuse to admit that God desires all nations excepting the Muslims to inquire into the laws most suited to their kind, religion and time, and that while their scientific and literary eminence is increased by this effort, His chosen nation is forbidden any resort to independent inquiry and experiment ; in a word, that its Providence deprives it of the means to achieve distinction in the contest of enterprising nations.'

The chief centres of Muslim modernism are in India, Egypt and Turkey, if, however, that of Turkey still deserves this name at the stage which it has reached in the wake of Kemalist laicism. All the modernists are united in the war against superstition. The most moderate amongst them have undertaken the mission of showing the complete agreement between Islām, sanely interpreted, and the progress and aspirations of modern times. They protest that misunderstanding alone has given rise to a belief in their antinomy and they are resolved to dissipate it. ' We have made the mistake of attributing absolute values to details of secondary importance, and of establishing as immutable and eternal laws rules inspired by the temporary necessities of a particular period.'

A theme on which they love to expatiate is the principle of ' historic evolution ', which governs human societies. They believe this principle to be found in the '*Sunnat Allah*', that is, 'the providential scheme observed in the history of nations' (*v.* p. 65), to which they assert the Qorān (**33**, 62) pays homage. The '*maslaḥa*', or *higher interest* of Islām, must even prevail over a '*naṣṣ*', a formal text, which has become a dead letter. This letter they intend to quicken with a new spirit; for God, author of the Qorānic revelation, cannot desire the stagnation of human society of which He is likewise the author. Except for the revealed dogmas there are no unalterable texts, and therefore no immutable laws. To govern the relations of social life, there is room only for regulations elastic enough to be adapted to the ever-changing exigencies of the times. Distinction must be drawn in the *Sharī'a* between the 'universal' rules and those that are 'specific', the latter being valid only for a particular period and set of circumstances.

This is an admission that the modernists, even those who are moderate in tone, imperiously demand the re-opening of 'the door of *ijtihād*', or liberty of discussion and independence of judgment with regard to the four orthodox rites. They are not to be countered by the agreement established between the teachers of bygone centuries. This understanding might advantageously be replaced by another agreement, a 'new *ijmā'*' which would take account of modern needs.

Some modernists liken Muḥammad to any other human legislator. In this capacity, the Prophet was entitled to obedience, but his successors, having inherited the same right, were qualified to amend or complete his legislative work. According to this theory, Islām is nothing more than a code of moral discipline, a collection of religious truths. It has no call to mingle in questions of politics and human legislation. 'Earthly things are of too little importance in the eyes of Allah that He should have deemed it expedient to confide their regulation to a prophet ; and the prophets have too correct an estimate of their trivial value to consent to deal with them.'

According to the learned 'Alī 'Abdarrāziq (*v.* p. 109), 'We search vainly in Muḥammad's career for the smallest trace of political organization.' Islām, a simple conception and ideal of the spiritual and religious life, does not as such form a State, still less a State-Church. So it cannot claim domination over civil society nor demand external jurisdiction or special tribunals. On the other hand, the government of the four first Caliphs had no religious character ; whence it follows that the legislation and *Sunna* attributed to them must be regarded as human institutions, that is to say, as transitory and capable of amendment.

After this brief sketch of the general tendencies of Muslim modernism, no one will be surprised to see the interest which it manifests, not only in sociology, but also in what it called 'the philosophy of religion'. Chairs are beginning to be founded and books written for promoting 'the critical and comparative study of religions'. Needless to say, this criticism is inspired by a spirit quite other than that to which we owe the ultra-conservative compilations of Shahrastānī and the early Muslim heresiologists (*v.* p. 140).

In India. India is the oldest centre of modernism in Islām. Its creators have judged it expedient to assume, as a distinctive badge, the appellation of Neo-Mu'tazilites. Their professed aim is merely the revival and renewal of early Mu'tazilite doctrine. To begin with, a gratuitous fiction enables them to annex to this system a theory dear to all modernists, to wit, historic evolution. The truth is that neither the Mu'tazilites nor the other Muslim theorists have ever dreamed of the theory of evolution.

One of the most active protagonists of Indian modernism was Sir Seyyid Aḥmad Khān Bahādur (1817–1898), founder of the *Muhammadan Anglo-Oriental College* at Aligarh (1875), which has since been raised to the status of a university. He is the author of a commentary of the Qorān and of numerous writings in which he defends the principles of the new school. 'Allah', affirm their adepts, 'has enclosed the precepts of Islām within the limits of a legislation, which is elastic and susceptible of further development.' Very eclectic in the matter of traditions, they do not trouble about the *ḥadīth*, when the latter fail to accord with modern progress; they then refute them unhesitatingly by recourse to inner criticism. Here again their line of argument, which is entirely subjective, is lacking in logic and does not shrink from distorting history, for instance, to suit their ends. They describe the life of Medina in the first century A.H. and the reign of the four first Caliphs as inspired by tendencies of the most advanced liberalism. A Persian newspaper, *Al-Ḥabl al-matīn* (27th of May, 1915), shows us Fāṭima and 'Ayesha in the intimate circle of the Prophet engaged in philosophical arguments.

According to them, Muḥammad was the declared adversary of slavery. If any mistake has been made on this subject, it is through misinterpretation of the Qorānic texts which appear to make this institution lawful. As for the *ḥadīth* quoted in its favour, Sir Seyyid Aḥmad accords them precisely the same degree of belief 'as the *Arabian Nights* and the legend of Ḥātim Ṭayy'. We can see from this example the method of argument adopted by the Indian school.

On the other hand, it admits the convincing value of the *ḥadīth* every time they harmonize with its evolutionist predilections. It refuses to recognize the authority of the *consensus* or *ijmā'*, if this happens to be urged against it. 'To accept the infallibility and immutability of *ijmā'* would be arbitrarily to admit a legislation independent of that of the Prophet.' Whence the conclusion, common to all modernists, that a new *ijmā'* can annul and reform the old.

From this Indian school sprang, in 1911, an English version of the Qorān. In it the *Sūras* are arranged, not, as in the official editions, according to their length and the number of their verses, but in chronological order; a daring innovation, since this can only be established by conjecture and approximation. But it testifies to the audacity and initiative of the innovators, who did not quail before the reproval of the orthodox. The *jehād* troubles them considerably, as it troubled the Aḥmadiyya (*v.* p. 149). Their theory is that the Qorān contemplated only defining warfare and that its recommendations were valid only in the Prophet's own time.

Their centre of learning is in the Muslim University of Aligarh. Since the death of Sir Seyyid Aḥmad, Seyyid Amīr-'Alī, author of *The Spirit of Islām* (1902), has shown himself one of the most active interpreters of their doctrines. In the liveliest terms he upbraids the reactionary *'ulemā* for their foolish desire 'to give permanent character to laws enacted for the use of a patriarchal society'—contrary to the intentions of the Prophet, 'that man of lofty intelligence, who has proclaimed the empire of reason and the law of social evolution'.

IN EGYPT. Much more recent, Egyptian modernism has a history very different from that of Indian modernism. It has sprung from the attempt of the

Salafiyya to bring about an Islāmic renaissance. The modernist party was founded in 1883 by the pan-Islāmic agitator, Jamāl ad-dīn al-Afghānī (1839–1897), and by his most brilliant disciple, the Egyptian Muḥammad 'Abdu, born in 1849, died in 1905, Grand-Muftī of Egypt.

Quite unlike Indian modernism, which pursues a policy of adaptation to the progress of the day, the Salafiyya school, in its reformist campaign, sets out to owe nothing to Europe and, apart from modern technique, to borrow nothing from that continent, whose encroachments it fears for their possible effects on the cohesion and independence of the Muslim races. It is a kind of Neo-Wahhābism. It proclaims the decline of Islām, and laments its 'doctrinal sterility since the days of Ghazālī', wrote Muḥammad 'Abdu, but professed to be able to find a cure by bringing it back to the spirit of the Qorān and authentic tradition. Dominated by hatred of the West, converted to the pan-Islāmic and pan-Arabian programme, it shows itself hostile to the nationalist currents which disturb the Muslim World. It recommends the fusion into one of the four great juridical schools, the reunion of the dissident Muslim sects in one vast Islāmic union or association, capable of opposing Europe and of 'resisting the encroachment of its culture and imperialism'.

Muḥammad 'Abdu began by expounding his progressivist programme in a course of lectures at the University of Al-Azhar, which attracted great attention. They were the first public manifestation of modernism in Egypt. Soon the opposition of the reactionary *'ulemā* forced the lecturer to give up. He then helped his favourite pupil, the Syrian Seyyid Muḥammad Rashīd Riḍā, to found (1897) the monthly review, *Al-Manār*, or, *The Lighthouse*, which was to serve as the doctrinal organ of the party. Rashīd Riḍā, who proclaims himself 'Arab and Quraish', is a fanatical admirer of Ibn Taimiyya and has done nothing but accentuate the Wahhābite tendencies of the school.

The *Manār* declares that 'true Islām admits all modern progress for those who do not insist on standing by a juridical rite. Everything is in the Qorān and the authentic *Sunna*.' The problem is confined to discovering in their text, more than a thousand years old, the equivalent of modern concepts and ideas. The Manārists excel in this delicate operation. We are familiar with the scruples occasioned among timorous Muslims by the prohibitive laws on images. A *fatwā* of the Sheikh 'Abdal-'azīz Shāwīsh declares that this interdiction retained its value only while the danger of a return to polytheism subsisted. The *Manār* (XX, 274–275) adds this reflection: Science cannot dispense with diagrams, neither can the art of war, the police, etc. How can the progress of electricity and machinery be imagined without the art of drawing and everything relating to it? Their use cannot, therefore, be other than legitimate.

The *Manār* condemns the subtleties and the whole casuistry of the four schools. It upbraids them for the levity with which they have enacted laws without any thought for the future. Their disagreement, their barren discussions, are compared to 'the quarrels of the Byzantine theologians while Muḥammad camped under the walls of Constantinople'. Its logic refuses to admit that the life of to-day can be bound hard and fast by a legislation built up during the three first centuries of the Hijra, or that research (*ijtihād*) can be forbidden in the presence of new problems and questions, which affect the very existence of Islām.

On this point, it tacitly separates from the Wahhābis

with whom it is associated in the war against superstition. Like them, it recommends the suppression of the '*maulid*', with their appearance of 'riotous fairs'. It proposes to employ the *Ṣūfī* fraternities on works of public utility: charity, teaching, etc. Its irony is especially directed against the cult of the tombs of santons and their visitors whom it calls '*qubūriyyūn*', or *tombolators*.

The Salafiyya, together with modernists of the various Muslim countries, have come to the conclusion that reform is necessary. The two bodies often differ in tone and in the choice of arguments. The Salafiyya would restrict themselves to a purification of the ancient religion freed at last from its vein of abuses and superstitions. As to the modernists, they sacrifice without regret the 'prophetic traditions', including the 'Six Books' (*v.* p. 77). The tactics of the Salafiyya are to make every effort to save them by means of pseudo-scientific glosses.

For example, 'the reality of the evil eye', attested in Bukhārī, is attributed by the *Manār* (V, 947) to 'magnetic effluvia'. If the Prophet denied 'the transmissibility of infectious diseases', it would be, according to the same review (V, 358–359), in order to maintain, in the face of the denials of the pagans, the direct intervention of divine action. When the *Sunna* forbids departure from an infected region, 'it must be with the object of circumscribing the extension of the epidemic centre'.

The *Manār* finds in the text of the Qorān the most daring modern theories, not excepting Darwin's natural selection. The *jinn* are alleged to represent the activity of microbic agents. Is not the etymological meaning of this word that which is *hidden*? The Qorān (**105**, 4) is supposed to have made another allusion to them in 'the birds in flocks (*abābīl*)' which annihilated the Abyssinian Army. When in this book lightning is mentioned, electricity must be understood. Muḥammad 'Abdu and his disciples are fond of quoting Leibnitz, Spencer, Auguste Comte, Berthelot, Tolstoi, Dr. Gustave Le Bon. They propose to substitute the gramophone for the 'two witnesses' required by the Qorān. According to them, recourse to an X-ray examination advantageously replaces the '*'idda*' or Qorānic respite (**65,** 4) of three months imposed on a divorced wife (*Manār*, XXI, 78).

It is not always easy, as may be seen, to establish a line of demarcation between the programme of the progressivists and that of the modernists. Determined never to lose touch with orthodoxy, the school of the *Manār* is anxious to distinguish itself by the novelty and unexpectedness of its interpretations. But where the Qorān is concerned the most advanced modernists never speak of it except with respect nor bring into question its character as a revealed book. All vie zealously with one another in the apologia of Islām. They often enhance the credit of Qorānic institutions, by pointing to the temperance campaign and the recrudescence of divorce among Christian peoples. Above all, the progressivists boast they can prove that as far as liberty of conscience, the *rights of man* and the other 'conquests' of modern civilization are concerned, Islām is several centuries ahead of Europe.

With meritorious energy they all take up arms against polygamy. But how is the text of the Qorān (**4,** 3), which allows four wives, to be circumvented? 'This passage', they reply, 'only contemplates an exceptional measure. There can be no question of anything beyond mere permission. Now, no one would venture to consider the right of the State to withdraw any permission when it is considered prejudicial to the public good.' The Qorān has, moreover, rendered this permissive clause invalid, 'since it has hedged it round with conditions which are, humanly speaking, unrealizable. Polygamy agrees very ill with domestic education; therefore it behoves the religious authorities to study this problem. Since religion pursues the good of society, it is beyond dispute that if an institution produces harmful effects it must be modified and adapted to the needs of the time. . . . Whence it follows', concludes the *Manār* (XII, 572), 'that polygamy is absolutely unlawful.' The Indian modernists had arrived at the same conclusion and those of Turkey have set it down in a legislative text. All are agreed in affirming that, judiciously interpreted, the Qorān not only proclaims the complete equality of the sexes, but that in its efforts to raise the status of woman, it has outstripped all other religions.

We have previously mentioned (p. 207) the opinion of the Egyptian modernists who liken Muḥammad to any other legislator or dispute the right of Qorānic legislation to regulate civil life.

IN TURKEY. Modernism was narrowly watched under the reign of 'Abdulḥamīd, and was not free to manifest its vitality until after the fall of the Sultan (July 1908). It is conspicuous among other modernist movements sprouting from Islāmic soil by reason of its strict subordination to a programme of nationalist claims, which, after the interlude of the Young Turks, were realized in their fullest degree by the Kemalists. Before the advent of the latter the attitude of the parties in Turkey towards the religious problem was as follows:—

The orthodox conservatives were opposed to all innovation and proposed to maintain Islām as it had been constituted by thirteen centuries of existence. This party was disarmed by the pressure of the *Nationalists* and *Reformists*. The Nationalists cherished vague sympathies for Islām, 'the historic religion of the Turkish people', but had the intention of modifying its political and social legislation in order to bring it into conformity with that of modern countries. They prepared the way for the extreme revolutionary changes of the Kemalists. The reformists desired improvements and professed to go back beyond traditional Islām to primitive Islām. Their programme corresponded, in broad outline, to that of the Salafiyya. Nationalists and reformists alike recognized the necessity for reorganizing the religious instructions of the people, with this difference, that the former proposed to entrust it to the State without the intermediate control of the Sheikh al-Islām.

The Nationalists have laboured gradually to 'de-Arabize' the Muslim religion; they have protested against the exclusive use of Arabic in the ceremonies of the cult and also against the importance attributed to Arab tradition and custom in the religious legislation of Islām. They place on the same footing as the *Sharī'a* the *Qānūns* (*v.* p. 92) or codes of law enacted by the Ottoman Sultans. 'Obscurantism alone could persist in denying them the same value, just as it had brought about the checkmate of the timid reforms attempted by the Tanẓimāt.'

For the Reformists, the religious problem took precedence over everything. Their best accredited representative was the Egyptian prince Sa'īd Ḥalīm Pasha, former Grand-Vizier, who died at Naples, whither he had retired after the world-war. 'In order to forestall the internal crisis of Islām,' he, too, proclaimed the necessity for religious reform. This reform was to be limited to 'a *re-Islāmization*; it will conform to the dogmas, the ethics and the social and political ideal of Islām.' Will the return to primitive Islām be a reaction? Presumably not, since the promoters pride themselves on 'adapting it opportunely to the needs of time and place'. Do they not possess a panacea? By the judicious use of *ijtihād*, 'it is possible to create indefinitely laws adapted to the progress of the ages and the needs of divers peoples'.

In a treatise entitled *Islāmashmaq*, or *Re-Islāmization*, the Egyptian prince sums up the aspirations of the reformist party. This treatise contains the apologia of Islām, presented as the final religion of humanity. 'Free from all external pressure, it entrusts to the most virtuous, the wisest and the most learned the guidance of their fellow-creatures.' In the opinion of the Reformists, the decadence of the Turks was the result of their *de-Islāmization*, of institutions borrowed from the West, and also of an exacerbated nationalism. On this question they are once again in agreement with the Salafiyya. If, they conclude, we understand aright the lessons of the last war, we must acknowledge the condemnation of nationalism. Back, then, to Islāmic internationalism! Since the Qorān contains the absolute truth, civil, social and political, this truth cannot bear a national stamp.

To this defence of the reformist programme, the literature of the Nationalists opposes its most audacious claims. The poets have undertaken the mission of popularizing them, and join issue with the preachers in the mosques. 'Why do they belittle material progress? Progress is life. Did steamers exist in the time of Noah? The law of evolution dominates everything. The world owes to it all progress. . . . God undoubtedly hurls the thunderbolt, but man has found the means to divert it; he has discovered the electric current and better still . . . aeroplanes'!

On the occasion of the Congress which met at Mekka (*v.* p. 205) one of the most eminent Turkish publicists, Agha Uglu Aḥmed-Bey, described the spirit in which the emancipated Turks of Anatolia will in future accomplish the pilgrimage.

'In kissing the Black Stone he will experience the sensation of venerating, not a piece of stone fallen from Heaven, but a sacred emblem of all the traditions, of the whole history of religion. In drinking the water of Zamzam, he will look upon it not as a panacea for all his ills, but as representing a communion with the religion which he reveres and with the saintly characters who founded it. In accomplishing the course between Marwa and Ṣafā he will not imagine that he is driving out the devil and obtaining pardon for his sins, but will dwell with emotion on what the Prophet and the saints suffered between these two hills for a faith, a conviction, a law. Finally, in making the sevenfold circuit of the Ka'ba, he will cast off the superstition of encircling a little house inhabited by God and will remember that in this very building monotheism superseded paganism. This is what the Turk will make known to the Muslim world; and this the religion worthy of the Divinity, into which he will breathe once more the breath of life.'

One of the foremost poets, Ziā Gheuk Alp, a former professor of sociology at the University of Stambul, who died recently, was entrusted with the task of preparing the popular mind for the Turkization of Muslim worship. This is apparently the aim of the poem '*Waṭan*', Fatherland. 'The fatherland of the Turk is the country where from the minaret the call to prayer re-echoes in the Turkish tongue, where the peasant understands the meaning of that prayer, where the Qorān is read in Turkish in the schools.' The Kemalists have taken upon themselves to realize all these poetical suggestions, including the translation of the Qorān into Turkish, which so greatly scandalizes the Salafiyya.

The poems of Ziā also deal with woman and the family. For woman he claims 'equality in the marriage contract, in divorce and in inheritance. So long as a young girl is worth only half a man in inheritance and only a quarter of a man in marriage, neither the family nor the country will be able to raise its head.' Progress 'can only in reason be expected from harmony between man and wife, from the union of two souls to create the fatherland. Formerly the sexes had to pray apart. Now both worship together a single God!'

Here again the Grand National Assembly of Angora has been content to give legal force to the nationalist poet's suggestions. In their reform of the personal statute, the Kemalists have ignored the Qorānic provisions on the subject of marriage and inheritance. They have just given fresh proof of this by adopting the civil code of Switzerland in its entirety. Now this code does not consider difference of religion as a nullifying cause in marriage. According to the canonical law of Islām, nothing stood in the way of a matrimonial union between a Believer and a Scripturary woman. But the inverse, the marriage 'of a female Believer with an Infidel', is explicitly forbidden by a Qorānic text (**60**, 10), and Muslim circles, even those most favourable to modernist ideas, had never consented to compromise on this prohibition. It is evident that the Kemalist government shows itself, by the adoption of the Swiss code, prepared to override all considerations of religious traditionalism.

In Albania, public prayer in several mosques is recited in Albanese. The Congress of Tirana (April 1923) imposed monogamy, abolished the veil for women and declared ritual ablution optional.

Some Statistical Data. The statistics of Islām can only be dealt with in approximations. We only possess the census of a few regions populated by Muslims—Egypt, British India, Dutch Malay, French Africa, Syria, etc. When we come to determine the total Muslim population of the world we are reduced to estimates of indifferent value and almost always exaggerated. We may recall the toast of Damascus (1898) when William II, Emperor of Germany, proclaimed himself 'the friend of 300 million Muslims', a figure to which the review *Al-Manār* (V, 605) hastened to add a further 60 millions. The highest total which has been alleged is that of a Muslim publicist in India, protesting in the name of '400 millions, his co-religionists', against the treaty of Sèvres. In the early European statistics, the estimates fluctuated between 260 and 175 million Muslims.

Strange illusions were formerly entertained concerning the density of the Muslim population in certain regions. In Morocco instead of 4 to 5 million inhabitants there were alleged to be 12 to 14 million; in China 40 million Muslims, instead of at most 7 million. It has also been confidently stated that the supremacy of Islām over the blacks was 'inexorable and decreed by fate', that in the course of the last century the whole of Africa north of the Equator had become Muslim. M. Delafosse, an expert on negro questions, observes that Islām 'has produced a deep and lasting effect scarcely anywhere except among the negro or negroid populations living on the edge of the Sahara. Its adepts become more and more rare in proportion as one advances towards the South, and even in the region which we commonly call the Sudan it is far from being the numerically dominant religion.' This is not all. Since we have become better acquainted with darker Africa, it has become evident that among the negro population Islāmic propaganda has remained stationary, and that tribes formerly converted by force have reverted in a body to their old animist beliefs.

The *Annuaire du monde Musulman* of M. L. Massignon records for 1926 a total of 240 million Muslims. The review *The Moslem World* (1923), correcting its statistical data of 1914, substitutes, for the original figure of 201 million Muslims, that of 235 millions. Of this number 106 millions live in the British colonies, protectorates or mandated countries, 94 millions are governed by other Western powers, 39 millions by Holland, 32 millions by France, etc. There presumably remains therefore a total of no more than 34 to 35 million Muslims completely independent of Western rule and scattered in China, Siam, Turkey, Arabia, Afghanistan, Persia, etc. If from the aggregate number of 235 million the sects are deducted it emerges that 210 to 215 million Believers profess the Sunni or orthodox religion. Of this number more than 90 millions belong to the Ḥanīfite rite.

Four-fifths of the Muslim population of the world is distributed over Asia. Oceania is the part of the globe which numbers fewest Muslims, perhaps about 40,000. America comes next with 170,000 to 180,000. Of the 19 million Muslims in Europe (the Balkan Peninsula and Russia), Western Europe numbers only 50,000, all immigrants. In England, some half-score or so of Anglo-Saxon families have adopted Islām, under the form of Aḥmadism (*v.* p. 188). In the other European countries the cases of individual Islāmization 'have not spread to the family nor been transmitted to descendants' (Massignon). The American Behāïs have been mentioned above (p. 195).

In regions which have remained independent, the figure of the Muslim population is stationary. It is only progressive in the countries governed under various titles by Western powers :—British and Dutch

India, French Africa, etc. In Egypt the population has increased fivefold in the space of a century. This growth has been especially rapid in the course of the last fifty years, that is to say, since the great works of public utility were undertaken by Westerners or under their patronage.

The percentage of illiterates remains high in Muslim centres remote from all contact with the West. We possess no precise returns on the subject except for British India and Egypt, the two countries where the war against analphabetism has been waged with the greatest steadiness and energy. In Egypt the proportion of Muslim men who can read is 10 per cent. and 0·60 per cent. for Muslim women. In India out of 72 million Muslims close upon three million are able to read. Taking as a basis the statistics which are available to us for other countries peopled by Muslims—95 per cent. of illiterates among the Muslims of Dutch India—*The Moslem World* believes itself in a position to affirm that in the whole world of Islām the number of Muslim men able to read 'would not amount to 8 millions, and that of Muslim women would be below 500,000'.

FUTURE PROSPECTS. As we have noted (p. 221) the Muslim population continues to grow, less by the progress of proselytism than by the favourable conditions which it encounters in the colonies and protectorates of the Western powers. Everywhere else, infant mortality, epidemics, political insecurity and instability arrest or retard its development. Contrary to certain too hasty asseverations, it is by no means unknown for more or less compact groups to abandon Islām, even after centuries of nominal profession. We have quoted the case of the African negroes. In British India, Hinduism strives, with success, to provoke apostasy among the early Muslim converts. We may recall the successful propaganda carried out by the Arya Samāj and the societies under its patronage. In Java and Sumātra (Dutch Malay), the missions number thousands of proselytes, former Muslims. In Europe, as a result of the late exchanges of population, the time can be foreseen when only Russia will possess important groups of Muslims, and on these Bolshevism is beginning to exert an influence.

With Sheikh 'Alī 'Abdarrāziq's book (p. 109), historical criticism burst rudely into the conservative circles of Islām. The condemnation of the Al-Azhar tribunal seems unlikely to stop the march of the ideas advanced by the Egyptian *'ālim.* Less than a year after (March 1926), appeared the no less suggestive book of Dr. Ṭāhā Ḥusain, Professor at the Egyptian University of Cairo, entitled *Fīsh-shi'r al-jāhilī.* In this treatise, which sets out to examine the degree of authenticity of *pre-Islāmite poetry*, the author finds occasion to reveal to his co-religionists the method of Cartesian doubt. He explains its operation and extols it as the sole path to scientific certitude. We must, according to him, 'forget race and religion. If our conclusions happen to be contrary to our national and religious opinions, so much the worse.'

Dr. Ḥusain defines the *Sīra*, or Life, of the Prophet, as 'a collection of stories and anecdotes which must be passed through the sieve of severe criticism'. In applying his method to them, he discovers that all the poetical quotations which appear in the *Sīra* are apocryphal, intended to show the noble extraction of the Prophet, the reality and universal expectation of his mission. The whole pre-history and proto-history of Islām which, for the most part, have their source in pre-Hijra poetry, would be found in like manner loaded with apocryphal documents. The mention of Abraham in the Qorān and his genealogical relations with the Arab people should not, according to Dr. Ḥusain, be considered as irrefragible historical arguments. It is evident that historical criticism on its first appearance in Muslim literature was resolved to outstrip the most advanced conclusions of European Islāmology. The Egyptian press gave this book the most resounding publicity.

A new spirit is breathing even in the very precincts of Al-Azhar. Here, in this citadel of conservative Islām, where the *'ulemā* of Egypt are trained, a strong group of students, *'ulemā* of the future, press for the revision of the rules and syllabuses governing the teaching of religious knowledge. Among their demands we may quote the following : ' The sending of students to European universities where they may perfect themselves in the subjects taught at Al-Azhar, especially in the philosophy (*sic*) of religion and in the sciences which bear upon religious beliefs.'

Islām has arrived at the cross-roads. With the exception of the old conservatives, all Muslims are conscious of the urgent need to carry out reforms and come to terms with modern progress. But each party envisages the transformation in its own way. On one point only are all instinctively agreed ; on no consideration will they approximate to Christian civilization.

To the Salafiyya or orthodox progressivists, reform is identified with a Muslim renaissance to which Western science will serve solely as a stimulus. They will merely borrow from Europe technique and material progress, since Islām contains in itself all the elements necessary to its own regeneration. Others confine their aspirations for reform to commercial development, and this tendency has produced in Islām types unknown a quarter of a century ago : big manufacturers, shipowners, bankers and stockbrokers. In these circles the general attitude is to ignore the restrictive stipulations of the *Sharī'a* in respect of money dealings (*v.* p. 63), to preserve to Islām the wealth of the Islāmic countries, and to substitute Muslim for foreign capital there.

Of the great mixture of peoples in Turanian Asia, the Russian Soviet has succeeded in constituting a whole gamut of small laicized and secularized States, among which every day it strengthens national consciousness and which it awakens to modern life at the expense of the Islāmic ideal. In Anatolia, Mustapha Kemal presides over a similar revolution. Angora and Moscow adopt, almost to a shade, the same methods in dealing with traditional Islām. Both appeal to 'pure reason' and to 'intellectual emancipation'. Over all the Turanian peoples to-day the wave of modernism is breaking.

Outside the Turanian territory modernist ideas advance more discreetly, but everywhere they are gaining ground. It is from the governing classes and the intelligentsia of Islām that they recruit the bulk of their adherents. Here again *The Moslem World* ventures to quote numbers. It speaks of '6 to 10 million Muslims who are alleged to have adopted Western culture, and to have broken with the traditional type of ancient Islāmic Orthodoxy so completely that they may be classed as modern Muslims'.

We do not know on what data these summary calculations are based, but it would be just as rash to deny the internal crisis through which Islām is passing as to attempt at the present time to prophesy its issue. 'Verily, a day with Allah is as fifty thousand years' (Qorān **22,** 46; **70,** 4).

A BIBLIOGRAPHY OF THE PRINCIPAL WORKS WHICH SHOULD BE READ OR CONSULTED

GENERAL INFORMATION

Victor Chauvin, *Bibliographie des ouvrages arabes ou relatifs aux Arabes publiés dans l'Europe Chrétienne de* 1810 *à* 1885. Liège, 1892, etc. Vol. X : *Le Coran et la Tradition* ; Vol. XI : *Mahomet.*

Carl Brockelmann, *Geschichte der arabischen Literatur.* Berlin, 1898–1902, 2 volumes.

Encyclopédie de l'islam (French, English and German editions). Leiden, 1907 (in course of publication).

Th. P. Hughes, *Dictionary of Islam,* 2nd edition. London, 1896.

A number of excellent articles in the *Encyclopædia of Religion and Ethics,* edited by J. Hastings, Edinburgh, 1908–1921. The same applies to *The Encyclopædia Britannica,* Cambridge, 1910–11, 11th edition.

Certain *jubilee* collections or ' Festschriften ' will repay examination, e.g. : *Orientalische Studien, Theod. Noeldeke zum siebzigsten Geburtstag gewidmet.* Giessen, 1806, 2 vols.

Revue du monde musulman. Paris (from 1907 onwards).

Der Islam, Zeitschrift für Geschichte und Kultur des islamischen Orients. Strasburg, 1910–19 ; Berlin, 1919–26.

The Moslem World. London (from 1911 onwards).

Die Welt des Islams. Berlin, 1913–19, vols. 1–7.

Islamica. Leipzig, from 1924.

Revue des études islamiques, directeur L. Massignon, Paris (depuis 1927).

Oriente moderno, Rome (from 1921 onwards), gives precise information as to events in the Muslim world.

To these reviews, more especially devoted to Islāmic questions, may be added *L'Afrique française,* Paris (from 1889, etc.), and *L'Asie française,* Paris (from 1899 onwards) ; as also the *Archives marocaines* (from 1904, etc.), and the greater number of the Orientalist reviews : *Journal asiatique,* Paris (from 1822) ; *Journal of the Royal Asiatic Society of Great Britain,* London (from 1834) ; *Zeitschrift der deutschen*

morgenländischen Gesellschaft, Leipzig (from 1847); *Mélanges de la Faculté orientale de l'Université S. Joseph* of Beyrout (from 1906); *Rivista degli studi orientali*, Rome (from 1907).
L. Massignon, *Annuaire du monde musulman*; statistical, historic, social and economic; first year, 1923, Paris.
The same, *Eléments arabes et foyer d'arabisation*: their rôle in the Muslim world of to-day (in *Rev. du monde musulman*, LVII, 1924).
Gius. Gabrieli, *Manuale di bibliografia musulmana.* Parte prima. bibliografia generale. Rome, 1916.
Gust. Weil, *Geschichte der Chalifen.* Mannheim, 1846, etc., 5 vols.
Aug. Müller, *Der Islam im Morgen- und Abendland.* Berlin, 1885, etc., 2 vols.
Leone Caetani, *Annali dell' Islam.* Milan, 1905, etc., 8 vols.
The same, *Studi di Storia Orientale.* Milan, 1911, etc., 1st and 3rd vols.
The same, *Chronographia islamica.* Paris, 1912, etc., 5 parts.
Theodor Noeldeke, *Orientalische Skizzen.* Berlin, 1892.
Clément Huart, *Histoire des Arabes.* Paris, 1912, 2 vols.
Abû'l Faraj of Ispahan, *Kitāb al-Aghāni.* Būlāq, 21 vols., 1st edition, 1868. It will be found that the substance of this work, as regards the pre-Hijra period, has been utilized in Caussin de Perceval's *Essai sur l'histoire des Arabes avant l'islamisme.* Paris, 1847, etc., 3 vols.
Alf. von Kremer, *Kulturgeschichte des Orients unter den Chalifen*, Vienna, 1875–77, 2 vols. (somewhat out of date).
Carra de Vaux, *Les Penseurs de l'islam.* Paris, 1921, etc., 5 vols.
Ign. Goldziher, *Muhammedanische Studien.* Halle, 1889, etc., 2 vols. (a fundamental work).
The same, *Vorlesungen über den Islam*, Heidelberg, 1910, 2nd edition, 1925. Translated into French under the title of *Le dogme et la loi de l'islam.* Paris, 1920 (translation by Félix Arin).
C. Snouck Hurgronje, *Verspreide Geschriften* (*Gesammelte Schriften*). Bonn and Leipzig, 1923, etc., 5 vols.
The same, *Mekka.* The Hague, 1888, etc., 2 vols.
C. H. Becker, *Islamstudien.* Berlin, 1924, 1 vol.
Duncan B. Macdonald, *Development of Muslim Theology, Jurisprudence and Constitutional Theory.* London, 1903.
The same, *The Religious Attitude and Life in Islam.* Chicago, 1909.
The same, *Aspects of Islam.* New York, 1911

T. W. Arnold, *The Preaching of Islam*, 2nd ed. London, 1913.
A. Mez, *Die Renaissance des Islām*. Heidelberg, 1922. (Ill-chosen title of an excellent monograph on Islām in the fourth century A.H.)
R. Dozy, *Essai sur l'histoire de l'islamisme*. Translated from the Dutch by V. Chauvin. Leyden, 1879.
C. Snouck Hurgronje, *Mohammedanism*. New York and London, 1916.
Martin Hartmann, *Der Islam : Ein Handbuch*. Leipzig, 1909.

I. THE CRADLE OF ISLĀM

Abū'l Faraj and Caussin de Perceval, mentioned above.
Ign. Guidi, *L'Arabie Antéislamique*. Paris, 1921.
Th. Noeldeke, *Geschichte der Perser und Araber zur Zeit der Sasaniden*. Leyden, 1879.
The same, *Die ghassānischen Fürsten aus dem Hause Gafna's*. Berlin, 1887.
Ign. Goldziher, the *Muhamm. Studien*, already quoted, and *Abhandlungen zur arabischen Philologie*. Leyden, 1896, etc., 2 vols.
René Dussaud, *Les Arabes en Syrie avant l'islam*. Paris, 1907.
Jul. Wellhausen, *Die Ehe bei den Arabern*. Goettingen, 1893.
The same, *Medina vor dem Islam* (in *Skizzen und Vorarbeiten*, IV). Berlin, 1889.
The same, *Reste arabischen Heidentums*. Berlin, 2nd ed., 1897.
Will. Robertson Smith, *Kinship and Marriage in Early Arabia*. Cambridge, 1885.
The same, *The Religion of the Semites*. London, 2nd ed., 1894.
G. Jacob, *Das Leben der vorislamischen Beduinen*. Berlin, 1892, 2nd ed.
A. Geiger, *Was hat Mohammed aus dem Judentum aufgenommen*. Leipzig, 1833 and 1902 (reprint).
Hartw. Hirschfeld, *Jüdische Elemente im Koran*. Berlin, 1873.
The same, *New Researches into the Composition and Exegesis of the Qoran*. London, 1902.
The same, *Histoire des Juifs de Médine* (in the *Revue des Etudes Juives*, VII and X, 1883 and 1885).
A. J. Wensinck, *Mohammed en de Joden te Medina*. Leyden, 1908.
R. Leszynsky, *Die Juden in Arabien zur zeit Mohammed*. Berlin, 1910.
D. S. Margoliouth, *The Relations between Arabs and Israelites prior to the Rise of Islam*. London, 1923.

C. Snouck Hurgronje, *Het Mekkaansche Feest* (in *Verspreide Geschriften*, I). In the same collection, numerous articles on Arabia (Vol. III).

Rich. Bell, *The Origin of Islam in its Christian Environment*. London, 1926.

W. Rudolph, *Die Abhaengigkeit des Qorans von Judentum und Christentum*. Stuttgart, 1922.

J. L. Burckhardt, *Travels in Arabia*. London, 2 vols., 1829. French translation by Eyriès. Paris, 1835, 3 vols.

Ch. M. Doughty, *Travels in Arabia Deserta*. Cambridge, 1888, 2 vols.

J. Euting, *Reise in Inner Arabien*. Leyden, 1896 and 1914, 2 vols.

H. St. J. B. Philby, *The Heart of Arabia*. London, 1922, 2 vols.

R. E. Cheesman, *In Unknown Arabia*. London, 1926.

Jaussen and Savignac, *Mission archéologique en Arabie*. Paris, 1909, etc., 3 vols.

H. Lammens, *Le berceau de l'islam. L'Arabie occidentale à la veille de l'hégire*. Rome, 1914.

The same, *La cité arabe de Ṭāif ā la veille de l'hégire*. Beyrout, 1922.

The same, *La Mecque à la veille de l'hégire*. Beyrout, 1924.

The same, *Le culte des bétyles et les processions religieuses chez les Arabes préislamites* (in *Bull. Inst. franç. arch. orientale*, XVII). Cairo.

The same, *Les chrétiens à la Mecque à la veille de l'hégire* (*Ibid.*, XIV).

The same, *Le caractère religieux du 'Tār' ou vendetta chez les Arabes préislamites* (*Ibid., XXVI*).

The same, *Les sanctuaires préislamites dans l'Arabie Occidentale* (in *Mélanges de l'Univ. S. Joseph de Beyrouth*, XI). Beyrout, 1926.

The same, *Les Juifs de la Mecque, à la veille de l'hégire* (in *Recherches de science religieuse*, VIII). Paris.

The same, *Les Aḥâbîch et l'organisation militaire de la Mecque, au siècle de l'hégire* (in the *Journal asiatique*, 1916²). Paris.

II. THE FOUNDER OF ISLĀM

Moḥammad ibn Hishām, *Sīrat ar-rasūl* (ed. Wüstenfeld). Goettingen, 1858, etc., 2 vols. German translation by Gust. Weil. Stuttgart, 1864.

Al-Wāqidī, *Kitāb al-Maghāzi* (ed. Von Kremer). Calcutta,

1855, etc. Abridged and annotated in German by Wellhausen under the title of *Vakidi's Kitāb al-Maghazi*. Berlin, 1882.

Ibn Sa'd, *Kitāb aṭ-ṭabaqāt al-Kabīr* (ed. by Ed. Sachau). Leyden, 1904, etc., 8 vols.

Ṭabarī, *Annales* (*Ta'rīkh ar-rusul wa'l- mulūk*), ed. de Goeje. Leyden, 1879, etc., 3 vols.

Tor Andrae, *Die Person Muhammeds in Lehre und Glauben seiner Gemeinde*. Stockholm, 1917.

Gust. Weil, *Mohammed der Prophet, sein Leben und seine Lehre*. Stuttgart, 1843.

Caussin de Perceval, work mentioned above.

William Muir, *The Life of Mahomet*. London, 1858, etc., 4 vols.

A. Sprenger, *Das Leben und die Lehre des Moḥammad*. Berlin, 2nd ed., 1869, 3 vols.

Theod. Noeldeke, *Das Leben Mohammeds*. Hanover, 1863.

Hub. Grimme, *Mohammed*. Münster, 1892, 2 vols. The first vol. is devoted to the life and the second to the doctrine of the Prophet.

D. S. Margoliouth, *Mohammed and the Rise of Islam*. London, 1905.

L. Caetani, *Annali dell' islam*. Milan, 1905, etc., 1st and 2nd vols.

The same, *Studi di storia orientale*. Milan, 1911, 1st vol.

H. Lammens, *Qoran et Tradition: comment fut composée la vie de Mahomet* (in *Recherches de science religieuse*, I). Paris, 1910.

The same, *Mahomet fut-il sincère?* (*Ibid.*, II), 1911.

The same, *L'âge de Mahomet et la chronologie de la Sîra* (in the *Journal asiatique*, 1911). Paris.

The same, *Le Triumvirat Aboû Bakr, 'Omar et Abū 'Obaida* (in *Mélanges de la Faculté orientale*, IV). Beyrout, 1909.

The same, *Fâṭima et les filles de Mahomet, notes critiques pour l'étude de la Sīra*. Rome, 1912.

Frants Buhl, *The Character of Mohammad as a Prophet* (in *The Moslem World*, 1911).

C. Snouck Hurgronje, *Mekka*, mentioned above.

III. THE SACRED BOOK OF ISLĀM

Louis Maracci, *Alcorani textus universus* (Arabic text, Latin translation and commentary). Patavii, 1698.

Gust. Fluegel, *Coranus arabice* (numerous editions, Leipzig, from 1834, of Fluegel's recension, reviewed by Maurice Redslob). We refer to this edition.

Le Koran. A new translation of the Arabic text by M. Kasimirski. Paris, 1840 (numerous reprints).

The best English version is *The Qur'ân.* Translated by E. H. Palmer, Oxford, new edition, 1900.

A. Fracassi, *Il Corano,* testo arabo et versione letterale italiana. Milan, 1914 (worthless).

The same verdict may be passed on all the early complete German versions of the Qorān. We may mention those of S. F. G. Wahl, Halle, 1828, and of L. Ullmann, Crefeld, 1840 (several reprints).

Several partial German versions where an endeavour has been made to preserve the original rhythm ; frequently quoted by German orientalists.

Der Koran. Im Auszuge übersetzt von Fried. Rückert, herausgegeben von Aug. Müller. Frankfurt a. M., 1888.

Mart. Klamroth, Die fünfzig aeltesten Suren des Korans, in gereimter deutscher Übersetzung. Hamburg, 1890.

H. Grimme, *Der Koran.* Ausgewählt, angeordnet und im Metrum des Originals übertragen. Paderborn, 1925

Gust. Fluegel, *Concordantiae Corani Arabicae.* Leipzig, 1842.

Gust. Weil, *Historisch-kritische Einleitung in den Koran.* Bielefeld, 2nd ed., 1878.

Theod. Noeldeke, *Geschichte des Qorans* (new ed. revised by Friedr. Schwally, 2 vols.). Leipzig, 1909 and 1919.

Hub. Grimme, *Mohammed.* Münster, 2nd vol. (introduction to the Qoran and dogma of the Qoran), 1895.

Stanley Lane-Poole, *Le Koran, sa poesie et ses lois.* Paris, 1882.

Ṭabarī, *Tafsīr al-qor'ān.* Cairo, 1901, etc. 30 vols.

Ign. Goldziher, *Die Richtungen des islamischen Koranauslegung.* Leyden, 1920.

Karl Vollers, *Volkssprache und Umgangssprache im alten Arabien.* Strasburg, 1906. (Deals with the language of the Qorān.)

Clément Huart, *Une nouvelle source du Qoran* (in the *Journal asiatique,* 1904).

Jac. Barth, *Studien zur Kritik und Exegese des Qorāns* (in *Der Islam,* VI, 1916).

Ed. Sayous, *Jésus-Christ d'après Mahomet.* Paris, 1880.

S. M. Zwemer, *The Moslem Christ.* London, 1912.

Otto Pautz, *Muhammeds Lehre von der Offenbarung*. Leipzig, 1898. (The book does not fulfil the promise of its title.)

Rud. Leszinsky, *Mohammedanische Traditionen über das jüngste Gericht*. Heidelberg, 1909.

Paul Casanova, *Mohammed et la fin du monde*. A critical essay on primitive Islām. Paris, 1911, etc. (An unfortunate theme.)

Miguel Asin Palacios, *La escatologia musulmana en la divina Comedia*. Madrid, 1919.

C. H. Becker, *Die Kanzel im Kultus des alten Islam* (in *Oriental. Studien, Th. Noeldeke gewidmet*, Giessen, 1906, I).

A. J. Wensinck, art. 'Ḥajj' (in the *Encycl. de l'islam*).

D. B. Macdonald, art. 'Jehād' (*Ibid.*).

Articles on the same subject in C. Snouck Hurgronje, *Verspreide Geschriften*, 3rd vol.

Heinrich Steiner, *Die Mu'taziliten oder die Freidenker im Islam*, Leipzig, 1865. (The epithet 'rationalists' has been badly chosen.)

Wilh. Spitta, *Zur Geschichte Aboă'l Ḥasan al-As'a-rī*. Leipzig, 1876.

D. B. Macdonald, art. 'Ash'ari' (in the *Encycl. de l'islam*).

Ludolf Krehl, *Ueber die koranische Lehre von der Praedestination und ihr Verhaeltnis zu andern Dogmen des Islam*. Leipzig, 1870.

C. H. Becker, *Christische Polemik und islamische Dogmenbildung* (in *Zeits. für Assyriol.*, XXVI, 1912).

IV. THE TRADITION OF ISLĀM

Victor Chauvin, work mentioned above, vol. X: *Le Coran et la Tradition*.

The *Muhammedanische Studien* of Ign. Goldziher, already quoted.

El-Bukhāri. The Islāmic Traditions, translated from the Arabic, with notes and index, by O. Houdas and W. Marçais. Paris, 1903–1914, 4 vols.

Tirmidhī, *Al-jāmi'as-saḥīḥ*. Cairo, 1872, 2 vols.

A. N. Matthews, *Mishcāt al-masabih*, or a collection of the most authentic traditions regarding the actions and sayings of Muḥammed. Calcutta, 1809–1810. (The *Mishkāt* is an abridged version of Baghawī, *Maṣābīḥ as-sunna*. Cairo, 1318 H., 2 vols.).

W. Marçais, *Le Takrib de En-Nawawi traduit et annoté* (in the *Journal asiatique*, Paris, 1900–1901).

Ign. Goldziher, *Neue Materialien zur Literatur des Überlieferungswesen bei den Mahomedanern* (in *Zeitschrift der deuts. Morgenl. Gesellsch.*, L, 1896).
The same, *Kaempfe um die Stellung des Ḥadīth im Islām* (*Ibid.*, LXI, 1907).
The same, *Neoplatonische und gnostische Elemente im Ḥadīṭ* (in *Zeits. für Assyriologie*, XXII, 1909).
The same, *Neutestamentliche Elemente in der Traditionsliteratur des Islam* (in *Oriens Christianus*, II, 1902).
Theod. Noeldeke, *Zur tendenzioesen Gestaltung der Urgeschichte des Islam* (in *Zeits. der deuts. Morgenl. Gesells.*, LII, 1898).
Joseph Horovitz, *Alter und Ursprung des Isnād* (in *Der Islam*, VIII, 1917).
Th. W. Juynboll, art. '*ḥadīth*' (in the *Encyclopédie de l'islam*).
H. Lammens, *Qoran et Tradition*, mentioned above.
The same, *Fāṭima*, etc.
For the tendencious use of the Tradition, see also:
H. Lammens, *Études sur le règne du calife Omaiyade Mo'āwia Ier*. Beyrout, 1907.
The same, *Le califat de Yazīd Ier*. Beyrout, 1921.
The same, *Ziâd ibn Abîhi, vice-roi de l'Iraq, lieutenant de Mo'āwia Ier* (in *Rivista degli studi orientali*, IV, 1912).
The same, *Mo'āwia II ou le dernier des Sofiānides* (*Ibid.*, VII).

V. JURISPRUDENCE OF ISLĀM

Th. W. Juynboll, *Handbuch des islāmischen Gesetzes*. Leyden, 1910. (A good introduction to the evolution of Islāmic law.)
C. Snouck Hurgronje, *Verspreide Geschriften*, vol. 2 (devoted to Islāmic law).
Ign. Goldziher, *Die Ẓāhiriten: Ihr Lehrsystem und ihre Geschichte*. Leipzig, 1884.
The same, art. 'fiqh' (in the *Encyclop. de l'islam*).
F. F. Schmidt, *Die occupatio im islamischen Recht* (in *Der Islam*, I, 1910).
Th. W. Juynboll, art. 'Abū Ḥanīfa' and 'Ḥanafites' (in the *Encycl. de l'islam*).
Ch. Hamilton, *The Hedaya or Guide. A Commentary on the Musulman Law* (ḥanifite). London, 2nd ed., 1870, 4 vols.
Khalil ibn Ishak, *Précis de jurisprudence musulmane selon le rite malékite*. Translated by A. Perron. 2nd ed. Paris, 6 vols.

An Italian and better version of the 'Muḥtaṣar' of the same Ibn Ishāk, by D. Santillana and Ign. Guidi, was published in Milan, 1919, 2 vols.

O. Houdas and Fr. Martel, *Traité de droit musulman (malékite). Le Tohfat d'Eben Acem avec traduction française.* Algiers, 1893.

M. Morand, *Avant-projet de code du droit musulman algérien.* Algiers, 1916.

Béshara El Khoury, *Essai sur la théorie des preuves en droit musulman.* Beyrout, 1926.

Eduard Sachaii, *Muhammedanisches Recht nach schafa'itischer Lehre.* Berlin, 1897.

Ferd. Wüstenfeld, *Der Imām el-Schāfi'ī, seine Schüler und Anhaenger bis zum Jahre 300 H.*

Walter Melville Patton, *Aḥmed ibn Ḥanbal and the Miḥna.* Leyden, 1897.

Ign. Goldziher, *Zur Geschichte der ḥanbalitischen Bewegung* (in *Zeits. der deuts. Morgenl. Gesells.*, LXII, 1908).

The same, art. 'Ibn Ḥanbal' (in the *Encycl. de l'islam*).

The same, *Zur Literatur des Ichtilāf al-maḏāhib* (in *Zeits. der deuts. Morgenl. Gesells.*, XXXVIII, 1884).

C. Van Arendonk, art. 'Ibn Ḥazm' (in *Encycl. de l'islam*).

J. Schacht, *Das Kitāb al-ḥial des Abū Bakr al-Ḥassāf.* Hanover, 1923.

The same, *Das Kitāb al-ḥiaḷ des Abū Ḥātim al-Qazuīni.* Hanover, 1924.

Ign. Goldziher, art. 'Ibn Taimīya' (in the *Encycl. of Religion and Ethics*).

C. H. Becker, *Bartholds Studien über Kalif und Sultan* (in *Der Islam*, 1916. Barthold's memoir in Russian on the Caliphate is a classic).

C. A. Nallino, *Appunti sulla natura dell califfato in genere e sul presunto califfato ottomano.* Rome, 1916.

Th. W. Arnold, *The Caliphate.* Oxford, 1924.

Études sur la notion islamique de souveraineté (a collection of memoirs relating to the Caliphate in the *Revue du monde musulman*, LIX, 1925).

'Alī 'Abd ar-Rāziq, *Al-Islām wa oṣūl al-ḥukm*, Cairo, 1925, several editions. (Cf. H. Lammens, *La crise intérieure de l'islam* in *Les Études*, 20 January, 1926, Paris.)

VI. MYSTICISM

The works of Dunc. B. Macdonald, given in *General Information.*

Alf. von Kremer, *Geschichte der herschenden Ideen des Islams.* Leipzig, 1868.
Ign. Goldziher, *De l'ascétisme aux premiers temps de l'islam* (in *Rev. hist. des religions*, XXXVII, 1898).
Reyn. A. Nicholson, *The Mystics of Islam.* London, 1914.
The same, *Studies in Islamic Mysticism.* Cambridge, 1921.
W. H. T. Gairdner, *'The Way' of the Mohammedan Mystic.* Leipzig, 1912.
Rich. Hartmann, *Zur Frage nach der Herkunft und den Anfaengen des Sūfītums* (in *Der Islam*, VI, 1916).
The same, *Al-Kuschairī's Darstellung des Sūfītums.* Berlin, 1914.
Louis Massignon, *Kitāb al-Ṭawāsīn d'Al-Ḥallāj.* Paris, 1913.
The same, *La passion d'al-Ḥallāj, martyr mystique de l'islam.* Paris, 1922, 2 vols.
The same, *Essai sur les origines du lexique technique de la mystique musulmane.* Paris, 1922.
H. Lammens, *Al-Ḥallāj, un mystique musulman au 3ᵉ siècle de l'hégire* (in *Recherches de science relig.*, 1914).
Maur. Bouyges, *Algazeliana, sur dix publications relatives à Algazel* (in *Mél. Université St. Joseph de Beyrout*, VIII, 1922).
Miguel Asin Palacios, *La mystique d'al-Gazzālī* (*Ibid.*, VII, 1914).
The same, *Algazel: Dogmatica, Moral, Ascetica.* Saragossa, 1901.
The same, *El mistico murciano Abenarabi*, monographias y documentos Madrid, 1925–26, 3 vols.
By the same, several penetrating studies in Spanish on the philosophers of Islāmic Spain.
Carra de Vaux, *Gazali.* Paris, 1902.
S. Zwemer, *A Moslem Seeker after God.* New York, 1920.
W. H. T. Gairdner, *Al-Ghazālī's Mishkāt al-Anwār and the Ghazāli Problem* (in *Der Islam*, V, 1914).
C. A. Nallino, *Il poema mistico d'Ibn al-Fāriḍ in una recente traduzione italiana* (in *Riv. degli studi orientali*, VIII, 1919).
Louis Rinn, *Marabouts et Khouan: étude sur l'islam en Algérie.* Algiers, 1885.
Oct. Depont and Xav. Coppolani, *Les confréries religieuses musulmanes.* Algiers, 1897.
C. Snouck Hurgronje, *Les confréries religieuses, la Mecque et le panislamisme* (in *Verspreide Geschriften*, vol. III).
A. Le Chatelier, *Les confréries musulmanes au Hedjaz.* Paris, 1889.

Margaret Smith, *Rābi'a the Mystic and her Fellow Saints in Islam*. Cambridge, 1928.

Ed. Montet, *Les confréries religieuses de l'islam marocain: leur rôle religieux, politique et social* (in *Rev. hist. des relig.*, XLV, 1902).

P. J. André, *L'islam noir*; a contribution to the study of the Islamic religious fraternities in West Africa. Paris, 1924 (lacking in precision).

D. S. Margoliouth, art. 'Abd al-Kādir' (in *Encycl. de l'islam*).

Georg Jacob, *Beitraege zur Kenntnis der Derwisch-Ordens des Bektaschis*. Berlin, 1908.

K. Voller, art. 'Aḥmed al-Badawī' (in *Encyc. de l'islam*).

VII. THE SECTS

Th. Haarbrücker, *Asch-Schahrastāni's Religionsparteien und Philosophenschulen übersetzt*. Halle, 1850, etc., 2 vols.

Rud. E. Brunnow, *Die Charidschiten unter den ersten Omayyaden*. Ein Beitrag zur Geschichte des I^en islamischen Jahrhunderts. Leyden, 1884.

Julius Wellhausen, *Die religioes-politischen Oppositionsparteien im alten Islam* (in *Abhandlungen der koenigl. Gesells. der Wissensch. in Goettingen*). Berlin, 1901 (important).

A. de Motylinski, art. 'Abāḍites' and ''Abdallah ibn Ibāḍ' (in *Encycl. de l'islam*).

M. J. de Goeje, *Mémoire sur les Carmathes du Bahrain*, 2nd ed. Leyden, 1886.

Israël Friedlander, *The Heterodoxies of the Shiites according to Ibn Ḥazm*. New Haven, 1909.

Ign. Goldziher, *Beitraege zur Literaturgeschichte der Schi'a und der Sunnitischen Polemik* (in *Sitzungsberichte der K. Akad. der Wissensch.*). Vienna, 1874.

The same, *Das Prinzip der Takiya im Islam* (in *Zeits. der deuts. Morgenl. Gesells.*, LX, 1906).

Th. Noeldeke, *Zur Ausbreitung des Schiitismus* (in *Der Islam*, XIII, 1923).

James Darmesteter, *Le Mahdi depuis les origines de l'islam jusqu'à nos jours*. Paris, 1885.

C. Snouck Hurgronje, *Der Mahdi* (in *Verspreide Geschriften*, I.).

Van Vloten, *Recherches sur la domination Arabe*. Amsterdam, 1894.

E. Blochet, *Le messianisme dans l'hétérodoxie musulmane*. Paris, 1903.

A. Noeldeke, *Das Heiligtum al-Husains zu Kerbelā*. Berlin, 1909.

R. Strothmann, *Die Literatur der Zaiditen* (in *Der Islam*, I–II, 1910–1911).
The same, *Das Staatsrecht der Zaiditen*. Strasburg, 1912.
The same, *Der Kultus der Zaiditen*. Strasburg, 1912.
The same, *Das Problem der literarischen Persoenlichkeit Zaid ibn 'Alī* (in *Der Islam*, XIII, 1923).
Corn. Van Arendonk, *De Opkomst van het zaidietisch imamaat in Yemen*. Leyden, 1919.
E. Griffini, *Corpus Juris di Zaid ibn 'Alī*. Milan, 1919.
L. Massignon, *Esquisse d'une Bibliographie qarmate* (in *Oriental Studies presented to E. G. Browne*. Cambridge, 1922).
Ign. Goldziher, *Streitschrift des Gazāli gegen die Bāṭiniya-Sekte*. Leyden, 1916.
W. Ivanow, *Ismailitica*. Calcutta, 1922.
Silvestre de Sacy, *Exposé de la religion des Druses, tiré des livres religieux de cette secte*. Paris, 1838, 2 vols. (a fundamental work).
Henri Guys, *La nation druse, son histoire, sa religion, ses mœurs et son état politique*. Paris, 1864.
Max von Oppenheim, *Vom Mittelmeer zum Persischen Golf*. Berlin, 1899, 1st vol.
Christ. Seybold, *Die Drusenschrift: Kitāb al-noqaṭ walda-wāir*. Kirchhain, 1902.
René Dussaud, *Histoire et religion des Noṣairis*. Paris, 1900.
H. Lammens, *Les Noṣairis: Notes sur leur histoire et leur religion* (in *Les Études*, 1899, Paris).
The same, *Les Noṣairis furent-ils chrétiens? A propos d'un livre récent* (in the review *L'Orient chrétien*. Paris, 1901).
The same, *Les Noṣairis dans le Liban* (*Ibid.*, 1902).
Wladimir Minorsky, *Note sur la secte des Ahlé-Haqq* (in *Rev. monde musulm.*, XL).

VIII. REFORMISTS AND MODERNISTS

Ign. Goldziher, his works cited above, *Vorlesungen*, etc.; *Richtungen*, etc.
C. Snouck Hurgronje, *Mohammedanism*, already cited (last chapter), *Mekka*, 1st vol.
S. G. Wilson, *Modern Movements in Islam*. New York, 1916.
Étude sur la notion islamique de souveraineté (in *Rev. du monde musulm.*, LIX).
Th. Lothrop Stoddard, *The New World of Islam*. New York, 1921.
Burckhardt, *Voyages en Arabie*, previously cited.

R. Laurent-Vibert, *Ce que j'ai vu en Orient.* Paris, 1922 (good observations).

H. L. Fleischer, *Briefwechsel zwischen den Anführern der Wahhābiten und dem Pascha von Damascus* (in *Zeits. deuts. Morgenl. Gesells.*, XI, 1857).

Jul. Euting, *Tagebuch*, previously cited, 1st vol.

Rich. Hartmann, *Die Wahhābiten* (in *Zeits. deuts. Morgenl. Gesells.*, LXXVIII, 1924).

H. St. J. B. Philby, work previously cited.

De Gobineau, *Les religions et les philosophies dans l'Asie centrale.* Paris, 1865.

Herm. Roemer, *Die Bābī-Behā'ī, die jüngste Muhammedanische Sekte.* Potsdam, 1912.

Edw. G. Browne, *A Traveller's Narrative written to illustrate the episode of the Bāb.* Cambridge, 1891, 2 vols.

The same, *Materials for the Study of the Bābi religion.* Cambridge, 1918.

Clém. Huart, *La religion de Bab.* Paris, 1889.

A. L. M. Nicolas, *Séyèd Ali Mohammed, dit le Bāb.* Paris, 2nd ed., 1908, 2 vols.

The same, *Essai sur le Chéikhisme.* Paris, 1910.

Hipp. Dreyfus, *Essai sur le béhaïsme, son histoire, sa portée sociale.* Paris, 1909.

Myron W. Phelps, *Life and Teachings of Abbas efendi.* New York, 1904.

M. Th. Houtsma, art. ''Abbās Efendi' (in the *Encycl. de l'islam*).

R. Mielek, 'Vom Bahaismus in Deutschland' (in *Der Islam*, XIII).

H. D. Griswold, *The Ahmadia Movement* (in *The Moslem World*, 1912).

M. Th. Houtsma, art. 'Aḥmediya' (in *Encycl. de l'islam*).

H. Lammens, *La crise intérieure de l'islam* (in *Les Études*, Vol. 186. Paris, 1926).

Le domaine de l'islam (in *Rev. du monde musulm.*, LV, 1923).

J. Castagné, *Russie slave et Russie turque* (*Ibid.*, LVI, 1923).

The same, *Le Bolchévisme et l'islam* (*Ibid.*, LI–LII, 1922).

Hubert Jansen, *Verbreitung des Islāms, mit Angabe der verschiedenen Riten, Sekten und religioesen Bruderschaften in den verschiedenen Laendern der Erde.* Friederichshagen, 1897.

S. Zwemer, *A New Census of the Moslem World* (in *Moslem World*, XIII, 1923).

M. Delafosse, *L'Animisme nègre et sa résistance à l'islamisation en Afrique* (in *Rev. monde musulm.*, XLIX).

Marshall Broomhall, *Islam in China, a neglected problem.* London, 1910.

Commandant d'Ollone, *Recherches sur les musulmans chinois.* Paris, 1911.

Ahmed Muhiddin, *Die Kulturbewegung in modernen Turkentum.* Leipzig, 1921.

Aug. Fischer, *Aus der religioesen Reformbewegung in der Türkei.* Leipzig, 1922.

Sheykh Mohammed Abdu, *Rissalat al Tawhid, exposé de la religion musulmane.* Translated from the Arabic with an introduction on the life and ideas of the Sheykh Moh. Abdu by B. Michel and the Sheykh Mustapha Ab-del Raziq. Paris, 1925.

John R. Mott, *The Moslem World of To-day.* London, 1925.

Max Meyerhof, *Le monde islamique.* Paris, 1926.

THE QORĀN

PRINCIPAL VERSES QUOTED OR EXPOUNDED

INDEX